NORTH AMERICA'S
Freshwater Fishing Book

NORTH AMERICA'S
Freshwater Fishing
Book

MIKE ROSENTHAL
ILLUSTRATIONS BY FRED WESSEL

CHARLES SCRIBNER'S SONS · NEW YORK

Copyright © 1982 Michael F. Rosenthal

Library of Congress Cataloging in Publication Data

Rosenthal, Mike.
  North America's freshwater fishing book.

  Includes index.
  1. Fishing.   2. Fishes—North America.   I. Title.
SH441.R795   1982   799.1'1'0951   82–10262
ISBN 0–684–17776–5

1 3 5 7 9 11 13 15 17 19   F/C   20 18 16 14 12 10 8 6 4 2

Printed in the United States of America.

To Minnie and the Judge

Acknowledgments

I am indebted to Norman Kotker, without whose help and encouragement I would never have started this book.

Thanks to Horace Lionel La Palm, for allowing me unlimited use of his warm-water research facility.

For their invaluable assistance, my thanks to the staff and management of the No Bullshit Bait Co. of Williamsburg, Massachusetts:

Alex Ghiselin
David Hale
Irma Hutter
Tracy "Lt. Gusto" Kidder
"Catfish" Martin Mahoney
Nancy Conway Martin
Gerald Morriss

Susan Parks
Bob "Blue Cricket" Riddle
Michael Steenburgh
Carol Sturm
"Calamity" Roy Superior
Fred "Kingfish" Wessel

And thanks to the many anglers I have met at stream and lakeside who have taken the time to discuss their fishing ideas and theories with me.

Contents

Introduction

What Is It about Fishing?

I have often heard fishermen say that 10 percent of the fishermen catch 90 percent of the fish. There is, of course, no way to substantiate these figures, but in truth many anglers catch very few fish. That they continue to fish testifies to their optimism and perseverance.

What is it about fishing that keeps even unsuccessful anglers coming back for more? After forty years at the sport, I still find myself too excited to sleep the night before a fishing trip. I laugh at myself for spending so many midnight hours, rain soaked and shivering, my back aching, pursuing nightcrawlers on the greens of the local golf course. I endanger my already failing eyesight tying bits of fur and feather on a tiny hook in hopes that the end result will fool some crafty trout. Obviously, I find much more in fishing than merely catching fish.

I like fishing partly because I can do it alone, and just getting away from it all has intrinsic value for me. But there is more to being alone on a lake or at streamside than the absence of the crowd. When quietly fishing all alone on a lake or stream, I seem to become a natural part of the ecosystem. I've looked up and found a doe so close that I could see her nostrils quiver as she tested the breezes. I've looked down and seen a mink chasing a trout, almost under my boot. I've been startled by a hawk brushing my fly line as it glided past with a chipmunk in its talons. When you go fishing alone in a beautiful spot, you put yourself in a position of being where magical things can happen. Watching a beaver slice cleanly through mirror-smooth water as the morning mists begin to burn from the lake, that hour when the line between water and air is indistinguishable, adds strength to my soul, and catching fish becomes incidental.

But we anglers do hope to catch fish, and that is the reason for this book. Many fishing books are written for the person who has never fished, but anyone beginning a new sport may have a hard time figuring out what to do just by reading about it. Other fishing books contain so much technical information that only a professional angler could gain anything from them. This book contains basic information for the beginner, but it is primarily designed for the person who knows what a fishing rod looks like and has held one in his hand—but hasn't caught many fish. This book is not full of forbidding technical data. It tells you what you need to know to catch fish, and it will be of assistance not only to the novice but to the moderately well-informed angler as well.

Beginning anglers should read Part One, "Equipment," before going on to the individual species of fish. As in all sports, a basic knowledge of the different kinds of equipment is essential. If you believe that all fishing rods, reels, lines, hooks, and lures are substantially the same, the first section explains why your choice of equipment will make a difference in your fishing. If you are an experienced angler with a good general knowledge of equipment but frequently find yourself coming home empty handed, Part Two, "The Fish and How to Catch Them," will make your sport more productive.

I would like to think this book represents an attempt to celebrate the sport of fishing, one of the most interesting, absorbing, and enjoyable things I do—and I'm not alone. At one time or another, about 100 million people in North America try their hand at fishing. Once they try it, many get hooked. It may be watching the line melt on the reel as a catfish or carp runs with the bait, or watching a dry fly disappear into the mouth of a brown trout, or feeling the soft change in pressure when a walleye sucks in your minnow or a bass lifts your plastic worm from the bottom in twenty feet of water. One thing remains the same: There is the same thrill every time you set the hook and feel the throbbing pressure that signals the "cosmic connection" between the aquatic and the terrestrial, between the fish and the fisherman. To those who have never hooked a fish, I hope this book will make you want to experience that sensation. To those of you who are well aware of the cosmic connection, I say, "one more time."

PART ONE

EQUIPMENT

1

Three Ways to Catch Fish

There are three basic techniques in sport fishing: spinning, baitcasting, and fly-fishing. Most fish can be caught using any of these methods.

SPINNING

Spinning became popular in the 1940s; considering the simplicity of the equipment, it is remarkable that it wasn't developed sooner. A spinning outfit is simply a reel with a fixed spool that is hung below a rod fitted with oversized guides. When the angler turns the handle of the reel to retrieve the line, a metal bail engages the line and neatly deposits it on the spool.

Medium-weight spinning tackle comes closest to being the all-purpose fishing outfit. A medium-weight outfit consists of a rod about 6½ feet long and a mid-sized reel loaded with six- or eight-pound-test monofilament line. This outfit allows for great flexibility and can be used to cast bait, lures, and even bass plugs. The one outfit can be used for trout, bass, the pikes, and panfish by simply changing the bait or lure for the specific fish sought. Spinning equipment makes it possible to easily cast light baits and lures, and the drag mechanism of the reel allows the angler to land large fish on line so light that it looks like thread from a spider's web.

When buying a spinning outfit you should stick with brand names. Today's spinning rods and reels are of very high quality and not expensive when you consider that a single outfit will last almost indefinitely if treated properly. A good spinning outfit will cost you less than fifty dollars.

Learning to cast with any fishing outfit is a matter of practice. No two outfits cast exactly alike. It is best that you do some practice casting with your new outfit before setting out for the nearest body of water; equipment problems on the first outing can easily dampen the fishing spirit beyond repair. A few hours of practice make the casting process almost automatic and allow you to concentrate on the action of your bait or lure.

FLY-FISHING

Even people who have never fished and have no desire to do so will stop to watch an experienced flycaster in action. An arc of line flashes through the sunlight, straightens, and drops to the water as gently as a snowflake. There is something mesmerizing about the process, and spectators often come away feeling hypnotized.

Fly-fishing is considered by many to be an unproductive esoteric pastime, but nothing could be further from the truth; it can be extremely productive and is more scientific than esoteric. But it isn't easy to learn to fly fish—not because the process is difficult, but because comparatively few fishermen take advantage of the sport. A person weaned on flies may find it difficult to use any other method to catch any species of fish, and other kinds of equipment will probably feel awkward in his hands. The person weaned on spinning or bait-casting equipment can quickly become frustrated when trying to learn to cast a fly.

I'm sure I would have eventually learned to use flies, but two totally unrelated events helped me along in the process. When I was twelve I won second prize in a fishing contest—a fiberglass fly rod, a reel, line, and three large cards filled with flies tied by the local expert. Disappointed with my award (first prize had been a small, wooden flat-bottomed boat I had wanted badly), I placed my prize in my bedroom closet, where it sat untouched for two years. Then, one early summer day, it became apparent that I would have to learn to use flies. I had fished a local river using my spinning rod and lures and knew there were lots of trout in it because I had caught more than my share, but that day I hadn't had a single strike. I was about ready to call it quits when I noticed a fisherman working his way downstream, casting a fly over water that I had just fished. I chuckled to myself, certain that he wouldn't catch a thing.

As I watched, he hooked a good-sized trout, fought it to net, and released it. Then he caught and released a second, and a third. The fisherman saw me watching him and called over that he had already taken his limit and was strictly fishing for fun. When he finished working that section of river we talked about fly-fishing and he explained that when the water was warm, most trout fed almost exclusively on insects that were represented by his fly. My spinning lure, which represented a minnow, was largely a waste of time.

The next morning I dug the fly rod from my closet, took the outfit to the backyard, and began to practice casting. I now find that it is my spinning and baitcasting equipment that most often sits in the closet. I have found fly-fishing to be effective for almost every species of fish, and when I can take them on flies that is my method of choice.

Flycasting is as easy as it looks. The major difference between flycasting and spinning and baitcasting is that in the latter two the lure or bait is the weight that carries the line from the reel. In flycasting it is the weight of the line that carries the fly. The angler is literally casting the line and the fly follows.

It's possible to spend a lot of money on flycasting equipment, but there are many inexpensive outfits that are perfectly adequate for most fishing. In fact, I have seen rods that sell for under twenty dollars that are every bit as good as rods selling for ten times that price. An adequate fly reel will sell for under ten dollars. Where casts of over thirty or forty feet are required, it is important that the weight of the fly line be matched to the rod. Most rods have the proper line number printed just above the handle. If no line number is present on the rod, most good tackle shops will have the equipment necessary to determine which line is best for the rod you have chosen. An adequate level fly line will sell for under five dollars.

A fly rod can be used to fish bait and small lures as well as flies. Many anglers use a small spinning reel on a fly rod to fish for trout with bait in brushy streams where there is no room for flycasting. The fly rod can also be used to fish popping bugs for bass and panfish and flashy streamer flies for members of the pike family.

The spinning or baitcasting angler should not be hesitant to try fly-fishing. It is not difficult to learn, offers great flexibility, and can be more productive under certain conditions than any other fishing method. Part One contains more detailed information on fly rods, lines, leaders, and flies, and their use and presentation.

BAITCASTING

Baitcasting is not suited to as many types of water and fish as are spinning and fly-fishing, but when heavy lures are to be cast or when a big fish must be dragged from weeds or other obstructions, the technique comes into its own.

Baitcasting was the earliest method to become popular for North American sportfishing, and while the equipment has changed dramatically, the principles remain the same. The earliest baitcasting reels were little more than a spool that turned when the handle of the reel revolved. When a bait or lure was cast, it was essential that the angler keep light pressure on the line with his thumb to prevent the spool of the reel from turning so quickly that it overran the line, creating a tangle known as a backlash. Today's reels have antibacklash devices and a drag (much like those on spinning reels) that allow a fish to take line even while the angler is reeling in. Modern baitcasting reels are also equipped with a free-spool mechanism that allows only the spool—not the handles—to turn when casting. The free-spool mechanism makes it possible to cast very light lures and baits and has added great flexibility to baitcasting. While it is still possible to have backlashes, today's equipment largely eliminates that problem.

Baitcasting rods are usually shorter and stouter than spinning rods. They have the backbone necessary for casting heavy lures and the strength to apply pressure on a big fish intent on burying himself in some underwater obstruction.

Baitcasting is the preferred technique for most southern bass fishermen, who have to contend with wrestling large fish in obstruction-filled waters. It is also popular with northern bass and pike fishermen and anglers using trolling techniques in deep-water impoundments. A modern quality baitcasting outfit will cost about seventy-five dollars.

Many anglers believe that the position of the reel above the rod in baitcasting allows for greater sensitivity to what is happening at the end of the line, which may be true. I instinctively reach for my baitcasting outfit when I am going to fish plastic worms for bass or jigs for walleyes because with it I can feel the gentle mouthing of a bass chewing on a plastic worm in fifteen feet of water, or the faint increase in line pressure when a walleye sucks in a jig, better than I can with spinning equipment. But many fishermen are able to detect the same subtle bites with spinning equipment, and their catches prove that point. Medium or medium-heavy spinning equipment can be used under the same conditions as baitcasting equipment, and in the last analysis the choice is strictly a matter of personal preference. Details about baitcasting rods, reels, and lines are included in Part One.

One of the biggest problems for the angler is determining which species of fish are present in any unfamiliar body of water. Looking at a lake or stream tells little about what is living under the surface of the water. You may assume that shallow lakes and ponds contain bass, pickerel, and panfish, and clear, cold streams contain smallmouths or trout, but that isn't always so. The shop where you purchase your equipment should be able to give you accurate information as to which species of fish inhabit local waters. Most state fish and game departments publish lists of waters and the fish they contain, but talking with other anglers is the best way to determine which species of fish are currently being taken and the methods that are being used successfully. You must also be sure to check state fishing laws before you start. Most states have regulated seasons and size limits for specific species of fish, and some limit the kinds of baits and lures and the number of hooks that may be used in various bodies of water. Once you have decided on a quarry and checked fishing laws, you should purchase a few basic lures known to be good for that particular species of fish—and go fishing.

2

Rods

When I was a kid, commercial fishing rods were made of a solid-steel alloy. They were heavy and awkward and if they had one saving grace, it was that they were virtually indestructible. I recall falling off my bicycle and landing on my two-piece solid-metal flyrod. I got up, dusted myself off, and carefully bent the rod straight (or nearly so) with my hands.

While metal rods were heavy and cumbersome, they were substantially better than earlier rods. The rods used by Izaak Walton and his contemporaries were made of solid fir and were so long and heavy that they resembled small flagpoles. The rods of Walton's day were followed by other wood rods. Lancewood and greenheart, also heavy and cumbersome, were used until the first bamboo rods were constructed. The latter were made of Calcutta cane, and while they were much lighter than solid-wood rods, Calcutta cane proved too pliant and soft for good casting. A major breakthrough in the construction of fishing rods occurred around the turn of the century with the discovery of Tonkin cane. Calcutta cane was a wild grass. Tonkin cane was cultivated in a small section of China and its straight, durable, elastic fibers made it superior in every way to Calcutta cane. When glued together in precise geometric patterns, sections of Tonkin cane result in a rod that is light, durable, and sensitive.

World War II saw the end of both steel and for the most part bamboo rods. Metal was needed for the war effort and the area of China that produced Tonkin cane was no longer accessible to the free world. A few American rod manufacturers managed to store a good supply of Tonkin cane before the war, and one story has it that at least one of them stored so much that it is still using the supply today.

The problem with Tonkin cane rods is that it takes approximately two months to create one. These fine rods will continue to be made by a few master craftsmen who have the necessary skill, but their price puts them beyond the means of the average angler. It is no longer necessary to spend a small fortune for a first-class rod, however. Even though the bamboo purists won't admit it, today's fiberglass, graphite, and boron rods are lighter, more sensitive, and easier casting than even the high-quality custom-built bamboo rods.

The first fiberglass rods appeared in the mid-1940s. They were heavy, solid blanks of glass fibers bonded together with plastics, and while their action left much to be desired, they were lighter than steel and much more durable than bamboo. Solid glass rods were quickly followed by the first hollow glass rods, and my first fiberglass rod was one of these hollow models. I remember that rod right down to its color and windings. Compared to today's models it was crude, but compared to steel, it was a lightweight dream. I paid twenty-nine dollars for that rod, and in the forties that was a lot of money to spend on anything, including a fishing rod. Today, as a result of modern technology, that same price will purchase a light, durable, first-quality fiberglass rod with excellent action.

Fiberglass rods are now made from woven fiberglass cloth, which is rolled, under extremely high pressure, around a steel mandrel. The rods are then heat-cured from the inside, leaving them with uniform action and no weak spots. They are then sanded smooth, finished with hard epoxy resin, and guides and handles are added. The process is very controlled and any combination of length, weight, and stiffness can be easily produced. This extremely simplified explanation essentially covers the way in which all fiberglass rods are made.

For almost forty years fiberglass was used to produce virtually every commercially made fishing rod; then graphite and boron came along. Graphite, in a form suitable for fishing rods, was a fringe benefit of the space program, in which strength with a minimum of weight is essential. Rods made with graphite cost almost twice as much as good fiberglass rods, but they are lighter and noticeably more sensitive. The longitudinal graphite fibers in these rods are bound together with special resins. It is these longitudinal fibers that determine the functional dynamics of the rod; the ability to "launch" a lure or bait when casting and to "feel" what is happening at the end of the line by vibrations transmitted to the hands of the angler.

Rods made of graphite have very thin walls and are not as strong as fiberglass. The tip of a graphite rod is extremely sensitive but is also very fragile and breaks easily if sat on, stepped on, or caught in a car door. The thin walls of a graphite rod also make it very notch-sensitive. This means that if the rod rubs on any sharp corner, such as a boat seat or gunwale, even a notch that is no more than a visible crease can cause the rod to break at that spot when you are casting or fighting a fish. Therefore, graphite rods must be treated at least as carefully as hand-crafted bamboo rods, and cannot be allowed to rattle around on the deck of a boat or in the trunk of a car; it is essential that they be stored in a rod case when not being used.

If graphite is too fragile for your fishing needs, you should consider purchasing a rod made of boron, a new substance in the construction of fishing rods. Boron is a common element found in deposits of borax, which was mined and transported by twenty-mule teams in frontier California and was a popular cleaning agent in the years before detergents. Today boron is used in airplane propellers, helicopter rotors, and Pyrex glassware.

The physical properties of boron are similar to those of graphite except that boron is considerably stronger. Its properties include a unique mix of strength, hardness, light density, and the ability to withstand distortion under both compression and tensile stress. It is a natural material for fishing rods, but costs about 50 percent more than graphite. Boron rods must also be treated with care, and like any good rod should be stored in a case except when actually in use.

Boron and graphite are forcing anglers to learn new concepts about fishing rods. In fact, when selecting one of these rods you can forget everything you have learned about fiberglass. You can't tell a thing about the casting action of a boron or graphite rod by hefting it in the sporting goods store. The only way to determine its action is to actually cast with it, because boron and graphite don't weigh enough to flex themselves. In other words, while these rods bend and unbend much faster than fiberglass or bamboo, they do so only when you are actually casting. In the store you can wave them back and forth all you wish, but they won't bend at all because their fibers are so strong and light.

Rod manufacturers have charts that compare the action and weight of fiberglass, graphite, and boron, and individual rods are marked showing the range of lines and weights of lures each will handle. You should select your graphite or boron rod using these numbers, and you can do so without fear of selecting a rod that is not adequate for your needs. These rods handle a broad range of line and lure weights, making them very adaptable to a wide variety of fishing conditions. Because of their fragility, however, anglers who want the lightness and sensitivity of graphite or boron should choose a rod from a reputable manufacturer who will stand behind his product with a warranty.

Reels and lines have also changed significantly over the past forty years; these changes are discussed in detail in the following three chapters, in the context of the specific functions of spinning, baitcasting, and fly-fishing reels and lines.

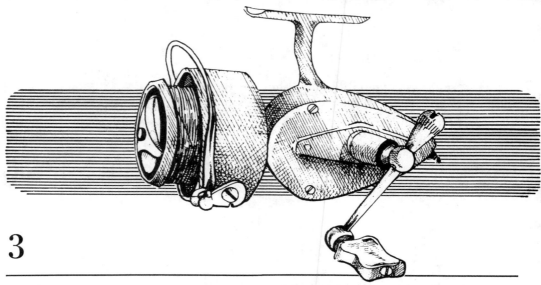

3

Spinning Tackle

Since its introduction to North America in the 1940s, spinning tackle has revolutionized fishing. The essential difference between spinning and other kinds of fishing equipment is that the spool of a spinning reel is stationary during the cast; the line flows off one end of the fixed spool. There is so little line friction that light lures and baits can be cast long distances with ease. In fact, casting with spinning gear is so easy that when it was first introduced, some anglers felt that it should be outlawed because it would result in the total depletion of fish from North American waters. Obviously, that hasn't happened, and spinning is now the most popular method of casting a lure or bait.

When choosing spinning tackle you should not look for inexpensive bargains. The equipment has been refined to the point at which even the best quality is not prohibitively expensive, and the few extra dollars you will spend for quality gear will repay you with years of effortless, trouble-free fishing.

SPINNING RODS

Most spinning rods are made of fiberglass, and while graphite and boron are becoming more popular, they are still comparatively expensive as of this writing. If you can afford these space-age products you will get a lighter and more sensitive rod, but fiberglass is almost as good, much less expensive, and much more durable.

The common feature in all spinning rods is the guides, which are widest at the butt end of the rod and gradually decrease in diameter as they go toward the tip. The large guides gather the loops of line as they flow from the fixed spool of the reel and gradually reduce them in size so that the casting distance will not be reduced by excessive friction between the line and the guides.

Spinning rods are made in lengths from tiny 4½-foot ultra-light models to heavy 14-foot surf rods. The most popular rod action is called omni-action, which is designed to handle lures of varying weights. There are also single-action rods that are designed for specific kinds of fishing. An example of a single-action rod would be a short, stiff trolling rod designed for use with lead-core line. Other examples of single-action rods are the so-called parametric rods, which are long, soft, and flexible and are designed for big, hard-fighting fish like steelhead.

In a good universal-action rod there are a few things you should look for. The rod should have a fair amount of backbone and a fast tip. Casting with spinning equipment is done with a snap of the wrist, and a rod with a fast tip will respond faster and cast easier. A rod with a soft backbone and slow tip will not have the action needed for casting light lures, and when you snap your wrist to launch the lure the rod will respond slowly and won't cast very far. The rod guides should not be very widely spaced, about twelve inches apart at the butt end and six inches at the tip. The windings that hold the guides to the rod should be even and smooth. The reel seat must hold the reel firmly, and both the seat and the ferrules should be made of rust-resistant material. The handle should feel comfortable in your hand. Most handles are made of cork rings, and on a good quality rod the joints between these rings will be barely visible while the cork itself will have few holes or pits.

The length of the rod is important. Lighter rods are better suited for light lures and baits; shorter, stiffer rods for heavier lures. A good rod will have the necessary information about the line and lure weights that should be used with it printed directly on the rod just above the handle. For instance, just above its handle, my favorite omni-action rod carries the following information: "Length—6½'; Action—medium/light; Lure Wt.—¼ to ½ ounce; Line Wt.—6 to 10 pound test." I use this rod for almost all of my spinfishing.

An all-around spinning rod must be able to cast lures as light as a quarter of an ounce with ease. The way you can test this is to hang a quarter-ounce lure from the tip of the rod. The weight of the lure should depress the rod tip just about an inch or two. If it doesn't depress the rod tip at all, the rod action is too heavy for quarter-ounce lures. If the tip is depressed more than a few inches, the action of the rod is too light.

SPINNING REELS

There are two types of spinning reels: open-faced and close-faced. On the close-faced reel the fixed spool is covered by a cone-shaped housing and the line runs out of a hole in the center of the cone. On an open-faced reel the spool is visible and the line flows off in large loops.

Close-faced reels sit on top of the rod handle and can be used on baitcasting rods. When casting, a button on the reel is depressed and held down with the thumb. When the button is released a lug or pin that holds the line is disengaged and the line flows from the spool. The lug engages the line for retrieving when the handle of the reel is turned.

Open-faced spinning reels hang below the rod. When casting, the bail that holds the line is pushed back over the face of the spool. The free line is then allowed to drape over the index finger, which is removed when casting. If you want to shorten the cast while the lure or bait is still in the air, you can "feather" the line by allowing the coils to lightly strike your index finger as they flow off the spool. Because it is impossible to feather the line with a close-faced spinning reel, I prefer to use open-faced reels.

When buying a spinning reel be sure you pick one that is balanced to the weight of your rod. For freshwater fishing a light or medium reel that holds at least 150 yards of six- to ten-pound-test line will cover most conditions. The reel should also be sturdy and well made. Good-quality reels use ball bearings in their anchor gear trains and are very smooth and quiet. The bail on an open-faced reel must be well constructed of stainless steel, since it takes a lot of punishment and on a cheap reel is the first thing to break. The drag of the reel must operate smoothly and should be convenient to reach and adjust. The spool should be easy to remove so you can have the convenience of changing to other spools filled with lines of different test weights.

Spinning reels are made with different retrieve ratios. Most reels have a retrieve ratio between three and a half to one and five to one. This means that the bail moves around the spool three and a half times or five times for each complete turn of the reel handle. The lower ratio is fine for most fishing, but the five-to-one ratio gives better control when fishing in streams, where a rapid retrieve may be necessary for proper lure action. The higher retrieve ratio is also easier when using lures that must be worked quickly. When you buy a new spinning reel, I suggest that you get one with a high retrieve ratio. You can still retrieve as slowly as you wish by reeling in gradually, and you will find situations in which the faster retrieve is a benefit.

The drag on the reel is one of its most important features. An improperly functioning drag accounts for more broken line and lost fish than almost anything else, yet many fishermen do not know the correct way to set the drag. When set properly, the drag allows a big fish to take line in a sudden rush even when the angler is reeling in at the same time. It takes almost twice as much pull to start the drag slipping from a spool that is not moving as it does once the spool has started to move.

The drag on most open-faced spinning reels is adjusted by a wing nut on the face of the spool. Close-faced reels usually have a micrometer wheel just above the cone. The best way to set the drag on either type of reel is to rig the rod and tie the line to some stationary object, close the bail, and back up while holding the rod at a forty-five-degree angle to the ground. If the line comes tight and refuses to slip, or if the line breaks, the drag is set too tight. By loosening the wing nut or micrometer wheel you will be able to find the drag position at which the line runs smoothly off the reel and doesn't break when the rod is yanked hard. It is very difficult to judge the drag setting by pulling line from the reel with your hand. I prefer to keep my drag set on the light side, and to hold my index finger against the spool to keep it from moving when setting the hook or trying to turn a fish away from an obstruction.

Besides the drag setting, the amount of line on the spool determines how much pull is required to make the drag work. It is therefore important to check the drag setting after adding new line or if a substantial amount of line is lost. The drag works best when the spool is filled to its proper capacity; the less line on the spool, the more pull required to make the drag slip. When I hook a very big fish, one that takes a lot of line, I sometimes adjust the drag setting during the fight. It takes practice to learn how to do this, and if you have never done it, don't wait until you hook a big fish to experiment. Practice by tying your line to a stationary object and backing away with the rod in your hands.

The drag must give line smoothly. A jerky drag that causes the rod tip to bounce and gives line unevenly will lose as many fish as one that is set too tight. In most cases a jerky drag is caused by washers that are worn or contain dirt, although in a new reel a jerky drag may mean that the drag needs to be broken in. Most drags are composed of alternating soft and hard washers, and the soft ones develop ruts if they are pressed too tightly together for a long time. After a day of fishing I release the tension on the drag by loosening the wing nut so the washers can relax and return to their regular shape. I have developed the habit of setting my drag every time I start fishing, and I know that this has saved me some big fish.

It is important to keep enough line on the spool for good casting. Too little line will result in very short casts because of the additional friction from the line rubbing on the lip of the spool. Too much line pulls many coils off the spool at one time, causing a bad tangle. The line on a properly filled spool should be wound on firmly and come to within one-eighth of an inch of the lip of the spool. I go through a lot of monofilament line each season and prefer to have new line put on my reels at a sporting goods store that has commercial spooling equipment. This guarantees that the new line will be wound on tightly and evenly without any twisting.

I used to have trouble putting new line on my spinning reels when I did this myself. Although I would sometimes do it perfectly, at other times I would twist the line so badly that coils would literally leap right off the spool. I have since learned how to avoid badly twisted line. In order to do this when filling a reel on which the bail moves around the spool in a clockwise direction—which is the case with most reels—lay the roll of new line flat on the ground in such a way that the line flows off the spool in a counterclockwise direction—the direction opposite to that in which the bail picks up the line. The reel should be on the rod when putting on the new line. The way to keep tension on the new line is to slide your hand up the rod about halfway to the first guide and allow the line to pass between your thumb and index finger as you are reeling it in. I also use this method for keeping tension on the line when I'm fishing and have slack line that has to be reeled onto the spool under tension.

Should you find that your new line is badly twisted, the twists can be removed by slowly letting most of the line out behind a moving boat, or by letting the line flow downstream and hang in the current for about a minute. When straightening line, do not tie any weight or lure to it; and when reeling it back onto the spool be sure to keep it under moderate tension by letting it pass between your thumb and index finger as described above.

MONOFILAMENT LINE

Spinning equipment is designed to be used with monofilament line, which is composed of synthetic resins that are melted and extruded into fishing line. Today's monofilament lines are inexpensive and durable, and while they do not lose any strength for over a year or more, they do become weakened by abrasion and by their continual stretching and relaxation during a season of fishing. I change the line on all my reels at the beginning of each fishing season and whenever necessary during the season. I consider new line a cheap form of fishing insurance.

There are many excellent monofilament lines and you should always pick a good one. Bargain lines don't wear or cast well, and their nonuniform diameter affects their strength.

There are over one hundred varieties of resins that are mixed in various combinations to achieve monofilament lines with different qualities of strength, stretch, visibility, and limpness, all of which are related. For instance, line strength, which depends in part on line diameter, is defined as the break load per diameter; the higher this load is per diameter, the greater the tensile strength of the line. Most monofilament lines are stronger than the pound test stated on their labels but lose up to 15 percent of their strength when wet. A quality line, even when wet, should break at a weight somewhat higher than its labeled rating. Also, different brands of line rated at the same strength will be of different diameters. A difference of just two-thousandths of an inch makes a difference in the way a line casts and how it feels when you fish with it. I prefer lines with the smallest diameter I can find that also have the pound test I desire.

When considering line strength you must also consider knot strength. Knot strength is the amount of tension on the line at which the knot will break. I have seen knot-strength comparisons done by line manufacturers, and most quality lines have a knot-breaking limit that approaches or exceeds the labeled strength of the line. A cheap line may have a test strength of eight pounds, for example, but a knot strength of only five or six pounds. Because the line is only as strong as its weakest point, a high knot strength is just one more reason to spend the additional money for a good-quality line.

Line stretch is also a consideration. A little stretch helps cushion the line when a powerful fish makes a break for a brush pile, but too much stretch makes it difficult to detect strikes on long casts and more difficult to set the hook securely. Also, the more a line stretches, the stiffer it becomes. Stretch can be a real problem in light lines with small diameters, so most good line manufacturers build in a little more stiffness into their light lines. If you find that your line is too stiff and springy, drop down to the next lower pound test or look for a line with a smaller diameter, but remember that after a few hours of fishing, the line will absorb water and lose some of its stiffness.

Where very precise casting is necessary, I pick the limpest line I can find. When I'm bottom fishing, or when the water is very weedy or brushy, I use a stiffer line, which will stand up better under abuse. As mentioned earlier, if your spinning reel has interchangeable spools, you can carry different lines to cover your needs for a variety of conditions.

I've found that high visibility lines make some kinds of fishing easier. There are many fluorescent lines that have been optically brightened; blue and yellow are the most popular colors. I like blue line because on a dark day when it is almost impossible to see an ordinary line, an optically brightened line will be seen to glow through a pair of polarized sunglasses. The yellow lines show up even better, but while line manufacturers claim the fish do not see these bright lines, I have always felt that the fish must be able to see their bright gold color, which is so visible that these lines diminish my confidence—and I catch fewer fish when my confidence level is low. But since many of my fishing companions use the bright lines and catch as many fish as I do, using optically brightened lines is strictly a matter of personal preference.

If you can walk and chew gum at the same time, you can be an expert at casting with spinning equipment. It is that easy, and there are only a few things you must know to become proficient at it. Open-faced spinning reels are made to hang below the rod. Every time I see someone trying to cast with the reel held above the rod, I have to resist the urge to suggest that he take up golf. The spinning rod is held with two fingers ahead of the reel leg and two fingers behind it. The lure should hang about ten inches from the rod tip. After the bail is opened, the line should rest across the first pad of the index finger on the rod hand. The line should not be held in the cleft of the joint, between the pads of the finger. The rod is then brought back and immediately forward with a snap of the wrist, with the forefinger being released from the line, allowing the rod to catapult the lure. To slow the lure while it is in flight, the forefinger is moved over the face of the reel so that the uncoiling line will slap against it. This feathering action gives excellent line control, and with a little practice you will be able to drop your lure exactly where you wish. In a short time the casting process will become automatic and you won't even think about it. No matter how you are casting—overhead, from the side, or backhand—the principles are the same and practice is the key to mastering the process.

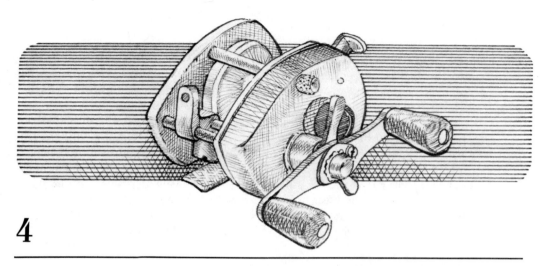

4

Baitcasting Tackle

Like many fishermen of my generation, I put my baitcasting outfit in the closet when spinning equipment became available in the 1940s. During the following fifteen years or so, I was exclusively a spin- and fly-fisherman, but there were times I missed my old baitcasting outfit. While spinning equipment is excellent for most kinds of fishing, baitcasting comes into its own when casting heavy lures, when a big fish must be pried out of the weeds, and where casting accuracy and control are essential.

Baitcasting equipment has improved so much during the past twenty years that the new rods and reels now compete with spinning in their ability to cast light lures for long distances, and with baitcasting there is the advantage of real pinpoint accuracy. Today's baitcasting reels have antibacklash devices, level-wind mechanisms that work smoothly, and a drag system that eliminates the burned thumbs and skinned knuckles of the past. These days it is my spinning equipment that most often sits in the closet. I believe nothing beats the light and delicate control possible with modern baitcasting equipment.

Selecting good baitcasting equipment is not difficult; it depends on the type of fishing to be done and the sizes and species of fish. I have two baitcasting outfits that I use with different lures. One outfit consists of a two-piece, six-foot, light/medium fiberglass rod that I use with a lightweight reel spooled with ten-pound-test monofilament line. This outfit handles lures between one-quarter and three-quarters of an ounce, and is ideally suited for fishing unweighted plastic worms, small crankbaits and spinnerbaits, and light topwater lures.

My second outfit consists of a one-piece, 5½-foot, medium/heavy rod that I use with a medium-weight reel spooled with seventeen-pound-test monofilament. I use this outfit with lures weighing from about one-half to one and a quarter ounces; it is ideally suited for fishing weighted plastic worms, large crankbaits and spinnerbaits, and big topwater lures. I stretch the limits of both outfits perhaps more than I should. For instance, I have taken muskies weighing over twenty pounds on the lighter outfit, and catfish over thirty pounds on the heavier rig.

BAITCASTING RODS

When selecting a baitcasting rod there are some basic guidelines to follow. Quality rods will be marked, just above the handle, with the manufacturer's suggested range of line and lure weights. I have found these suggested weight ranges to be accurate, although somewhat conservative. The number of guides, their placement, and material of which they are made are also important. I prefer guide spacing of no more than ten inches at the butt end of the rod, decreasing to about three and a half inches at the tip. I also like a rod that has at least six and preferably seven guides. Rods with few guides don't cast well because the line slaps against the rod. The guides should be made of aluminum oxide, carbaloy, ceramic, or titanium dioxide. These very hard substances prevent the guides from being scored by dirt and grit that adheres to the line. Inexpensive rods have soft metal guides that quickly develop grooves from the abrasive action of the line, and these grooves, or scores, will quickly weaken or fray even the best line.

When buying a new rod for a reel you already own, it's a good idea to take the reel with you to the store to see how it will fit on the rod. A reel seat that does not hold the reel firmly on the rod can become more than a nuisance. The last thing you want is to have your reel drop off the rod into your lap while you are fighting a big fish. For the same reason, it is also a good idea to bring along the handle of a rod for which you are buying a new reel, since some of the newer reels do not fit older model rods.

For many years I preferred one-piece baitcasting rods because I felt they had better action. But modern baitcasting rods have glass ferrules and I can no longer tell the difference in action between a one- and a two-piece rod. I now prefer two-piece models because they are much easier to travel with and to get

safely in and out of vehicles. Also, two-piece rods are more convenient and safe for shipping long distances. A fishing trip can be ruined if, upon opening your rod case, you find your rod in pieces.

At the beginning of Part One I discussed the characteristics of the new graphite and boron rods. These modern materials combine strength with lightness and sensitivity. Baitcasting rods are constructed with comparatively few graphite or boron fibers that are, at this writing, competitively priced with top-quality fiberglass rods. If you are someone who is careful and not very hard on your equipment, you're a good candidate for a boron or graphite rod. If you break rods in car doors and trunks and by sitting on them, you'll want to stick with the more durable fiberglass.

BAITCASTING REELS

The early baitcasting reels had no antibacklash adjustment or level wind. With a heavy lure good distance and accuracy were possible for the expert caster, but light lures were a problem. Today's fine reels, and there are many, have made casting easy with lures as light as a quarter-ounce.

The problem with the earlier reels was that when the lure was cast, the reel spool, gears, and handle also revolved. Once all of these things got moving it was difficult to stop them, and if the timing and thumb pressure on the spool weren't perfect, the resulting backlash was accurately described as a bird's nest. I can remember coming home early from more than one outing because of a backlash that required hours of work with a crocheting needle to untangle.

The advent of modern, free-spool baitcasting reels, on which only the spool revolves when casting, is attributed to Swedish craftsmanship; these reels began to appear in North America in the late 1950s. Fishermen were waiting to buy them. There were a few attempts to develop a free-spool reel in this country. One of the earliest, called the Blue Grass Simplex Free Spool reel, was produced in the 1930s by the Horton Manufacturing Company of Bristol, Connecticut. For some reason the reel never became popular, and anglers had to wait for almost thirty years before the free-spool reels were perfected.

Modern baitcasting reels are computer designed and constructed like a fine watch. Most have two sets of brakes, which control spool rotation. One is an internal centrifugal brake, which applies pressure in the same way as an automobile brake-shoe as the spool turns. The other brake mechanism allows for adjustable friction to be applied directly to the spool through a control knob located on the palm plate of the reel. There have also been other, recent improvements in reel design, such as floating bushings that support the spool axle and result in smooth, silent casting. Level-wind mechanisms have been improved, and sophisticated star drags enable the angler to fight large fish with

light line without burned thumbs from braking and bruised knuckles from the flying reel handle. Other recent improvements include reels that automatically shift from a two-and-a-half-to-one retrieve ratio to a four-and-a-half-to-one ratio when pressure is taken off the spool. This feature is a real benefit when a large fish charges the boat because it allows the angler to take up the slack line at a much faster rate.

Most improvements in reel design have been done to enhance the smoothness and efficiency of operation and to eliminate backlashes, but even with these refinements, the angler still needs an educated thumb. No matter what reel manufacturers state, every baitcaster knows that there is no way to completely eliminate the backlash.

Backlashes happen in two situations. The first is at the beginning of the cast when so much power is applied that the spool moves faster than the lure can take out line. This results in an overrun of line and a nasty tangle. Backlashes also occur at the end of the cast if the spool isn't stopped with the angler's thumb the instant the lure hits the water. This also results in an overrun of line. If the brake mechanism is set properly, you will be able to cast with a minimum of thumbing and few backlashes.

The way I set the brake on my reels is to tie onto my line the lure I am going to use, and put the reel into the free-spool setting. I hold my rod at a forty-five-degree angle to the water, remove my thumb from the spool, and let the line flow as the lure falls to the water. I adjust the brake on the palm plate of the reel to the degree of tension at which, after the lure hits the water, the spool immediately stops without tangling. When I switch to a lighter or heavier lure I adjust the brake accordingly. This brake setting will minimize backlashing, but you must still learn to use your thumb to keep the spool from overrunning the line when casting.

A good way to educate your thumb is to use the same technique mentioned above for setting the brake, but also to apply enough thumb pressure to stop the lure just as it barely touches the water. With a little practice you will be able to stop the lure at this point every time. When you can do this fifteen times in a row, you are ready to start casting.

Baitcasting is more difficult than casting with spinning equipment, but with practice the process becomes automatic. Once you have mastered stopping the lure just before it hits the water, select a target about forty feet away and cast at it. Imagine that you have a rubber ball stuck on your rod tip and that what you are trying to do is throw the ball from the rod tip to the target. Let the lure, weight, or practice plug you are using dangle about four inches below the rod tip. Keep your eye on your target, and with one smooth motion (no stops) lower the rod until the lure seems to touch the target, bring the rod back past your ear until it is parallel to the ground, then immediately bring the rod forward in a direct line with the target. Remember that you're trying to gently

throw that imaginary rubber ball on the rod tip to the target. Your thumb must stay in light, continual contact with the spool and must stop the spool the instant the lure touches the water. Thumb pressure is applied at the start of the cast, relaxed while the lure is in flight, and reapplied with increasing pressure to slow and stop the lure at the target. Don't be discouraged when you get backlashes. Everybody has them, and the more you practice the easier the process will become.

Backlashes are caused as much by forcing the cast as by improper thumbing. Your casts should be gentle and the rod should do most of the work. If you force the cast and apply too much power, the reel spool will revolve too quickly for the amount of line that is going out, and the overrun will wind the line back on itself.

It is not difficult to untangle a backlash, especially with monofilament line, if you work slowly and patiently. If you yank at the line you will accomplish nothing. Study the line where it enters the spool. You will see that the backlash is composed of loops of line that encircle the main strand. These loops should be located and pulled out one at a time, at which point the snarl will simply fall apart.

BAITCASTING LINES

Most anglers, myself included, use monofilament line on their baitcasting reels. The physical properties of such lines are discussed in Chapter 3, "Spinning Tackle"; it will suffice to say here that the softer and less wiry the line, the easier it will cast.

Braided lines, used exclusively before the development of monofilament, are once again gaining in popularity with many baitcasters. Not only does braided line lie flat on the reel spool, making for easier casting, but it is also more sensitive than monofilament and transmits vibrations more readily to the hands of the angler. Modern braided lines are far superior to those used in the years before the advent of monofilament, and although they cost more than mono-filament lines, many anglers will use nothing else.

The most popular braided lines are made of nylon, the same material used to make monofilament—or single-filament—line. The several filaments of a braided line are composed of tiny threads .001 inch or less in diameter. Single nylon filaments of .002 inch in diameter or more are called monofilament. Some lines are constructed of very fine strands of polyester, which are braided together to form lines called Dacron or Micron.

One of the most desirable qualities of braided line is its low stretching property, which gives the advantage of a better sense of feel, better striking power, and the ability to restrain a fish that is headed for an obstruction. Braided lines also lie flatter on the spool of the reel and hold a knot better than monofilament, which has a tendency to slip, especially in the larger diameters. Some braided lines float on the surface of the water and give better feel and control when a surface lure is being used. A floating line is also an advantage when you're fishing bait under a bobber, because you don't have to deal with the problem of the line's sinking to the bottom between the bobber and the rod. Braided lines are also easier to cast than monofilament lines; even the softest mono lines have a "memory" and come off the spool in coils that require a much more educated thumb to prevent backlashing.

There are also disadvantages to braided lines. For one thing, they have a larger diameter than mono lines with the same test strength, and are more visible in the water. Moreover, most anglers use a monofilament leader with a braided line, and this means more knots, each of which is a potential weak spot in the line. Braided lines also wear faster than monofilament lines. The wear is primarily in the first two feet of line and is caused by friction against the tip guide at the beginning of the cast when there is the greatest amount of line stress. A periodic snipping of the first three feet of line will ensure full line strength. Guides wear faster with braided lines because the rough surface of these lines picks up tiny bits of dirt and grit from the water, which can cut grooves into a rod guide in a short time. Therefore, braided lines should be used only on rods with hardened guides.

Another factor with braided lines is that they are more expensive than monofilament lines, but unless you use huge quantities of line, this isn't a problem. One line manufacturer contends that although you pay more for braided line, its ability to transmit vibrations is so superior when compared to monofilament line that using it with a fiberglass rod gives the angler the same sensitivity as using a graphite or boron rod.

One other thing that must be kept in mind when baitcasting is that the level-wind mechanism of the reel travels many miles during a day of fishing. Putting a couple of drops of high-quality reel oil on the worm gear at the bottom of the level-wind assembly each day that you fish will help keep the reel running smoothly and quietly.

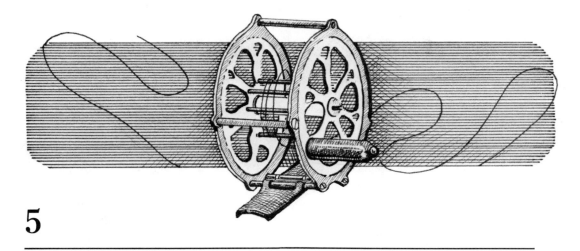

5

Fly-fishing Tackle

Each spring, after the first few weeks of really warm weather, I catch trout easily on wet flies. The bait- and spinfishermen I meet at streamside haven't had a strike, and there is a look of disbelief when I show them the trout in my creel and attribute my success to the tiny bit of fur and feathers tied to my leader. I have never been certain whether their doubtful expressions mean that they think I'm lying or whether they're questioning their own ability to learn the alleged intricacies of fly-fishing.

Many fly fishermen have been guilty of perpetrating a hoax—that the art of fishing an artificial fly is terribly difficult, that flycasting requires the coordination of a professional athlete, and that the successful fly fisherman needs a degree in biology to successfully match the hatching aquatic insects with an artificial fly. Nothing could be further from the truth. Fly-fishing is not difficult, the equipment is not expensive, and when conditions are right there is no easier way to take trout. In addition, while fly-fishing is generally associated with trout and salmon, it is equally effective for bass, pike, and many other species of freshwater fish.

For as long as anglers have set out after trout, some of them have done so using artificial flies. The first mention of fly-fishing was made by a second-century Roman author who wrote about catching trout on a hook of some sort that was adorned with cock's hackles and red wool. He called his fly the False Hippourous and I'm sure I have one somewhere in my fly box.

The *Treatyse on Fysshynge with an Angle*, by Dame Juliana Berners, was printed in 1496 and contains the earliest information to which the modern fly fisherman can relate. The treatise discusses rods, lines, and hooks, and describes the dressings of over a dozen different flies. I have always liked the fact that there were so few fly patterns in those days. Today there are literally hundreds.

One of the best-known early works on fly-fishing is *The Compleat Angler*, by Izaak Walton, which was published in England in 1653. Walton was a bait fisherman. In the ten years following its publication the original work was revised and combined with the writings of two other men, Charles Cotton and Colonel Robert Venables. Writings by Walton, the bait fisherman; Cotton, the fly fisherman; and Venables, the early master of casting and fly presentation, make up *The Compleat Angler* as it is known today.

The rods of Walton's day had no reels. Lines were tied directly to the end of the rod, which was between eighteen and twenty feet long. The rods were constructed of from six to twelve sections of tapered wood that were spliced together. The weight of these rods could be measured in pounds, and their action was as soft as a buggy whip. Over the years, rods became shorter and lighter as new woods were tried. In 1854 the first split bamboo rods were made, and about one hundred years later fiberglass was introduced. The graphite and boron that have more recently been introduced have become popular rod materials and are far superior to any other rod substance.

The early fly lines were hand-braided horsehair with as many as twenty or more hairs tapering down to only one or two. Silkworm gut followed horsehair and was in turn followed by braided silk. Today's fly lines are made from synthetics and are scientifically tapered in a variety of shapes to meet a variety of conditions. Modern fly rods, reels, lines, and leaders will be discussed later.

The first commercially made hooks were produced in the mid-1500s by the needle makers of Redditch, England. These hooks were needles from which the temper was removed by heating. The hooks were then bent and barbed and the temper was restored. The hooks were extremely brittle and many fish were lost when the hook simply broke in half during the fight.

The first mention of fishing a floating fly came in 1850, but it wasn't until 1886 that Frederic M. Halford published his work *Floating Flies and How to Dress Them*, which marked the development of modern dry-fly fishing.

FLY LINES

In fly-fishing it is the line itself that is cast. The line is, in effect, a very long flexible sinker. For this reason, many different shapes of lines have been developed for different conditions.

A few years ago, when fly lines were made of braided silk, the line had to be dried between outings to keep it from rotting. Today's synthetic lines can be stored on the reel. They don't rot, and except for occasional cleaning with soap and water or commercially prepared line cleaners, they are maintenance free.

Early braided silk lines were classified by letters that indicated their diameter. Today the American Fishing Tackle Manufacturers Association (A.F.T.M.A.) has developed a far superior classification system for modern lines. Under the new system, fly lines are given a number between 1 and 12 that indicates the weight in grains of the first thirty feet of line. For example, a No. 6 line weighs 160 grains; a No. 10 line weighs 280 grains. Under the A.F.T.M.A. code there are also letters used before the line weight that illustrate the shape (taper) of the line. After the weight number is another letter that describes whether the line floats (F), sinks (S), or sinks very slowly (I). This new system has brought order out of chaos and has made it an easy matter to determine the exact characteristics of a fly line.

The A.F.T.M.A. classification code is as follows (the first letters indicate line shape):

L   Level line
DT   Double-tapered line
WF   Weight-forward tapered line
ST   Shooting tapered head

A number from 1 to 12, indicating the weight of the line, is printed in the middle. The last letter describes the floating characteristics of the line:

F   Floating line
S   Sinking line
I   Intermediate (slow-sinking) line

The combination of numbers and letters identifies the shape, weight, and flotation characteristics of the line. For example, a line marked DT-6-S is a double-tapered, 6-weight, sinking line.

The level line (L) is usually seventy-five feet long. It is the same diameter from one end to the other. A level line is excellent for trolling and for making short casts where a very delicate fly presentation is not important, such as when fishing a streamer or bucktail in fast water. Level lines are also good where wind resistance is a problem, such as when casting a bulky hair bug or popper for bass. Level lines cast well up to about thirty-five feet, after which their uniform weight tends to make longer casts difficult. A level line costs less than half as much as a tapered line.

A double-tapered line (DT) is, in effect, two lines in one. It is a level line that has the same taper at each end, and you can reverse the line and use the other end after the first one becomes worn. The standard double-tapered line is ninety feet long. The level center section is sixty-six feet long. At either end of the level line there is a ten-foot section that gradually tapers to a two-foot level tip. This taper allows for a very gentle delivery of a fly, which will "paint" lightly onto the water. The double-tapered line is excellent with smaller flies that do not have great wind resistance, and its most effective casting range is about forty to fifty feet. Some anglers, myself included, snip the first two feet of level line off their double-tapered line. This still allows for a delicate delivery but increases the casting distance by about 20 percent.

A weight-forward tapered line (WF) is the easiest to cast. It allows for the delicate presentation of a small fly as well as the use of wind-resistant hair bugs and poppers; it is also good where long casts are required. There are differences in weight-forward lines, but the standard WF line is composed as follows: for its first twelve feet, the line is identical to a DT line, having a two-foot level tip followed by ten feet of gradual taper. The center, level section of a WF line is twenty feet long, after which it tapers immediately to about sixty feet of light level line known as the running, or "shooting," end. The advantage of a weight-forward line is that it will deliver a fly on short casts with the delicacy of a double-tapered line, while on long casts the twenty-foot center section will easily carry the lighter running end to the target, making the WF line the popular choice for distance casting. I feel that a good WF line is the best all-around fly line, and if I had to pick a single line, a weight-forward would be my choice.

With a shooting-head line (ST), tournament casters are able to cast up to 200 feet. A shooting-head line is simply 30 feet of fly line with a 6-foot taper at one end and a loop at the other end. The shooting line is attached to the shooting head and is so named because it shoots quickly through the guides when the cast is released. Many anglers use monofilament as a shooting line, but I prefer a very small diameter fly line that is made for shooting. The ST line is the easiest way to cast wind-resistant lures long distances, but handling large amounts of shooting line requires practice.

FLY RODS

My basic fly rod is a Fenwick fiberglass eight-footer weighing three and a half ounces and taking a No. 6 line. It has a universal action, which means that during casting its strength flows in an even arc from the middle of the rod to the tip. This type of action is the most common and desirable, and a rod with universal action can be used in most fishing conditions. Some other rod actions are the so-called steep action, in which all of the action is in the tip of the rod, and the parabolic action, in which the rod is very soft and has all of its action in the butt.

Quality fly rods have a label just above the grip indicating the line weight recommended by the manufacturer. In most cases the recommended weight is best. If you are selecting a very inexpensive beginner's rod—and there are some good ones that sell for about ten dollars—the rod may not indicate a suggested line weight. You can find the proper weight by bringing the rod to any good sporting-goods store that specializes in fly-fishing equipment. They can easily determine the correct line weight by placing the rod in a specially designed rack that fits over a chart. A weight is put on the rod tip that corresponds with the weight and length of the rod; the tip weight will depress the rod to a spot on the chart that will indicate the proper line weight for that rod. It is a good idea to test any rod you buy, regardless of its quality, for line weight. Sometimes even a high-quality rod will cast better with a different weight line than the one suggested by the manufacturer, and the rod-testing rack will show which weight line will perform best on that particular rod.

You should select your fly rod on the basis of the kinds of flies you will be fishing and the distances you will be casting. My eight-footer is a bit light for tossing big, air-resistant bass bugs all day, and it is a bit heavy for delicately presenting a tiny nymph in a small stream, but it does handle both situations moderately well. I can cast bass bugs for a few hours without needing a brace for my arm the next day, and I use this outfit for bream, trout, shad, and pike, and have even taken a few big carp on it.

If most of your fishing is going to require short casts, about forty feet or less, and you will be using small flies for trout and panfish, pick a rod from six to seven feet long that will take about a No. 4 line. If you are going to fish more often for salmon, bass, or steelhead, you will want a longer, heavier outfit that can cast big flies long distances. For this kind of fishing a rod between eight and a half and nine and a half feet that takes a No. 9 or 10 line is not too heavy.

No single fly rod is suited to all kinds of fishing, but the new rods made with boron fibers combine lightness and strength in such a way that they can be used for a much wider range of fishing conditions than a fiberglass rod. Unfortunately, at this writing, boron fly rods remain very expensive because they use many boron fibers, but if you can afford one, you will have as close to an all-purpose fly rod as has yet been developed.

FLY REELS

The fly rods of Izaak Walton's day had no reels. The line was the same length as the rod and was tied directly to the tip. Even these days, when casting for stocked trout or panfish, the reel used in fly-fishing does little more than store line. But when casting for big trout, steelhead, bass, or shad—fish that are going to make long runs—a well-made fly reel that has a drag mechanism is required.

Fly reels come in a few basic varieties: conventional, single-action reels that take in a set length of line with each revolution of the handle; multiplying action reels that take in two or more set lengths of line with each turn of the handle; and automatic reels that are spring-loaded and retrieve small amounts of line with a flick of the finger. I prefer a good single-action reel with a drag mechanism. Automatics are heavy, and those I've tried have barely enough capacity to hold a fly line and no room for backing. It is also difficult to play a large fish with an automatic reel, and the only time I've found one to be useful is when I'm fishing for small fish, where my casts are very short and where any excess line ends up tangled in the brush or underfoot. There are some automatic fly reels advertised that are claimed to have solved the problems of the older automatic reels, but I have yet to try one.

If you are going to be fishing for large fish such as salmon or steelhead, you will want a multiplying reel that has a two-and-a-half-to-one retrieve ratio. This kind of reel is essential for the quick recovery of line when a big fish rushes the boat, or when after a long upstream run the fish heads quickly downstream.

For most freshwater fishing a good single-action reel with a one-to-one retrieve ratio is fine. The reel should have a drag, which should be set on the light side. I don't use the drag on my reel to tire a fish; I use it to keep the line from overrunning itself when a fish makes a long run and I apply pressure on the line with my hand to tire the fish. A good reel should have easily changeable spools so you can move from a floating to a sinking line, and it should hold at least 100 yards of backing. I have 150 yards of Dacron backing on all my fly reels and have never lost a fish because it took all my line and backing.

LEADERS

In fly-fishing the leader is more important than in other kinds of freshwater fishing. The transition between the line and the fly must be tapered or, when casting, the leader will not straighten out and will drop on the water in coils, the fly on top. When I first started fly-fishing it was in the days when silkworm gut leaders were being replaced by synthetic monofilament. The early monofilament left much to be desired. Most of it was so stiff that it was almost impossible to straighten out. Even soaking it in water didn't help much, and to top it off, the stuff was almost impossible to knot.

Silkworm gut had a few problems of its own. It had to be soaked in water for a few hours before it was usable, and it deteriorated quickly, but gut leaders did have a few nice qualities. When properly soaked and softened, they would cast beautifully and were excellent for floating a dry fly. Gut material also seemed to reflect less light than monofilament. I know a few die-hards who still swear by gut leaders, but it is difficult to find gut in this country and they must be ordered from fly shops in England. The fact is, the modern monofilaments are as good as gut, do not deteriorate, knot well, and can be purchased in a number of colors and shades that reflect little light. I see no reason for going to the trouble to find and use gut leaders.

Today you can purchase relatively inexpensive, knotless, ready-made leaders that are tapered to almost any length and strength. However, most fly fishermen prefer to build their own leaders.

Building tapered leaders is one of those areas in which fly fishermen like to get technical. They pull out their micrometers and start talking in numbers, with statements referring to "6X at .005" and "7X at .004." But it isn't necessary to carry a calculator and micrometer with you to build a fine tapered leader.

First, I'll discuss leader length. Some fishermen claim they use very long leaders, up to sixteen feet or longer. But there are few situations in which a leader that long is necessary, and it's a good thing, because it is difficult to cast with a very long leader. My basic trout leader is about eight feet long, and I find I rarely need one that is longer. When I'm going to fish a fly on a sinking line in very fast water, a shorter leader gives me better control of my fly and is easier to fish deep. For fast water, a five- or six-foot leader is long enough. When fishing a dry fly on a glassy stream I might use a leader that is ten feet long. I have never used a leader longer than about twelve feet and can't imagine a situation in which I would need a longer one. When you build a leader for fishing in very clear water, build one that allows you to make a very gentle presentation. If you can deposit the fly gently on the water with an eight-foot leader, and you find that a leader longer than this makes presenting the fly difficult, stick with the shorter one.

At the beginning of the season I tie a three-foot length of twenty-five-pound-test monofilament to my fly line using a nail knot. This heavy butt section stays on my line all season, and I build different leaders from it using blood knots. These knots are described in Chapter 17, "Knots." I then add about twelve inches of fifteen-pound-test leader, twelve inches of ten-pound test, and then twelve inches of eight-pound test. This gives me a basic leader about six feet long to which I add the length and weight tippet I desire for the kind of fishing I am doing. The tippet is the term used to describe the last length of a tapered leader—the one to which the fly is attached. For readers interested in numbers, the approximate diameters of the sections are, in inches: twenty-five-pound butt section, .018; fifteen-pound second section, .016; ten-pound third section, .014; eight-pound fourth section, .012. These diameters are approximate because different brands of monofilament have different diameters even though the pound test may be the same.

The last, tippet, section of the leader is traditionally expressed with a number and the letter X. For instance, a 1X leader tests at approximately eight pounds, a 2X leader tests at six pounds; a 3X at five pounds; 4X at four pounds; a 5X at three pounds; and a 6X at two pounds. The smallest tippet is an 8X, which equals approximately one-half-pound test. The "X" designation is based on the diameter of the old silkworm gut and is one more confusing technicality in the fly-fishing jargon. I select my tippet on the basis of its pound test and not its X rating.

While my approach to leader building may not be terribly scientific, it works well and I rarely have a leader problem when casting. The thing you should remember when building leaders is that you are creating a gentle taper with gradually decreasing strength and diameter. The heavy butt section, which is attached to the fly line, should be about one-third the length of the entire leader. Some of my fishing companions like to build a very gradual taper and use as many as nine or ten different sections. I don't like that many knots in my leader, since they are potential weak spots, and while the knots do help the leader sink, I prefer to apply a commercial leader-sink solution and have a leader with fewer knots.

There are a few situations in which a level leader is better than a tapered one. When I'm casting a heavy bass bug I use a level, four- or five-foot, ten-pound-test leader. When I'm using a tiny jig on my fly rod for shad, I use a level, five-foot, eight-pound leader and simply lower the jig (dart) over the side of the boat into the current.

FLYCASTING

Every fly rod casts differently from every other one. But with all rods, the line moves in waves or humps as it flows toward the target. These waves are caused by undulations in the rod as it straightens itself. The waves create air resistance on the line, and the fewer the waves the faster and farther the line will travel.

The more flexible the rod the greater the number of waves that will occur during casting. For this reason, soft fiberglass rods with a parabolic action are the most difficult ones to cast with. Fiberglass rods with a universal action cast better, and graphite and boron, which are stiffer still, are the easiest-casting rods.

Flycasting is simpler to learn than to describe. Most of the time a cast longer than about 40 feet is not needed, but for some kinds of fishing, such as for summer steelhead, it may be necessary to toss the fly almost 100 feet to keep from scaring the fish. I would guess that over 90 percent of all the fish I take on flies are hooked on casts of 40 feet or less.

The essentials of flycasting include only two casts; the overhead cast and the roll cast. For the sake of description, I will use the traditional "clock positions" when describing the positions of the rod during the casting. The position when the rod is held parallel to the water is called nine o'clock. The position when the rod is held pointing straight up is called twelve o'clock.

The first thing the beginning flycaster should do is rig up the rod and start trying to cast. You don't have to tie on a leader and fly, just step into the backyard or go to the nearest park and start tossing the line around. The process is natural, and within a few minutes you will get the feel of the rod and develop an understanding of what it means to be casting the line and not a lure as in spinning or baitcasting. There is no way to familiarize yourself with any kind of fishing equipment except by trying it out. You can read about it forever, but you won't have any idea what you are reading about until you have actually tried it.

Once you have tried it, you will immediately realize that flycasting isn't very difficult. By manipulating the rod in almost any fashion, it is easy to throw the line fifteen or twenty feet. As I stated earlier, for most fishing you will rarely need a cast over forty feet, and an understanding of the basics can have you casting forty feet in a few minutes. It really is that easy.

There are three essentials to the basic overhead cast. First, when bringing the rod back, stop the backward movement when your wrist reaches your right ear. At this point the rod should be straight up in the air, the twelve-o'clock position. The tip of the rod will naturally drop back a little as the line straightens out behind you, but the lifting action should stop when the rod reaches the vertical position. You will find it easy to stop the backward motion of the rod if you move your arm in the way that you would if you were trying to throw the line straight up over your shoulder. Many anglers try to throw the line as far behind them as they can, which is a mistake. They should be throwing the line up, not back. Second, start moving the rod forward just as the line straightens out behind you. When practicing this step, you should look over your shoulder and watch the line until you perfect your timing. You will notice that if you wait too long before starting your forward movement, the line will drop. When this happens, your fly will end up hooked to something on the ground behind you. If you start your forward cast before the line straightens out, you will have created a whip of your line and you will snap the fly off the leader. Third, stop the forward motion of the cast abruptly at the ten-o'clock position. The best way to accomplish this is to attempt to bring the line from behind you up into the air over your shoulder. If you try and throw the line forward, the resulting cast will slap very hard on the water. The forward cast is the same as the back cast. You are attempting to throw the line up rather than out.

The roll cast is exactly what the name implies, a rolling out of the line without taking it from the water. This cast is essential when trees or other obstructions make a back cast impossible, and I also use it to bring a sunken line to the surface before making my next overhead cast. The roll cast is difficult to practice anywhere but in water because it is the resistance of the water on the line that makes the cast possible.

In order to make a roll cast you will need about twenty feet of line in the water. To begin the cast, bring the rod back to a position at about one o'clock. With the line now hanging slightly behind and to the side, make a downward thrust of the elbow and a forward snap of the wrist and forearm. This will send a roll of line out across the surface of the water. If the first roll doesn't cast far enough, strip some line from the reel and repeat the cast, but this time release the slack line you have stripped from the reel as soon as the forward motion of the rod reaches the nine-o'clock position. That's all there is to the cast, and it is much easier to do than to describe.

Casting a shooting-head line (ST) requires only a bit more practice than the basic overhead cast. The casting technique is the same as for the overhead cast except that when the cast is released its power carries many feet of shooting line out over the water. When casting a shooting head, work out all thirty feet of fly line by false, or roll, casting, then strip additional shooting line from the reel. The shooting line can be held in loose coils in the line hand or dropped at your feet in loose coils. Make a back cast and a forward cast in the regular way, but as soon as you apply power on the forward cast, release the shooting line. The shooting tapered head will easily pull out thirty feet or more of shooting line.

I enjoy fishing with a shooting head, especially when I'm using big deer-hair bugs for bass. When I'm showing other anglers this technique, I notice that they make far too many false casts before releasing the shooting line. Once the whole fly line is out beyond the tip of the rod, one good back cast is all you need before releasing the shooting line and sending it on its way.

There are two basic methods used to retrieve a fly line and hold it for the next cast. The stripping method is good when making relatively fast retrieves and when large amounts of line are to be retrieved. In this method the forefinger of the hand holding the rod presses the line loosely against the rod grip to keep control. The hand holding the line strips in about two feet of line, making large coils that are draped in the palm of that hand. It is a very natural process and easy to do. The large coils are easily released for the next forward cast.

The other basic line retrieve is popularly called the hand-twist retrieve. It is good for working a fly slowly but doesn't conveniently handle as much line as the strip retrieve. With the hand-twist retrieve, the line is held between the thumb and index finger of the line hand. The remaining three fingers are brought over the line and down, so that the line passes under the little finger. By continuing this motion you will gather a handful of small coils. When you get a handful of small coils you can drop them and continue to collect another. This process sounds much more difficult than it is; just a few minutes of practice will make you proficient in it.

One of the nicest aspects of fly-fishing is that the casting process is just plain fun. I like to watch my line float through the air as the line and leader straighten and the fly drops gently to the water. It is a graceful, gentle process and even people who don't fish (poor souls) will stop to watch an experienced flycaster in action.

Be sure to experiment with your casting and become proficient with sidearm and backhand casts. Once you have the basic overhead cast down pat, the others will be easy. Also, try turning your forearm and wrist to the left or right as the forward cast is ending and you will discover that you can throw a curve to one side or the other. It won't be long before you'll be able to drop your fly exactly where you want it.

The various kinds of flies are discussed in Chapter 12, "Artificial Flies."

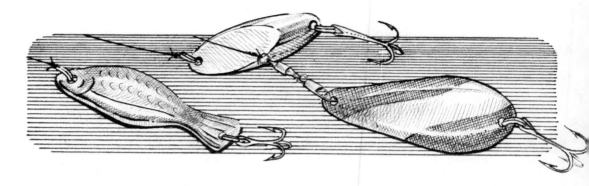

6

Spoons

The story goes that the fishing spoon was invented by the angler who dropped a teaspoon overboard and saw a fish strike it as it fluttered to the bottom. That may be the origin of the name, but the spoon-shaped lure design was developed long before our mythical angler made his discovery. Spoon-shaped fishing lures of bone and ivory have been unearthed by archeologists digging on archaic Indian sites that date back many thousands of years. Of course, those artifacts were equipped with bone hooks, but their shapes are little different from today's metal wobbling spoons.

Spoons are meant to imitate baitfish and can be used to catch every species of freshwater game fish; they come in a wide variety of shapes, sizes, colors, and hook arrangements. There are tiny spoons less than an inch long that are designed for use with ultra-light spinning equipment. At the other end of the scale are spoons over ten inches long weighing upwards of six ounces.

The typical spoon is a tapered, shaped metal blank to which a set of treble hooks is added by means of a split ring. There are far too many variations of this to discuss, but the same basic principles apply to all; anglers are primarily concerned with the size, weight, and thickness of a spoon.

Heavy or thick spoons can be cast long distances, offer little wind resistance, and sink very fast. They are used most often in lakes and in deep rivers with strong currents.

Thin spoons do not cast as far and have the disadvantage of being blown off course when being cast on windy days. They are used for fishing shallow waters and for trolling. Many of the trolling spoons are paper-thin and are designed to dart widely and erratically.

It is important to always use a good-quality, ball-bearing snap swivel when fishing a spoon. All spoons spin in the water, especially when worked quickly, and without the aid of a good swivel the line will become badly twisted in just a few casts. Spinning reels are most vulnerable to bad line twists because, besides the effect of the action of the spoon on the line, there is a built-in twist imparted to the line as it flows off the fixed-reel spool. Baitcasting line will also become badly twisted if a swivel is not used.

While there is a basic action built into each spoon, the angler can greatly vary that action by varying the speed of retrieval and with different rod movements. Spoons are most effective when worked with a slow fluttering action signifying a wounded baitfish. In deep lakes and slow-moving rivers the spoon should be allowed to sink before the retrieve is started. Many times a fish will take the spoon while it is sinking, and by allowing the spoon to sink on a tight line the fisherman can feel these strikes. In waters without many obstructions it is possible to let the spoon sink all the way to the bottom and retrieve it slowly just off the bottom. If no fish are found near the bottom, it is a simple matter to vary the sinking time and speed of retrieval to cover different depths until the fish are located.

The size and general shape of a spoon should represent those of the common forage fish in the particular body of water being fished. Color and surface finish can also be important. In very clear water on a bright sunny day, a spoon with a bright silver or gold finish may actually scare the fish. My general rule is to use bright spoons on cloudy days and in discolored water, and duller finishes and darker colors on bright days or in very clear water. For instance, I have taken some excellent smallmouth bass out of crystal-clear streams using a coal-black spoon. A shiny spoon sent the fish for the nearest cover. When fishing waters where silver-colored baitfish are common, I have found that spoons with a genuine silver plate will outfish chrome- or nickel-plated models. Silver plate produces a white flash that is almost identical to that made by forage fish such as smelt, and while these spoons are both difficult to find and comparatively expensive, they are well worth the investment.

Spoons of brass and copper are usually covered with varnish to attract fishermen while on display in the store. I have found that taking off the varnish with nail polish remover will gradually dull and darken the spoons in the air. These tarnished spoons can be extremely effective in clear water, and their flash is easily restored when necessary by using a polishing cloth.

Although the traditional way to fish a spoon is to cast it out and retrieve it at various speeds, there are times when jigging with a spoon is much more effective than casting. Many thick, solid, Hopkins-type spoons are made for jigging and have no action when retrieved in the traditional manner. These spoons should be fished straight down, lifted, and allowed to flutter back down. They can be very effective when fishing deep water, and have the advantage of not requiring heavy trolling equipment to be fished deep.

One of the most effective lures for fishing weed-choked waters is the Johnson weedless spoon. This spoon has a single weedless hook, to which most anglers add a piece of pork rind or a plastic worm. The Johnson spoon can be cast right into holes in the weeds and be allowed to settle right to the bottom without becoming badly tangled. It can also be crawled right over the tops of the thickest vegetation. Johnson-type weedless spoons come in many sizes and colors and are extremely effective for any species of gamefish that inhabit weedy waters. The secret is to fish them very slowly, the slower the better.

When using a spoon don't be afraid to experiment. Vary the speed of your retrieve, lift the rod tip to give the spoon a darting action, and try allowing the spoon to sink around weedbeds and other obstructions before starting your retrieve. In rivers, try casting directly upstream to work the bottoms of deep pools, or cast across stream and let the spoon flutter in the current as you work it around obstructions. It will take a little experimenting to learn the best sizes and shapes of spoon for the fish you're seeking, but once you learn to fish them, you will find spoons to be among the most versatile of all artificial lures.

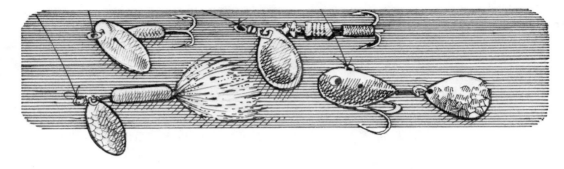

7

Spinners

Spinners are lures that consist of a blade attached to a central wire shaft with a clevis—a U-shaped piece of metal with a hole in each end of the U that allows the blade to spin as the lure is retrieved. Spinners are not new; many of the older models were designed to be fished in front of a snelled hook on which a bait, usually a minnow, was impaled.

Modern spinners are most often used without bait, and they come in a wide variety of sizes and blades. Spinners with round blades, called Colorado, Hoosier, Indiana, or June Bug spinners, rotate at almost a right angle to the wire shaft and provide extreme water resistance. They work best in streams with a slow current, or in lakes and ponds. In streams with a fast current these water-resistant blades will pull the lure out of the water. Long narrow blades like the Willow Leaf, Rhythm, or Swedish Swing styles provide minimum water resistance and can be used in fast water or fished deep in lakes.

Most of the blades on spinners are polished gold or silver, but they can be painted any color, and dull copper, and dull brass, and mother-of-pearl are also popular. Spinners also come equipped with metal bodies that add weight and flash, and many have colored beads or other attractors on the shaft. The various types and styles are too numerous to classify.

The blade on a good-quality spinner starts revolving the instant the retrieve is started. Poorly made and designed spinners have to be twitched into motion and retrieved rapidly to keep the blade turning. When buying spinners it is worth paying the extra money for good quality ones. Cheap spinners simply don't work well. The blades don't spin, have a tendency to get tangled in the line, and become more of a hindrance than an attractor.

Spinners come in sizes from tiny one-half-inch models to large, long lures that weigh over two ounces. The smaller sizes are excellent for stream fishing for trout and smallmouth bass, and in ponds for panfish. The larger sizes are used for large game fish such as pike, bass, and muskellunge.

Spinners attract fish by the flash of their revolving blade and by their underwater vibrations. They differ from spoons in several ways. First, in order to keep the blade revolving, a spinner must be fished with a constant retrieve and cannot be fished erratically like a spoon. Second, each different shape of spinner must be retrieved at a different rate of speed, and just fast enough to keep the blade turning. Finally, a spinner cannot be jigged like a spoon.

When a spinner is being used to fish a river or stream, it should be cast across or slightly downstream. Spinners cannot be fished directly upstream like wobbling spoons, because without constant tension on the line they lose all their action. They are most effective when held in the current, where their water resistance allows them to be worked deep and slow around rocks, downed trees, and other obstructions.

In lakes, spinners with round blades can be easily fished in shallow water or over the tops of submerged weeds, where a spoon or crankbait would become snagged. For fishing deep in lakes, spinners with longer, thin blades can be fished slowly and more deeply than those with round blades. The water resistance of round-bladed spinners tends to bring them to the surface when they are retrieved.

Spinners such as the Mepps and Panther Martin are among the most popular. They come in a variety of sizes and are most effective when the water is slightly discolored and the fish are finding their food more by sound than sight. In clear water, the same color rules apply to spinners as to spoons: those with dull copper, brass, or painted black blades are more effective than those with shiny blades, which will actually scare the fish. Spinners are very effective in late spring when the baitfish fry have grown to a length of about an inch, and if there are many small baitfish a shiny lure may be productive, even in clear water.

Many spinners, like the popular Rooster Tail, have a treble hook dressed with bucktail or hackles. These lures are often much more effective than those with plain hooks. Sometimes it helps to add a minnow, a piece of nightcrawler, or a triangle of cut bait to the treble hook of a spinner. A large Rooster Tail fished with a large dead minnow hooked through both lips with one of the hooks is often better for big bass, pickerel, and pike than either the lure or minnow fished by itself.

Most of the time spinners are used for casting, but they can also be trolled. In northern lakes, just after the ice goes out in the spring, almost any of the popular spinners can be trolled near the surface for trout and landlocked salmon. Color or finish doesn't seem to make much difference in the early spring, and I like to use lures with slender Willow Leaf blades because they offer less resistance in the water and are much easier to troll at different speeds.

When the waters warm and many species of fish go deep, many trollers prefer the popular Davis or Webertroll spinners. These rigs come in a variety of sizes and are composed of series of blades and glass beads strung on a wire leader. Some trolling rigs are constructed with six or more large blades and require the use of heavy tackle and lead-core line because of the extreme water resistance of the blades. These rigs are frequently trolled at depths of eighty feet and more. At such depths there is little flash generated by the spinners because there is very little light, and the lures probably attract fish by their vibration. The blades are used as fish attractors and are strung ahead of a long leader, at the business end of which is a wobbling spoon, crankbait, minnow, or piece of cut bait.

Spinners have proven to be very effective lures, but most of the time they must be worked deep to be effective. This means more fish, but it also means lost lures because the treble hooks of most spinners catch very easily on snags. Unfortunately, these small hunks of metal are expensive, and if you find that you are losing many, you should consider making your own. Many companies sell kits containing all the parts needed to build your own spinners. Quality sporting-goods stores carry these kits or will be able to give you the address where you can send for them. Most of the kits sell for under twenty dollars and contain enough parts to make about 100 lures. This puts the cost of the individual lures at less than twenty cents each, while the same commercially produced spinners often sell for almost two dollars each. Making spinners is easy and enjoyable, and well worth it if you are losing many lures.

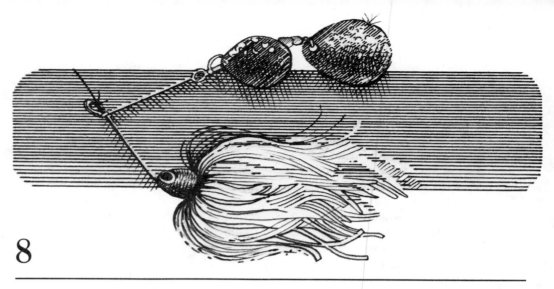

8

Spinnerbaits

Take the blade of a spinner, add a jig, and you have a spinnerbait, one of the very best all-around lures for largemouth bass. At times they are also excellent for pike, and in smaller sizes they can be effectively used for panfish.

Spinnerbaits differ from ordinary spinners in that they are rigged on a safety-pin wire that separates the blade from the jig. The first lure of this design was introduced in the 1940s and was called the Howser Helldiver. Many other spinnerbaits followed as the lure gained in popularity, and today there are literally dozens of different combinations of spinners and jigs. They range in size from tiny, one thirty-second of an ounce panfish models to those weighing over two ounces.

In a spinnerbait, the spinner blade is attached to one end of the bent safety-pin wire. The other end of the wire is molded into the head of the jig. The line is tied at the bend of the safety-pin. Spinnerbaits may have from one to three blades, which may be in line on a single wire or attached to two wires that extend from the eye. The jig bodies may be adorned with feathers, bucktail, rubber or plastic skirts, or plastic split-tail grubs.

Baitcasting or medium-weight spinning tackle is required to fish the larger spinnerbaits because of their weight and water resistance. The methods of their presentation are many. One of the most effective techniques for bass is called "buzzing." Buzzing requires retrieving the lure fast enough to keep the blade running just on or under the surface of the water. Some spinnerbaits are designed for buzzing only and will immediately rise to the surface when retrieved, but any spinnerbait can be worked on or near the surface if it is retrieved at a fairly rapid rate. Buzzing is most productive in warm summer waters when done around cover such as weedbeds, brush piles, stumps, or any structure that might hold bass. You should not be hesitant to toss your spinnerbait into thick cover. As long as it is moving, it is almost snagless.

Spinnerbaits used for buzzing should be "tuned" to keep them from rolling over as they are moved through the water. If a new bait doesn't run true, the wire with the spinner blade should be bent so that it is centered with the point of the hook. If the lure still rolls over, bend the wire in the opposite direction from the roll until it runs properly.

Buzzing a spinnerbait is easy and fun. I cast my lure beyond the obstruction I suspect harbors a bass and begin my retrieve the instant the lure touches the water. I keep my rod tip high and, as the lure passes the obstruction, slow it down for an instant and then resume my retrieve. There is no doubt when bass hit a buzzed spinnerbait; they do so with authority. If a wake appears behind the bait, don't slow your retrieve. Keep it moving at the same rate of speed, and hang on.

Another effective way to fish a spinnerbait is to buzz it over the tops of weeds, but to stop the retrieve and allow the lure to settle into holes or pockets in the weeds. The fish will often hit the lure as it flutters down into the opening.

In cooler water the lure can be fished at different depths by varying the speed of the retrieve. It can be moved steadily through the water or, in deep water, allowed to fall to the bottom, pumped, and allowed to fall again. How fast you pump the lure and how far you let it fall are decisions with which you must experiment. A slower retrieve is usually best in discolored or cold water, while warmer or clear water usually calls for a faster retrieve. For this kind of pump-and-drop fishing I prefer a spinnerbait with a single blade because it has less water resistance and is easier to work slowly than lures with two or more blades.

When water temperatures get very cool, below about 50°F, spinnerbaits should be fished slowly and deep for big bass. They are an excellent cold-water bass lure when the fish are suspended over submerged islands, old creek beds, or in the tops of standing timber. Under these conditions, I retrieve the lure with a very slow pumping action that barely moves it forward as it falls. It is necessary to keep a tight line because in cold water the strike of a bass can be nothing more than a faint tap on the line.

When fishing around fallen trees, try and work your spinnerbait in the same direction in which the limbs of the tree are pointing. It will easily pass over limbs as long as it is moving and won't hang up as much as it will if fished against the grain of the tree. Always be prepared for a strike after your spinnerbait bounces off a limb or other obstruction.

When fishing very heavy cover, try making a few casts to the clear edges of the cover before tossing the spinnerbait into the brush. The vibrations from these lures will often draw a fish from the cover, making it easier to fight and land the fish than if it was hooked in the middle of the brush.

Spinnerbaits are quite versatile lures that can be fished at all seasons and under all water conditions. At any time of the year, any color spinnerbait might work. I prefer yellow or chartreuse in discolored water, and white or green under clear, bright conditions. If I had to pick a single color, however, I would stick with solid black. It is also important to remember that there is no single most effective way to use these lures. The best approach for each fishing day is to let the fish tell you what they prefer. Don't spend hours using the same technique if it isn't producing. Vary the color of your spinnerbait, change from a single- to a double-blade lure, and try adding a pork rind or plastic worm to the hook. Most important, vary your retrieve. Crawl the lure over the bottom, buzz it on the surface, and run it at the mid-depths. Don't get into a rut and forget to experiment.

There are times when you will get skunked using a spinnerbait, just as with any other lure, but these lures are among the most consistent bass producers. Knowledgeable bass fishermen never leave home without a few in their tackle box, and when other lures aren't producing, a spinnerbait frequently will.

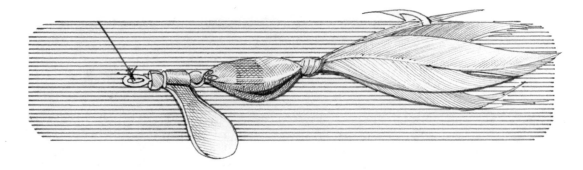

9

Jigs

Jigs are single-hook lures consisting of a lead head that is molded around a hook with a turned-down eye. The heads come in many different shapes including flat, round, and tapered, and weigh from as little as one thirty-second of an ounce to over three ounces or more. Many have a skirt of fur, feathers, or plastic, and some are plain-hooked for use with bait or plastic worms or grubs. The variety of jigs and their colors is virtually unlimited.

The jig is one of the most versatile of all lures. I find it remarkable how few anglers use them, but those who do know that there is no species of freshwater game fish that can't be taken on a jig.

These lures have no built-in action of their own; it is up to the angler to add the action using the rod and the speed of the retrieve. A jig can be bounced along the bottom, crawled through weeds, and will swim through the water at almost any depth, depending upon the speed of the retrieve. It can also be used on the surface over weeds with a plastic worm or a pork rind, and many jigs are designed with a weedless hook for this purpose. The beauty of these lures is that they cast easily, and with a single lure you can cover the same water you can with a spinner, spinnerbait, plug, or spoon. The jig can also be worked to imitate almost any kind of forage fish at any depth, and is the closest thing to the universal lure.

Each of the different-shaped jig heads, and there are dozens, is designed for a different purpose. Most designs are created to attract the angler more than the fish, and there are actually only two real differences in shape; round or flat.

Round- or bullet-headed jigs are general-purpose lures. They sink quickly and for this reason are used for deep fishing or when the angler wants the lure to swim through the water at a particular depth determined by the speed of the retrieve. Flat-headed jigs sink more slowly than round- or bullet-headed ones and are designed for swimming near the surface or at medium depths when seeking suspended fish. On the bottom, the flat-headed jig will skim over rocks and many other obstructions. When at rest on the bottom, the head stands on its flattened underside with the bend of the hook pointing straight up. This hook position makes the flat-headed jig an excellent choice for use with minnows or other natural baits. It also displays a hair or feather body slightly off the bottom where it can easily be seen by the fish.

Tapered jigs are commonly called darts and are used most often for shad fishing. Readers interested in shad darts are referred to Chapter 39, "Shad."

Jigs have long been dressed with a variety of materials ranging from feathers and fur to plastic and shiny strips of Mylar tape. When bottom fishing, I favor jigs with marabou feathers, which have a "breathing" action and expand and compress as the jig is hopped and stopped. When I am going to use a jig with a swimming action near the surface, or at medium depths, I prefer one dressed with bucktail or barred rock hen feathers.

When jig-fishing it is essential to learn how to keep a tight line when the jig is sinking. Many strikes come at this time, and if there is too much slack line, the fish will inhale and reject the lure before the angler realizes he has had a strike. To maintain line control, raise the rod tip at the completion of the cast, then lower it while very slowly reeling in slack line as the jig sinks. The same effect can be had by lowering the rod at a rate that matches the sinking speed of the jig. This is easiest with heavier jigs, and the round-headed jigs will sink much faster than the flat-headed ones. After a few casts you will get the feel and timing of the sink, the timing being essential. Most strikes on a sinking jig are no more than a faint tap or a hesitation in the sinking speed of the jig. Once you have the feel and timing of the sinking rate of your jig, strikes will become obvious.

A good way to slow the sinking rate of a jig is to use a slightly lighter jig on a slightly heavier line. Another way to reduce the sinking rate is to add a minnow, nightcrawler, or pork strip to the jig. If you use a light line with a heavy jig, you will find it difficult to keep the lure from dropping to the bottom like a stone. On the other hand, a heavy line with a very light jig will make it sink much slower and makes line control difficult. I use six- to eight-pound-test line with jigs up to about one-half ounce, and ten- to seventeen-pound-test line with heavier jigs.

Light jigs are fished best with a long, light spinning rod. For heavy jigs fished in deep water I prefer baitcasting equipment, but that is my choice and, with practice, you can use almost any weight or type of equipment to fish any size jig.

When casting, it isn't necessary to impart a lot of action to the jig. Many times, simply lifting the jig from the bottom and letting it fall back is the best way to work it. I believe this bottom-hopping action closely resembles that of a crawfish to many species of game fish. Slowly crawling a jig over a bottom with few obstructions can also be very effective, and I have taken some big walleyes by still-fishing a jig-and-minnow combination.

I like to use a bobber or spinning bubble to fish tiny jigs that are too small to cast without some additional weight. The bobber will hold the jig at a fixed depth where it can be worked very slowly with slight twitches of the rod. Spinning bubbles can be partially filled with water to make them sink slowly, allowing the jig to be worked at medium depths at a crawl. The tiny jig-and-bobber combination is excellent for crappie and bream, and can also be very productive for walleyes in the weeds.

Many anglers buy unpainted jigs of various weights, tie on their own body materials, and paint the heads with their favorite colors. I enjoy painting my own jigs with quick-drying enamel paint. I usually stick with white, black, yellow, and brown, and if I had to pick one color, black would be my choice.

The weight of the jig I select usually depends on the depth of the water and the fish I am seeking. It is easier to control a heavier jig in deep water, but a large jig does not always take big fish. For example, while fishing the St. Lawrence River in New York State one weekend, looking for smallmouth bass, I was using a quarter-ounce black jig tipped with a piece of nightcrawler and bouncing the rig off rocky ledges in about twelve feet of water in a spot where I had taken many smallmouths. That day I didn't catch a single bass, but I couldn't miss with pike. They would take the small black jig as it was falling and I caught them one after another, the largest going over ten pounds. The tiny jig hooked the pike lightly in the upper lip and I had a fine time playing and releasing them without having to take the fish from the water. I have taken many large pike, walleyes, and bass on very small jigs, and my general rule is to use the smallest jig that still gives me good control of my line.

In some ways jigs are like spoons. A spoon that sinks slowly and flutters as it drops will ordinarily take more fish than one that plunges to the bottom. The same is often true with a slow-sinking jig, the exception being under warm summer conditions when the fish may prefer fast-moving lures. Sometimes in the summer heat I will do best using a round-headed jig that drops quickly.

Every angler should carry an assortment of jigs in his tackle box and should learn to use them. When your favorite crankbait, spinnerbait, plastic worm, or spoon isn't producing, try a jig. If you give it the same chance to produce as you do your other lures, it will produce just as well, and many times even better.

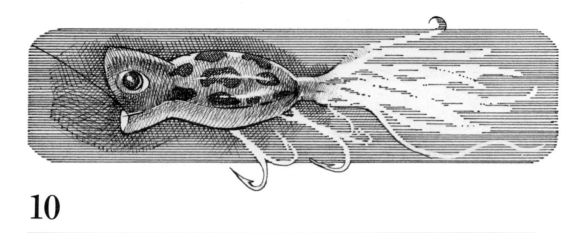

10

Plugs

Plugs are lures that run on top of or through the water at various depths; they generally resemble minnows, crawfish, frogs, or other forage. All have an eyelet at their head for attaching the line, and most are equipped with from one to three sets of treble hooks. Plugs vary greatly in size, shape, and weight, coming in sizes from tiny one-eighth-ounce ultra-light spinning models barely an inch long to eight-inch-long or longer models weighing over three ounces.

Plugs also come in a wide range of colors and finishes. The newer photo-finish models are extremely accurate representations of popular forage fish; but while they are very appealing to the angler, I haven't found them more productive than the older, surrealistic models. Today, nearly all plugs are made on plastic-injection molding machines that turn out solid and hollow models, with some of the latter having sonic chambers or sound cavities filled with splitshot that rattle as the lure is moved through the water. A few wood plugs are still made, but they are becoming harder to find and many are now considered collector's items.

There has been extensive research into fishing lures. Soon to come, if you believe some equipment manufacturers, are lures that will be able to seek out preselected water temperatures, finding the water with the correct temperature for a particular species of fish. When the lure reaches this water, it will release a dose of fish pheromones (hormones) that will, theoretically, drive any fish in the area into a feeding frenzy. Biologists have already developed chemicals that will attract fish from dozens of yards away, and primitive sonic lures have been improved to the degree that they can now give off vibrations almost identical to those made by a fleeing or injured baitfish. Perhaps it is inevitable that some basement genius will eventually develop a lure that can find a fish, pursue it, hook it, and bring it back to the angler. This electronic retriever will probably be called Rover or Spot.

There are three basic types of plugs: topwaters, floater-divers, and subsurface plugs, which are popularly called crankbaits.

TOPWATER PLUGS

As their name implies, topwater plugs float at the surface of the water, and their retrieval creates a disturbance on the surface that attracts fish. This disturbance is a result of the shape of the plug head, various attachments such as propellers at the head or tail of the plug or both, and the action given the plug by the angler. Among the most popular topwater lures are the chuggers and poppers, the wobblers, stickbaits, and propeller lures.

The chugger is actually the name of a specific lure, but most bass fishermen use this name for any plug that has a cup-shaped mouth and a tapered body. The popper is a chugger with a wider mouth. Many are equipped with rubber skirts on the tail hook and are designed to represent a frog swimming on the surface. These lures make a loud "pop" when jerked through the water. With a little practice you can make these concave-faced lures chug, pop, gurgle, and dart from side to side in a multitude of routines.

All surface lures should be cast near likely cover and allowed to sit, especially when you're looking for bass. How long you let the lure sit depends on your patience, but many of my biggest largemouth bass have hit the lure after it had been lying motionless for more than a minute. If you have the patience, allow the lure to sit for a minute or longer. If you don't get a strike, reel the slack out of your line and give the lure a gentle nudge, just enough to barely move it. If nothing happens, give a sharp jerk with the rod that makes the lure chug or pop, and then let it sit quietly again. Remember, no matter how the lure is designed, you're trying to make its action look like that of a frog or an injured baitfish, or the struggles of some other creature that has fallen into the water. If you still don't get a hit, try reeling it just fast enough to create a surface wake, then stop, chug the lure, and let it sit quietly. It really pays to experiment. One of my fishing friends discovered that, at times, reeling in a surface lure almost as fast as possible really turns the bass on. When I first saw him fishing a topwater that way I thought he had tired of casting and was fooling around. Then he hooked a nice bass. I kidded him about the technique, but a few casts later he took another, even bigger bass. I stopped kidding him and tried it myself. I took some very nice bass and that technique has since worked many times for me when slowly moving the lure has produced nothing.

Pickerel and muskies like a topwater lure that is jerked or popped loudly and then allowed to slow down, but not stop. They will often turn away from a lure that stops moving.

Jerk plugs—very large topwaters used exclusively for muskies—are discussed in Chapter 32, "Muskellunge."

Stick plugs are cigar-shaped lures with no built-in action. They rely completely on the skill of the angler to make them appealing to a fish, and the methods of working them are limited only by your imagination.

Wobblers are lures with a pronounced side-to-side action. The most popular of these lures are the Jitterbug and the Crazy Crawler. These lures should be retrieved at a constant speed that brings out their best action. The fish find them by their vibrations as well as by sight, and for that reason they are excellent for night topwater fishing.

Propeller lures are skinny stickbaits with a propeller at either or both ends. They should be pulled through the water in short bursts that are fast enough to keep the propellers turning. For bass they should be retrieved with a jerk-pause-jerk action; for pickerel and muskies, with a continual jerking motion with no long pauses.

Topwater lures are ordinarily most effective when fished around weedbeds and other comparatively shallow structures, but I have taken some big bass by working these lures in deep water. I've done best at dawn, dusk, and night, and the best deep-water locations I've found are adjacent to rocky points or on the deep sides of dropoffs near shallow flats with heavy aquatic growth. These same deep areas can be fished with topwaters on a day that is heavily overcast or even when it is clear if the wind is blowing hard enough to make some real waves. In fact, any day you aren't having any luck with traditional daytime lures, it doesn't hurt to tie on a topwater and give it a go. Sometimes, when conditions indicate that the bass should be lying in deep water because it is clear, sunny, and hot, a topwater lure will take them when nothing else seems to work.

FLOATER-DIVERS

Floating-diving plugs float when not being moved. They have short, slanting bills that cause them to run beneath the surface when retrieved. The depth at which they run depends on the size of the slanted bill and the speed at which

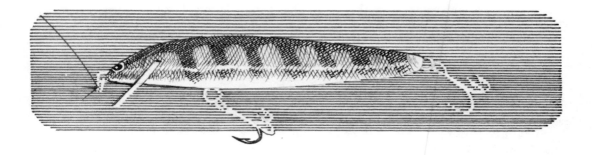

they are retrieved. My favorite floater-divers are the jointed Rapala, Bagley's Bang-O-Lure, and the Heddon Cobra, all of which come in a variety of sizes and colors. I prefer floater-divers that are about five inches long and have three sets of treble hooks and a bright silver finish.

Floating-diving lures are particularly good for spring and fall conditions when you need a shallow-running lure that can be worked quickly around standing timber, shallow man-made structures, and along shallow weedbeds. When retrieved at a steady speed, they run just under the surface and wiggle seductively. When moved with fast sweeps of the rod, they dart frantically and produce vibrations that can be felt right down the rod into your hands. This fast retrieve is sometimes an excellent way to take big northern pike.

Floater-divers can also be used as topwater lures. If twitched gently, they will stay in almost one spot. This makes them an excellent choice for fishing inlets and holes in the weeds, but you have to be a good caster for this kind of fishing because a cast that is off the mark will usually collect three sets of treble hooks full of weeds. One way to avoid the weed problem is to make short casts into the open pockets and work the lure until you're sure you aren't going to get a strike. Then point the rod at the lure, take up all the slack line, and give the lure a full overhead jerk to one side. The lure will usually be flipped right over the boat into the open water on the deep side. Obviously this is not the way to work a lure when you're fishing with a companion, and you must be certain to flip the lure to one side so you don't hook yourself in the process.

An excellent way to fish a floater-diver for walleyes is to add a fixed weight, just heavy enough to sink the lure, about eighteen inches above it. This allows the lure to be suspended in the water and worked very slowly. Although this rig can be a bit cumbersome to cast because the sinker will occasionally get tangled with the lure, it is an excellent way to take walleyes in shallow water and bass over moss beds.

Some floater-divers have an extra-long lip, which increases the angle and depth of their dive. If worked quickly, they can reach depths of five or six feet. An effective way to fish these lures is to cast beyond some underwater obstruction such as a stump or a rock pile, then to reel fast enough to bring the lure to the bottom near the obstruction, stop reeling, and let the lure begin to float up toward the surface. The lure is then twitched to keep it deep, and a fast retrieve is resumed away from the obstruction. Many times when the lure stops and starts to float up, or when it quickly moves away, a fish will rush from the obstruction and grab it.

SUBSURFACE PLUGS

Sinking plugs or crankbaits come in as many varieties, sizes, shapes, and colors as any of the artificial lures. The science of subsurface baits has developed lures designed to run at specialized depths. As an example, Rebel produces crankbaits that run at depths of from zero to two feet all the way to over fifty feet, and at every depth in between, at two-foot intervals. I find it remarkable that with only a half-dozen lures the angler can fish from literally the top to the bottom of a lake fifty feet deep.

I prefer the "countdown" method when fishing sinking plugs. Suppose the top of the weedbed is twelve feet deep and I want my crankbait to run just over the top of it. I cast beyond the weedbed and let the lure sink for a count of twelve seconds before retrieving it. I find that many of my sinking plugs fall at a rate of about one foot per second, but each is slightly different. If my lure catches in the weeds after sinking for twelve seconds, I reduce the count on the next cast to about nine or ten seconds. Once I find the count that allows the lure to pass over the top of the weeds without getting fouled, I fish the top and the sides of the weedbed.

Many anglers cast their sinking plugs and just reel them in. This is an easy way to fish these lures and it can be effective, but I find that it helps if I vary the retrieve with pauses and twitches of the line. As with all artificial lures, experimentation with the retrieve is the key to success with crankbaits. If a steady retrieve isn't producing for you, try working the lure at different rates of speed, add a frantic darting action, or pause and let the lure sit motionless for a few seconds. The way in which crankbaits are retrieved is more important than the choice of lure.

Deep-diving crankbaits with oversized bills are designed for hard, fast fishing and require more than a little energy to work properly. They dive almost straight down with a tight, fast wiggle and nose the bottom, sending up tiny puffs of mud much like a crawfish. Their large bills also have the advantage of allowing these lures to strike objects without becoming snagged. They bounce off stumps and rocks at an angle that resembles that taken by a panicked minnow, and I find that many strikes occur immediately after the lure bounces off some underwater object.

When retrieved steadily, some diving plugs will run as deep as fifteen feet. If you crank the lure back with the tip of the rod in the water, you can even get a few more feet of depth out of it. These deep-running lures are excellent for reaching bass, walleyes, and pike when they are in deep water. I prefer medium-sized deep-divers about three or four inches long. Color doesn't seem important, although I do find myself using dark-colored lures more often than bright ones.

The real deep-divers, many over eight inches long and weighing almost two ounces, are made to be trolled. The beauty of these lures is that they allow the angler to fish at depths of fifty feet or more without the need for using lead-core line or a downrigger. But the plug itself offers a lot of water resistance and must be trolled on a long line to reach its maximum depth, and a fairly stiff rod is necessary to maintain line control and to be able to firmly set the hooks when a fish strikes. These very deep-divers are excellent for going into the depths for summer trout and also for big largemouths in deep-water impoundments.

Many subsurface lures are made with hollow chambers filled with splitshot that give off vibrations as the lure is retrieved. I have found that these rattle-lures work well in muddy or discolored water where the fish are forced to feed by sound more than by sight. In very clear water I have never taken a fish on a rattle-lure. I believe that under very clear conditions these noisy lures scare rather than attract the fish.

There are so many styles and varieties of plugs that it would be almost impossible to own one of each—and if you could, you would need a dozen tackle boxes to carry them all. I don't carry a box full of plugs. I own just a few of the most popular models that I've mentioned; a few surface plugs, floater-divers, and deep-runners. I have become familiar with the actions of these plugs and know how they will run as I retrieve them at various speeds. I believe that knowing how to use a few plugs well is better than having a boxful of lures, many of which run at the same depth and are simply different colors or shapes.

Color and shape have never seemed to make much difference in my experience, and most of my plugs are silver or gold. What is important is the depth and speed at which the lures run best, and my ability to exercise enough patience to carefully and methodically work the various depths until I find the

fish. I'm not saying that there won't be days when a particular species of fish
will strike only a certain lure that is a certain color, but I have found this to be
the exception rather than the rule. When an angler shows me his tackle box
overflowing with lures, I usually assume that he spends all his time changing
lures, looking for the one that is "magic." The fact is, the magic is in the hands
of the fisherman, and a few lures that you know well and can be worked at
different depths are all you need.

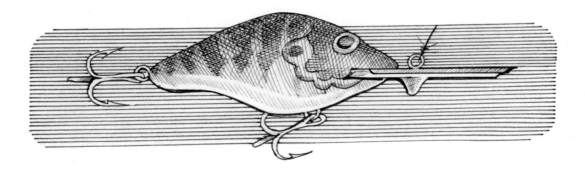

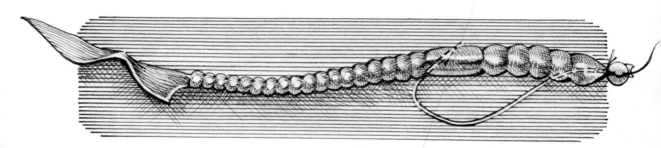

11

Plastic Worms

Plastic lures became popular in the late 1940s. The early models were of comparatively hard plastic, making it difficult to hook fish that took the lure. The plastic lures of today, however, are very soft and pliable; they are molded from liquid plastic, and their degree of softness and flotation is controlled in the manufacturing process. Scents and colors are also molded into these lures.

While worm shapes are the most popular plastic lures, crawfish, salamanders, grubs, and curly-tailed lures that ripple in the water can also be used with good results. The worms come in sizes from barely one inch long to over fifteen inches, but the most popular are the six- to nine-inch lengths.

The manufacturers of plastic worms use plasticizers to keep them soft, and these chemicals can be harmful to some plastic tackle boxes and lures, as well as to the finish on some crankbaits and spoons. If you find that your plastic worms are damaging your tackle box or lures, you can purchase a "worm-proof" box for your plastic baits. Keeping these lures in a plain plastic sandwich bag will also eliminate danger to your tackle box and other lures.

While plastic baits can be used for every species of freshwater game fish, they are most often used for largemouth bass.

There are many ways to rig a plastic worm. Most come without hooks, and while there are models that can be purchased with built-in hooks, usually on a leader with a spinner blade or brightly colored beads for additional attraction, most anglers prefer to rig their own worms.

I prefer to hook my plastic worms using the Texas rig, although some anglers find fault with this method. The Texas rig is simply a matter of passing the hook through the head of the worm and back through the body in such a way that the point and barb of the hook are buried in the worm. I use stainless steel, southern Sproat-style hooks in a 4/0 size for eight-inch worms and a 3/0 size for six-inch worms. Many anglers use slip sinkers above the worm, but I feel I have better control by using a single splitshot attached to the line right at the head of the worm. With all methods of rigging, it is important that the worm be absolutely straight. If it has even a slight bend it will twist as it runs through the water. Hooked Texas-style, the worm is almost snagless and can be fished in heavy weeds, brush, and downed timber.

A variation of the Texas rig is to hook a floating worm in the traditional Texas style, but to add a leader by using a swivel. Above the swivel is added a slip sinker. The advantage of this rig is that the worm will float as far off the bottom as the length of the leader. This is an excellent way to rig a worm when you want to keep it floating off the bottom, such as when you're fishing above a grassy or moss-covered bottom.

Some anglers feel that by burying the point of the hook in the worm many strikes are missed. They use a plain jig head that moves through the water in a hook-upward position and leave the hook exposed after running it through the head of the worm. I don't use this method unless the waters I'm fishing are relatively snag-free, because I find that the exposed hook tends to snag easily. No matter how you rig your plastic worms, there are methods of fishing them that have proven to be very effective.

The first action to consider with a plastic worm is sinking. Because I find that many of my strikes happen on the initial drop of the worm, I always let it drop right to the bottom, on a slack line, before starting my retrieve. I then watch the line carefully. Most strikes that occur while the worm is falling are little more than slight hesitations in the rate of the fall; often, however, a bass will take the worm and head immediately for the nearest deep water. I set the hook with authority at any unnatural action in the sinking rate of the worm. The speed at which the worm sinks can be varied by using a floating worm and adjusting the weight to allow the worm to sink slowly or quickly.

If the fish are not taking the worm on the drop, there are a number of ways to retrieve it. In clear water I find that fish will often turn away from a worm that hops quickly along the bottom. Under clear conditions I allow the worm to sit motionless on the bottom for up to one minute, and then I barely crawl it, a half-inch at a time, along the bottom. It takes patience to work a lure this slowly, but under clear water conditions I have found it to be the best method.

In muddy or discolored water I have my best results by hopping the worm. I do this by twitching the rod tip in such a way that the worm jumps a few inches off the bottom, and I maintain this steady hopping action for the entire retrieve. Sometimes the speed of the retrieve should be varied, and it pays to experiment. Many anglers work a worm too quickly, although there are times when the fish do prefer a worm that is moving quickly through the water.

A Texas-rigged sinking worm without any weight can be very effective when fished over the tops of thick weeds. I like to drag the worm slowly over the tops of the weeds and let it sink into holes and pockets. This technique is effective for walleyes, pike, and pickerel as well as bass. At times a worm fished in a rapid swimming motion over the weed tops or lily pads will result in explosive strikes.

When worm fishing it is essential to watch the line and concentrate on what is happening at the end as the worm sinks or is being retrieved. Converting "taps" into fish can be a problem if you don't concentrate on what is going on at the end of your line. Some anglers let a fish run with the worm, but I find I catch many more fish if I set the hook as soon as possible. It isn't necessary to set the hook with all your strength; this will result in broken lines and lost fish. When setting the hook, I extend my arms and take up slack line, and then reel in and lift the rod with a solid snap. I set the drag on my reel so that it gives grudgingly on the hook set.

The color of a plastic worm usually isn't very important. Blue is my favorite color, but I also use purple, black, and brown. Many days I've taken good fish using a blue worm while my fishing companions were doing as well with red or orange ones. There are times, however, that the fish will show a real preference for a particular color, so it doesn't hurt to carry a variety of colors and change from time to time if the old standbys aren't producing.

Some bass fishermen consider the plastic worm a one-lure arsenal and refuse to use anything else. As with every other lure, there are days when I've been skunked on plastic worms, but they are consistent producers, and there is no doubt that they are among the deadliest bass lures yet developed.

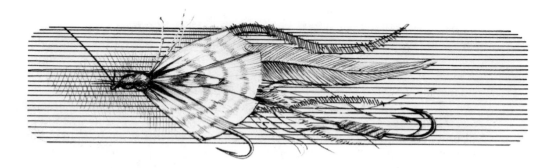

12

Artificial Flies

Artificial flies are bits of fur, feathers, and other materials that are tied on a hook in a fashion representing the insects or minnows that comprise the food of game fish. The general classifications of flies are wet flies and nymphs, dry flies, bucktails and streamers, and bass bugs. Wet flies and nymphs are made to sink below the surface of the water and represent the various subsurface stages of aquatic insects. Dry flies float on the surface of the water and represent terrestrial insects and the adult stage of aquatic insects. Bucktails and streamers represent minnows and other forage fish. Bass bugs represent frogs, moths, or any small creature that falls to the surface of the water.

BUCKTAILS AND STREAMERS

The minnows represented by bucktails and streamers number over 200 known species in North American waters. It is difficult to identify the many species because they often look alike, but almost every body of water contains some species of minnow that constitutes part of the forage of the larger fish in that location. Bucktails and streamers (see the illustration at the opening of this chapter) are tied on long-shanked hooks in sizes ranging from tiny one-half-inch flies to ones over six inches long. The difference between a bucktail and a streamer is that bucktails have wings made of deer hair while streamer wings are made of feathers. Bucktails are more durable than streamers, which have a tendency to get chewed up by sharp-toothed species of fish.

I don't carry a large assortment of bucktail patterns. My preferred colors are brown and white, red and white, red and yellow, and the all-brown Muddler Minnow. For large bass and trout I use these bucktails in sizes from 2 to 6. For small trout and panfish I use sizes 8 to 14.

I tend to use streamers most often for larger fish, and I like those tied with marabou feather wings. When dry, marabou feathers look like a ball of fluff, but in the water they become long and slim and pulsate during pauses in the retrieve. In waters where small yellow perch are a primary forage food, I like to use yellow marabou streamers that have a few barred rock feathers in the wing. If I had to pick a single pattern of streamer, I would select the popular Ghost pattern. I have found the Grey, Green and Black Ghosts to be close to a universal streamer fly pattern, and have taken almost every species of fresh-water game fish on these streamers.

There are some differences in the streamers and bucktails used in the West and the East. Western fly fishermen prefer large, bushy flies, while easterners prefer smaller flies tied very sparsely. But East or West, the methods of presentation are identical.

Fishing bucktails and streamers in fast-water areas of streams and rivers is easiest with a comparatively short leader. The fly should be cast directly across the current and retrieved rapidly. It can be allowed to hang in the current near obstructions or worked rapidly across the surface. The depth at which the fly is worked is determined by the cast. To work the fly deep, cast well above the area to be fished and allow the fly to settle before starting the retrieve. When a trout takes a streamer or bucktail in fast water, it does so with authority and usually hooks itself.

In areas with more moderate currents, the angler has the advantage of being able to slowly fish likely looking locations. As discussed in the chapters on trout, likely obstructions are rocks and logs, undercut banks and ledges, and brush piles. During my first few casts to such locations with a streamer or bucktail, I impart no action to the fly, letting the current take it through the area. Sometimes when the fly finishes its downstream swing and hangs in the current at the end of the drift, a fish that has been following it will strike. After a few casts I start to work the fly, casting to the same area and retrieving the fly with a darting action. If that produces nothing, I will try retrieving the fly very quickly just under the surface of the water. It pays to cast to an area many times, especially if the river holds big brown and rainbow trout. Often a big trout that is not feeding can be tempted into striking if you make many casts to the same location.

When you are wading a river and have finished casting to an area, make a few casts directly downstream before moving to a new location. Wading a stream dislodges aquatic insects from rocks on the stream bottom and frightens minnows, which swim downstream. I have taken big trout by making a few casts directly downstream before moving to a new spot.

One experience with bucktail fishing that I will never forget is of the day I first interested my dad in fly-fishing. Dad had always been a bait fisherman: worms for trout and different-sized minnows for everything else. I took a lot of good-natured kidding from him when I first started fly-fishing, and even after I began to bring home some decent trout, dad still kidded me and maintained that I was adding a worm to my fly.

One warm June day I took him to one of our favorite rivers to show him how trout could be taken on flies. I had planned this trip for a long time, and waited until the fly-fishing conditions were perfect. I didn't want to get skunked and have to suffer more jokes. The spot I picked was a large, deep pool with a huge flat ledge about four feet above the water that extended well into the pool. There was no room for a back cast so I made a roll cast about thirty feet upstream and about two-thirds of the way across the pool. As the fly drifted downstream it was clearly visible from where we were standing. When the line straightened at the end of the drift and the fly hung in the current, two trout rushed at it. In my excitement, I pulled the fly right away from them. Dad had seen the trout and was very interested. On my next cast I hooked a chunky fourteen-inch rainbow and after a nice fight led it to the net. I handed dad the rod and told him it was his turn. It took a few minutes of instruction to show him how to roll cast, but he picked it up quickly and took a nice trout on his third or fourth cast. We kept taking turns and in less than an hour had six nice fish. That did it, and the next day dad came home from work with a fly rod of his own. We did a lot of fly-fishing together after that and it became a standard joke, every time we broke out the fly-fishing gear, to ask each other if we had remembered to bring the worms.

When fishing deep pools and runs I use a sinking line and a longer, lighter tippet that isn't as visible in the slower-moving water. It is often necessary to fish these deeper areas right on the bottom, and I cast almost directly upstream and let the current take the fly deep. When the line reaches a cross-stream position I start my retrieve and give the fly gentle twitches with the rod tip. It is important to keep a fairly tight line when fishing these deep areas because the fish in them often strike with little more than a faint twitch of the line. Deep-fishing a streamer or bucktail is great practice for fishing wet flies and nymphs.

Bucktails can also be fished in lakes and ponds, where they can be cast or trolled. When casting for bass, pickerel, or pike I like to work a big streamer quickly along the outside edges of weedbeds and into inlets and pockets in the weeds. A floating line and a short, stout leader are best for this kind of fishing because you frequently have to be able to pull a big fish out of the weeds. Casting large streamers for bass, pike, and pickerel is a very effective technique that is often overlooked even by experienced fly fishermen.

Streamers and bucktails can also be trolled with good results. I like to troll a four-inch Grey Ghost streamer in northern lakes in the early spring, right after the ice has gone out; in such cool waters, lake trout, rainbows, and land-locked salmon can comfortably pursue smelt and other forage fish near the surface and at the mouths of feeder streams. When trolling a large streamer for spring trout and salmon I use a sinking line and a level, eight-pound-test leader about eight feet long. I have found that I get many more strikes if I work the fly with long sweeps of the rod while trolling at about six miles per hour, or about the speed of a very brisk walk. The fish inevitably strike when the fly hesitates as the rod is dropped back, and they really smack the fly. I find that I miss fewer strikes with a streamer that has tandem hooks. With streamers having a single hook, short strikes can be a problem.

One postscript to fishing bucktails and streamers is that trout feeding actively on flies on either a lake or stream surface will often eagerly take these artificials. There have been many days when I have seen trout taking flies on the surface or nymphs trapped just under the surface film but can't generate a strike on a wet fly, dry fly, or nymph; when I have knotted on a bucktail, however, I have caught a trout on almost every cast. I think that a lot of dry-fly fishermen walk away frustrated on days that would have seen them take some nice fish if they had tried a bucktail or streamer.

WET FLIES AND NYMPHS

There are over five thousand species of insects in North America that spend all or some of their life in water. To the fly fisherman, the most important orders of these insects are the mayflies, dragonflies, stoneflies, caddis-flies, and dobsons. It would be impossible to discuss the life cycles of all of the aquatic insects, but the mayfly has a cycle that is similar to most of the others.

Mayflies (Ephemeroptera) are common to most lakes and streams throughout North America. The adults have four almost transparent wings and two or three long filaments projecting from the rear end of the abdomen. The aquatic nymphs (naiads) have rows of leaflike gills on both sides of their abdomen. The nymphs burrow into the mud or live under rocks where they feed on small plants and animals and organic debris. They may live in the nymph stage for a

few months to as long as three years, depending on the species. When they mature they swim to the surface, shed their skin, and change into a dull-colored flying dun. Most of the mayfly's life is spent in the larval stage. The pupal stage lasts from one day to about two weeks, depending upon the species. I have seen what have looked like millions of mating mayflies swarming above the surface of the water, and piles of dead females inches deep floating on the water after the hatch is complete.

With so many aquatic insects living in our waters, it might seem impossible to determine which artificial fly would best represent whatever the trout are feeding on. But the sheer number and variety of insects is actually a benefit to the angler, for while trout can sometimes be maddeningly selective in their feeding, much of the time they will sample anything resembling an aquatic insect that drifts into their area. I have experimented with different wet flies and nymphs on days when the fishing was good and have taken trout on different flies that were shades of red, black, brown, and gray without changing my position in the river. Most of the time I find that the pattern is not nearly as important as the size and presentation of the fly.

Wet flies were the very first artificial flies, and while there are hundreds of patterns, most fly fishermen find a few that produce consistently and stick with these. My own favorites are traditional patterns and include the Dark and Light Cahill, Olive and Ginger Quill, Quill Gordon, March Brown, Leadwing and Royal Coachman, and the Black Gnat. I have probably taken as many trout on the Cahill patterns as on all the rest combined. My color rule, which is not hard and fast, is to use brown or dark-colored flies in the spring, lighter browns and grays in the summer, and light-colored flies in the fall.

Most of the time I use size 10 or 12 wet flies, although there are times when larger or smaller flies work better. I find that a good way to determine the size of the fly I'm going to start fishing with is to turn over some small stones in the river to determine the sizes of the aquatic insects clinging to the rock bottoms. Another good way to take a sample of the prevalent aquatic life in a stream or river is by using a screen. This technique is described in Chapter 13, "Natural Baits," under aquatic insects. A sample of the aquatic life in a body of water is also a good way to determine the color of the predominant insects. Nevertheless, a change in water temperature of just a few degrees will dramatically change the variety of insects that are maturing and hatching in a given location, and just because a particular size and color of fly are effective on one day does not guarantee that they will be good the next day.

My favorite way of fishing wet flies is what I call the natural drift. I take my casting position opposite the area I suspect holds fish and cast upstream at about a forty-five-degree angle. As soon as the fly hits the water, I drop my rod tip and point it directly at the fly as it sinks and is carried downstream. I slowly tighten the line using a hand-twist retrieve so that the slack is kept to a minimum. I answer any hesitation in the drift of the line by gently lifting the rod tip. It is not necessary to actually strike a fish that has taken a wet fly. Most of the time the fish will hook itself if the line is fairly tight. If the line is too tight, or if I strike aggressively, I inevitably pull the tiny hook right out of the trout's mouth.

It is important to completely fish out each cast. Sometimes the trout will take the fly as it drifts to them; at other times they will follow it and not strike until the line comes tight at the end of the drift and the fly begins to move toward the surface. Often the fish will strike only when the fly has completed its drift and is directly downstream, hanging in the current. I've also taken many trout by slowly retrieving the fly after it has completed its drift, and I have hooked many fish at the very end of the retrieve just when I'm lifting the line to make another cast. It is essential in wet-fly fishing to be prepared for a strike from the moment the fly touches the water until it is lifted from the water for the next cast.

When a natural drift is not producing, I vary my retrieves. A speedy, jerky movement of the fly will often generate a strike, as will a gentle jigging action. Remember, there is a multitude of insect life in every body of water, and the "insect of the day" may have a particular swimming motion all its own. In fly-fishing, as in all other fishing, it pays to experiment with the speed and action of the retrieve.

NYMPHS

I don't pretend to be an expert nymph fisherman, but I do take my share of trout on nymphs. Fishing artificial nymphs became popular in the early 1900s

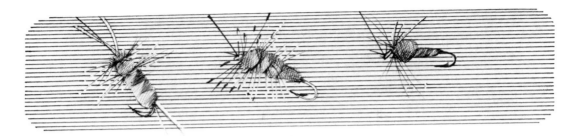

when an Englishman named G. E. M. Skues experimented with, and wrote about, his experiences in fishing these flies.

Nymphs must ordinarily be fished very slowly, almost on the bottom, to be effective. They represent the larval stages of aquatic insects, which crawl along the bottom rather than swim through the water. The only times most nymphs swim through the water is when they are headed for the surface before emerging as adults and mating.

There are at least one hundred different nymph imitations available to the angler. Some look like nothing more than a tiny ball of fur while others are lifelike representations of real aquatic insects. Most nymphs are designed to represent the larval stages of mayflies, caddis-flies, or stoneflies, but the variety and number of aquatic nymphs are so large that the presentation is usually much more important than the pattern of the fly.

In fast water, nymphs can be fished with a natural drift, exactly like wet flies. In slower water, I find the best way to fish them is directly upstream, and this technique requires some practice. When I'm fishing a river where most of the water is less than about six feet deep, I use a floating line and a weighted nymph. In fact, except for very shallow streams, I use weighted nymphs all the time. I cast up and slightly across the stream. As the nymph drifts toward me, I retrieve line fast enough to keep control and minimize the slack in the line. The advantage in using a floating line is that by watching the tip of the line during the drift, I can see strikes that I can't feel. The floating tip of the line acts somewhat like a bobber, and when I see the line twitch or stop, I immediately, but gently, raise the rod tip to set the hook. Because the nymph must drift along the bottom with little or no action, strikes can be difficult to detect. I believe that recognizing a strike when fishing an artificial nymph is as difficult as anything in fishing that I've done.

To help detect strikes, I often use a dry fly as an indicator. I select a heavily tied dry fly that has good floating qualities and attach it to my leader on a six-inch dropper. I like to attach the dropper right at the nail knot that holds the leader to the fly line, but many anglers like to attach the indicator closer to the nymph. The depth of the water should be used to determine where the indicator is attached. Remember, the nymph must be on or very close to the bottom to be most effective. The dry fly acts as a tiny, sensitive, bobber. At times it will disappear quickly beneath the water when a trout takes the nymph. At other times it will just slow down and move a bit more slowly than the flow of the current. Although the nymph may only have bumped a rock or momentarily hung up on an obstruction, I always set the hook immediately when the indicator fly makes an unnatural movement. I've also had the bonus of taking trout on the dry indicator fly.

The reason extreme sensitivity is required when fishing a nymph is that trout continually take many bits of drifting matter into their mouths, sample them, and swallow or reject them. Thus the angler has only a few seconds to set the hook before the trout detects the sham and exhales the artificial fly.

Fishing a nymph in deep water is even more difficult than fishing it in shallow water. In order to reach bottom in deep water a sinking line is necessary, and this precludes the use of an indicator fly. The technique is the same as in shallower water: the fly is cast directly upstream and allowed to tumble along the bottom at the same speed as the current. The rod tip should be pointed at the fly and slack line should be gathered to maintain control. Many anglers like to hold the rod at a forty-five-degree angle to the water and watch the line. I prefer to point the rod directly at the fly as I take in slack line. A strike is usually little more than a brief hesitation in the drift, which is why fishing nymphs in deep water requires a good knowledge of water currents and a sense of judgment of when the fly is drifting naturally and when a trout has taken it. I believe that expert nymph fishermen probably take more trout than anglers using any other technique, but fishing a nymph properly takes real concentration and practice.

DRY FLIES

The techniques for tying and fishing floating flies were developed in the late 1800s by English angler and author Frederic M. Halford. Dry-fly fishing was introduced to North America in 1890 by an angler named Theodore Gordon when he received, upon request, a selection of Halford dry flies.

Dry-fly fishing is comparatively easy because the fly is clearly visible as it floats on the surface of the water, and there is little doubt when a trout takes it. Of course a tiny dry fly fished in fast water is difficult for the angler to see, but the splash of a fish taking that fly is ordinarily easy to see—much easier than detecting a strike when fishing a nymph in deep water.

Dry flies represent mature aquatic insects or terrestrials such as grasshoppers or crickets that have fallen into the water. Except when the trout are feeding

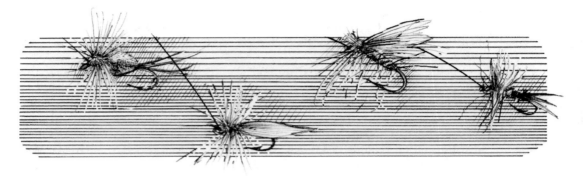

very selectively, it is the size of the fly, its presentation, and how it floats on the water that are of primary importance. The exact fly pattern is usually of secondary importance.

When presenting a dry fly a delicate cast is essential if the surface-feeding fish are not to be put down. This delicacy is achieved through good casting techniques and a rod, line, and leader that are properly balanced. It is possible to use a level fly line when very short casts are needed, but for most dry-fly fishing a tapered floating line will facilitate a delicate presentation. Forget about trying to fish a floating fly with a sinking line; after a very short drift the fly will be pulled under the surface by the weight of the line.

A properly tapered leader is also necessary for the delicate presentation of a dry fly. The building of a tapered leader is discussed in Chapter 5, "Fly-fishing Tackle." I ordinarily use a leader that is about the same length as my rod, but when the water is very clear, a leader as long as twelve feet will sometimes be necessary to keep from scaring the trout. The tippet of the leader should be as light as is convenient and comparatively long. I use a three-foot tippet for most of my dry-fly fishing, and prefer from about two- to four-pound test depending on the size of the fly and the clarity of the water.

While the line and the fly must float, the tippet of the leader must sink when fishing a dry fly because a floating tippet casts a shadow. Rubbing mud on the tippet will cause it to sink, but I am a firm believer in any of the commercial leader-sink preparations. Many of these preparations come in a tiny bottle with a brush built into the cap, which makes their application easy. Leader-sink solutions should also be used on wet flies and nymphs to assure that they sink as soon as they hit the water.

It is also important to keep the fly floating high and dry. When I first started using dry flies, this was a problem. I tried following instructions for mixing gasoline and wax to make a fly floatant, and the resulting concoction left a lot to be desired. Today there are many commercially prepared dry-fly floatants.

My favorite is a preparation that contains silicone and comes in a small, very convenient spray can. This floatant dries almost instantly and makes a fly almost unsinkable.

I fish a dry fly by casting it up and slightly across the stream so that the line and leader will not pass over the area to be fished. In many ways dry flies are fished exactly like nymphs, being allowed to drift naturally at the same speed as the current. The difference, of course, is that the line and the fly are floating on the surface rather than along the bottom of the stream. Effective dry-fly casting requires a knowledge of water currents so that each cast will allow the fly the longest possible drag-free drift.

Most of the time the fish will respond to a dry fly only if it is floating naturally at the same speed as the current, but sometimes trout—and Atlantic salmon in particular—will rush to a fly that is dragging across the surface; however, this is an exception. A drag-free drift can be difficult, especially when casting across currents that are moving at different speeds. The popular technique used to help assure a drag-free drift is called "mending." Mending is simply throwing a loop of line in the direction of the floating fly. It is actually a partial roll cast and its purpose is to create enough slack line to allow the fly to continue its natural, drag-free drift. There is no way to describe the many different kinds and speeds of currents you will encounter; only experience and observation will teach you how to properly mend your line to give you the longest natural drift. But before you start casting, study the currents to determine where you should stand in order to be casting across currents that are nearly equal in speed.

I haven't found it necessary to have a boxful of different patterns for successful dry-fly fishing. My favorite patterns are traditional: the Light Cahill, Ginger Quill, Adams, Royal Coachman, and Black Gnat. I also have a selection of bivisibles, which are flies that have a body completely covered with hackle feathers. These heavily hackled flies are excellent floaters, and I like to use them in fast water where flies with less hackle have a tendency to get dragged under the surface by the heavy current.

I use sizes 10 to 16 for most of my dry-fly fishing, although I do carry a few No. 18 and 20 flies for days when the fish are taking tiny natural midges. Fishing a tiny dry fly is difficult because it is hard to see the fly on the water, and the light tippet required for tiny flies is very fragile. Moreover, a good-sized fish hooked on a tiny fly requires skillful handling if it is eventually to be brought to net. I also carry a few flies that represent terrestrial insects. The Hornberg pattern is an excellent grasshopper representation and I also use small ant and beetle patterns, which frequently produce well after a summer rain that washes terrestrials into the stream.

It can be difficult to tell if the trout are taking insects from the surface of the water. There have been many days when the area I'm fishing will have many flies on the surface of the water and trout rising everywhere, but on which I'm unable to get a rise on a floating fly. Sometimes during an insect hatch the trout will be feeding on nymphs as these struggle to break through the surface film and emerge into adult insects. It is important to watch the rising fish. If I see only their backs and tails breaking the surface of the water, I start by fishing a nymph on a floating line just under the surface. If I see the head of the trout coming out of the water, it usually means the fish are taking a floating insect, and I begin my fishing with a dry fly. The fly fisherman is well advised to study the rising fish and the insect life of the stream before starting to fish.

BASS BUGS

Bass bugs are large floating "flies" with deer-hair or cork bodies. They represent frogs, small birds, large moths, beetles, or anything else that is likely to fall into the water. These lures have a lot of air resistance and are more difficult to cast long distances than smaller flies, but they are very effective for smallmouth and largemouth bass.

I use an eight-foot fly rod and a weight-forward six-weight floating line for fishing bass bugs. The outfit is a little light for the job, and if I were going to do all my fishing with bugs, I would get a rod that handles a nine-weight line that will carry these bulky artificials long distances through the air without collapsing. Bass are rarely leader-shy and I prefer a short ten-pound-test tippet. The shorter the leader the easier it is to cast, and I have had good fishing with one as short as four feet.

Bass bugs can be worked around weedbeds, along shorelines, over shallow humps, off rocky points, and in any other place where you would work a surface lure for bass. I can comfortably toss a bug about forty feet with my outfit, and that is all I need for most of my fishing. I let the bug sit motionless on the water for about a minute and then gently twitch it a few times. If I don't get a strike, I retrieve the bug quickly with a jerking action and toss it back into the same spot. For some reason, repeated casts into the same spot will not spook the bass the way repeated casts with a large topwater lure will. Some of the biggest bass I've taken on bugs have inhaled the lures after six or seven casts.

When fishing bugs I have found it important to keep the rod pointed at the bug. This allows me to set the hook firmly with a full lift of the rod. A bass will usually hold the bug in its mouth and chew it for three or four seconds or more, and I hook more fish if I resist the temptation to strike the instant the fish takes the bug. When I have a strike, I tighten up on the line until I can feel the weight of the bass, and then I sock it to him.

The best times to use bass bugs are at dawn and dusk, but bugs will frequently draw strikes in the middle of a hot summer afternoon when a topwater lure fitted with treble hooks would be a waste of time. No matter when you hook one, a big bass on a fly rod is more than a handful. Most of the time the bass will immediately head for the nearest obstruction or dive into the weeds. I get more strikes and land fewer bass on bugs than with any other lure, but I don't mind. Fishing bass bugs is fun and most of the time I'm satisfied if I get a good jump out of the fish before he tosses the bug or wraps me around brush or weeds. If you're a bass fisherman who has never tried bass bugging, you're missing some exciting sport.

13

Natural Baits

As a kid I started fishing with natural baits. My first forays into the world of artificial lures were made with much hesitation. I found it difficult to believe that any fish, regardless of size, would take a huge plug fitted with sets of treble hooks. I remember laughing out loud the first time I saw the lure called a Hawaiian Wiggler, a precursor of today's spinnerbaits. My laughter was cut short when the fellow using the lure took a four-and-a-half-pound bass from the very spot where my large minnow had sat under a bobber all afternoon. Of course I eventually learned to enjoy the process of casting and retrieving artificial lures, but when the going gets tough, I return to natural baits. There is no doubt in my mind that natural baits, properly presented, will consistently outfish artificials no matter how well those artificials are presented.

AQUATIC INSECTS

Most stream fishermen use natural baits in spring, when the waters are cold, and at other times such as when the water is discolored after a summer rain. Worms are the most popular natural bait, but there is something even better.

Throughout the year, regardless of the season, there is continual underwater activity by aquatic insects. This activity is most noticeable when the insects hatch and rise in clouds from the surface of the water to mate, lay their eggs, and die. But this above-water phase is brief; aquatic insects spend most of their lives clinging to underwater debris and crawling over the stream bottom where they make up the bulk of the diet of many fish. When fished properly, these insects are a much more effective bait than a worm for most stream fish.

Collecting aquatic insects for bait is interesting. The best collection method requires two people, one of whom stands in a rocky, shallow, flowing area of the stream holding an old window screen against the stream bed, with its top above the water and tilted slightly downstream. The other person wades back and forth above the screen, turning over rocks and gravel with his feet. The aquatic insects attached to the bottoms of the rocks will be dislodged and carried downstream into the screen. When large nymphs have collected on the screen, it should be raised from the water and the nymphs removed and placed in a covered container with damp leaves or grass. A remarkable display of insect life will appear on the screen, from tiny, barely visible creatures to some over two inches long. The stream life will vary according to the climate, location, and season of the year, but any nymph or other aquatic insect that is large enough to put on a hook is an excellent bait.

I fish aquatic insects on light spinning tackle. I pass a small hook through the tail of the insect, add enough weight to bounce the bait along the bottom, and fish this rig across and downstream. The insects, being the familiar food of the fish in the stream, are usually taken with little or no hesitation.

Ponds and lakes also contain a wide variety of aquatic insects. Among the most popular fishing baits are the "perch bugs," which are the nymph stage of the dragonfly. Perch bugs look something like crickets, except that they move much more slowly and are easier to gather than crickets. They cling to weeds and grasses in the warm, shallow water, and it is an easy matter to pull a handful of weeds up on the shore and look for tiny legs kicking in the mud and vegetation. Be sure to push the weeds back into the water after you have gone through them because they are literally full of microscopic creatures that compose the food supply for many small fish and other creatures. If not put back in the water, these tiny insects will die when the vegetation that is their home dries out.

Perch bugs and other pond insects are easiest to fish on a small hook under a bobber near weedbeds. They are natural forage for every fish in the pond and are among the best baits for panfish and trout. They can also be fished on the bottom in deep water for trout.

WORMS

There are hundreds of varieties of earthworms and they are without doubt the most popular fishing baits. When I was a teenager, one of my early business experiences was selling nightcrawlers, and more than one new fishing rod came from the receipts of this venture.

When the weather gets hot and the ground dries, worms and nightcrawlers become as scarce as hens' teeth. The summer angler will pay well over a dollar a dozen for crawlers and will often be glad to get them at any price. Few baits are more effective for almost every species of fish, and a nightcrawler kicking on the bottom of a cool spring hole is a top summer trout bait.

Catching crawlers is easy and fun. The only equipment you need is a flashlight, the traditional coffee can to hold them, and fast hands. You probably won't have to go any farther than your front lawn to find all you need. Pick any warm rainy night and move slowly around the lawn, taking care not to let the beam of light fall directly on the light-sensitive worms. When you grab a crawler, pull on it with steady pressure and it will release its hold on its burrow in a few seconds. After a very rainy period, the crawlers will be completely out of their burrows and it is a simple matter to just pick them up.

Garden worms can be dug from any damp area with rich soil. Both garden worms and nightcrawlers keep well and there is no reason to run out of bait in the middle of the summer. They keep best in temperatures below 70°F. As a bachelor, I have plenty of room for them in my refrigerator. If your mate refuses to go along with that plan, store your worms in a wooden flat at least sixteen inches deep. Put about six inches of bedding in the flat and store it on the floor in the coolest part of your basement or in a shed or outbuilding. Damp topsoil and leaves make excellent bedding, and when the worms are used up the bedding can serve as a top dressing for house plants that will really make them sit up and take notice. Inexpensive worm bedding preparations are also available at sporting-goods stores, and some even contain food for the worms.

Worms and crawlers should be fed every few weeks by scattering coffee grounds, leaves, grass clippings, or cornmeal over the surface of the flat. When putting worms in the flat, pour them over the top of the bedding. The healthy worms will quickly disappear into the bedding; those remaining on the surface should be discarded. Once they are in the bed, leave the worms alone except to feed and water them. The bedding should be kept damp, not wet, since too much water will drown the worms. Also, don't save pieces of worm or return unused worms to the flat after a day of fishing. Worms are like apples—a single rotten one can eventually spoil the whole barrel.

In streams, worms should be fished by letting them drift with the current just off the bottom. In lakes, they can be fished on the bottom, under a bobber, trolled behind a spinner, or pulled over the surface of weeds in the same way as with a plastic worm. The only problem with live crawlers is that every single fish in the lake loves them. It can be difficult to keep small panfish from stealing a worm by grabbing its tail and pulling it from the hook. For this reason, I don't use live worms for bass fishing in shallow water or around weed beds; for such fishing, a plastic worm is better than a live one.

One unusual technique that is growing in popularity involves pumping an air bubble into a nightcrawler with a hypodermic needle. The best needle to use is one of the disposable insulin needles available at any drugstore; these come in packages of ten costing a couple of dollars. One package will last many seasons.

To use the air-bubble technique, first put the nightcrawler on your hook, making sure you hook it through the head, not the flat tail. Hook it in at least two places and let the tail hang down. Lay the tail of the worm in the palm of your hand, pull the plunger of the needle all the way to the end, insert the needle into the tail of the worm, and slowly press the plunger. The worm will swell up immediately. You will have to experiment with how much air should be injected to keep the worm floating off the bottom. I add a splitshot or two about eighteen inches up the line, toss the rig out, and let it sit on the bottom. A crawler with air in its tail stands up like a wiggling strand of spaghetti, and there is no way it can bury itself in silt or weeds where it would be invisible to the fish. When a fish grabs the worm, I give line and let the fish run for at least five feet before setting the hook. If you fish these inflated worms on a tight line they will be torn right off the hook.

I have had excellent results using an air-filled crawler for trout and walleyes. I haven't yet tried the technique for bass, but several bass fishermen have told me it works well, and one fellow swears by the inflated-worm technique for big catfish.

MINNOWS

All game fish feed on minnows, and most artificial lures are meant to represent one species or another of these small forage fish.

Minnows can be netted in the shallows in lakes and the backwaters in streams. They can also be caught in a minnow trap using breadcrumbs for bait. Wire minnow traps are available at all good sports shops, and if you do a lot of fishing with minnows, you will find it much less expensive to trap your own. When collecting minnows that are to be used in a body of water other than the one from which they were taken, be sure that it is legal to do so; many states have stringent laws concerning the use of minnows and you should always check these before transporting the fish from one body of water to another.

Minnows can be used as bait for almost all freshwater fish. I use minnows two or three inches long for panfish and trout and large ones for pike, pickerel, and bass. I have used them up to eight inches long when seeking lunker bass.

When using minnows in summer, it can be difficult to keep them alive and active. It is essential that the water in the minnow bucket be kept cool and well oxygenated. There are many commercial tablets, capsules, and mechanical devices designed to keep minnows alive, but I have found nothing that beats ice cubes. Water at 32°F holds exactly twice as much oxygen as water at 77°F (which is why ice floats), and minnows can be held in blistering summer heat if their water contains enough ice.

Every minnow fisherman has his favorite way of rigging these baitfish. When still-fishing with a bobber, I like to hook them lightly just under the back fin, being careful not to hit the backbone, which will immediately kill them. This hooking method allows the minnow to swim actively, and permits me to set the hook, which is in the center of the bait, as soon as I have a bite. Most fish hooked quickly on a minnow will not have had time to swallow the bait and can be released, unharmed, when desired.

When bottom fishing, trolling, or fishing in rivers and streams, I hook a minnow through both lips by running the hook through the lower jaw and out through the upper one. When hooked this way, the minnow can close its mouth to breathe and will not suffocate the way it will when hooked through one lip. Also, lip-hooked minnows offer less resistance in the water than those hooked under the dorsal fin, and are not as easily torn from the hook by currents or underwater obstructions. When using lip-hooked minnows it is necessary to allow a fish to run with the bait before setting the hook, unless the fish is big enough to inhale the whole minnow. Most game fish grab a minnow across the middle of its body, turn it, and then swallow it head first. Trout are an exception; my experience is that they immediately grab a minnow by the head, and for this reason I hook all of my minnows through the lips when going after trout and set the hook as soon as I have a bite.

There are many other ways to rig minnows, some so involved that the end result looks like a ball of yarn that has been played with by a kitten. I don't use any of these rigs. The only baiting method I use other than hooking under the dorsal fin or through both lips is to hook a large minnow near the base of the tail. Hooked in this way the minnow will usually stay on or near the surface, and I have found this to be the best rig when trying to get a minnow to swim under a mat of floating vegetation.

Be sure to experiment when fishing with minnows. One friend of mine told of fishing for bass using large minnows dangled under a bobber. Small pickerel were killing his expensive bait as fast as he could cast them out. He tossed the

dead shiners into a bucket and when the live ones were gone, began to experiment, coming up with a technique that has proven very effective for a big
bass. He fished a large dead shiner hooked through both lips on a three-
quarter-ounce purple Rooster Tail spinner. The small pickerel were intimidated by the total size of the lure, and in a few hours my friend took three
largemouths over five pounds each. I wouldn't go out and kill a bucketful of
minnows to try this technique, but it pays to save dead minnows and experiment by fishing them in different ways when the live ones are gone.

CRICKETS AND GRASSHOPPERS

Grasshoppers and crickets are great baits, but catching them can be difficult.
They are easiest to catch early in the morning when it is still cool. The night
chill immobilizes them and they can be picked up easily, whereas once the sun
hits them it's a different story. During the day some sort of a fine-meshed net is
needed and it is just a matter of chasing them down, which is harder than it
sounds. One good daylight technique is to spread a fluffy wool or acrylic
blanket on the ground and chase grasshoppers onto it. The hoppers have small
spines on their feet which will catch in the fluffy finish of the blanket, trapping
the insects for a few seconds.

Crickets are easily picked up before the sun warms them. They don't like to
get wet and will be found in numbers in corn- or haystacks. They can be
caught by hand, but a fine-mesh net will make catching them much easier.

Grasshoppers and crickets should be kept in a commercially made cricket
cage. These cages, which are inexpensive, have an opening with a plug that is
just large enough to let a single insect crawl out, making it easy to grab one
without all the rest escaping. Hoppers and crickets can be kept in a cage for
about a week if a few weeds are added and they are not overcrowded. I find
that they keep best in the refrigerator, where the cold keeps them sluggish,
but any cool, dry place will do.

Crickets and hoppers are great bream baits, and are also excellent for trout,
bass, walleyes, and catfish. I've found hoppers to be one of the best summer
trout baits when the streams are low and clear. In summer lots of grasshoppers
fall into streams, especially where large fields line the banks.

I like to fish summer streams by drifting a hopper like a dry fly. I hook the
hopper by passing the hook through its body, which kills it, but that doesn't
seem to make a difference to the trout. When drifting a grasshopper in a clear
summer stream, give the trout plenty of time to chew on it before setting the
hook. For some reason trout seem to mouth these baits for a long time before
swallowing them, and if you set the hook too quickly you will pull the hopper
right out of the fish's mouth.

In lakes and streams, hoppers and crickets can also be fished right on the bottom like any other bait. A couple of big hoppers threaded on a hook are an excellent catfish bait, and adding a hopper to a jig will occasionally turn on the walleyes.

Grasshoppers and crickets are available to all North American anglers. If you haven't tried them for bait, especially during the heat of summer, you're missing a good bet.

CRAWFISH

Crawfish are among the very best natural baits for bass, trout, walleyes, and catfish. In some areas there are limits on their use and you should be sure to check local laws before collecting or using them for bait.

The best way I've found to catch crawfish is to tie a piece of fish to a line and throw it into the water where you can see a few of these crustaceans. They are nocturnal and most easily gathered at night, but you can also catch them during the day; it just takes a little longer. Once the crawfish find the piece of fish and begin to feed on it, it can be gently lifted from the bottom and a fine-meshed net slid under it. If your movements are slow, the crawfish will hang onto its meal until it is lifted from the water, and if you are cautious, you can easily gather all you need.

Crawfish shed their shells as they grow, and when they are soft, just after shedding, they are better bait than when they are hard-shelled. I like to store a bunch of crawfish and select the soft ones for my fishing. I take an old galvanized washtub, put about four inches of water in the bottom, and add five- or six-dozen crawfish. I liberally sprinkle corn meal into the water and cover the crawfish with a piece of burlap. In a few days they will start shedding their shells and you can pick the soft ones for that day's fishing. Some crawfish die when shedding, and the dead ones should be removed from the tub.

For bass I use a whole crawfish hooked through the tail, with the point of the hook facing upward so it won't get hung up as easily on the bottom. It is difficult to keep a live crawfish from diving under the nearest rock or log, and it must be tugged every few seconds and kept moving. Some anglers break off the large pinching claws, which they claim prevents the crawfish from grabbing on to bottom debris, but I don't believe this is necessary.

You can't use too large a crawfish for bass. I like to use one about four inches long and drop it near stumps, weeds, or big rocks. I don't let it sit long, just a second or two, and then I lift it off the bottom about a foot. This is when a bass will usually grab it. I let the fish move off with the bait in its mouth for about five feet before I set the hook.

Crawfish can also be fished deep off rocky points for summer smallmouths. It is essential that you keep the bait moving slowly or it will bury itself under rocks. Hooking it through the tail will let you pull the crawfish from under rocks, but you will still lose a lot of bait. I never take fewer than three dozen crawfish with me for an afternoon's fishing.

In rivers and streams crawfish should be drifted through riffles, runs, and deep pools. You have the opportunity of catching any gamefish living in the stream, and I have taken trout, smallmouths, and channel catfish from one short stretch of river using a live soft-shelled crawfish for bait.

Crawfish tails are also excellent bait. They can be fished with the shell left on or off, and should be threaded onto the hook from the forward end. Crawfish tails should be fished in lakes and streams exactly like live crawfish, except that they can be allowed to sit on the bottom. The tails can also be added to small jigs. Crawfish are a staple food of walleyes, and adding a crawfish tail to a jig is one of the very best ways to take these fish. Readers are referred to Chapter 37, "Walleyes," for the specifics of jig- and baitfishing for these fish.

FROGS

Frogs are an excellent bass bait and will also take pickerel, pike, and even muskies. Many states have limitations on taking frogs, and you should consult the local fish and game laws before beginning your frog hunting. As a kid I would catch my frogs by chasing them around in the shallow weedy areas of a lake or pond and catching them in my hands. It was great fun and in a short time I would be covered with mud and slime, which was also great fun. As an adult, I have managed to control my frog-hunting exuberance and am much more civilized about the process. These days I use my fly rod and gently dangle any small fly in front of a frog. They may miss it a few times but will eventually grab it and can be swung onto shore or into the boat. A lot of frog hunters gather their bait at night. I usually get all I need during the day, and have always had an aversion to walking around the swamps at night anyhow. It's not that I'm afraid of snakes, I just like to treat them with great respect.

Frogs can be kept for a short time in a damp burlap sack, but they keep better in a cage that is partially submerged in water and has a few rocks in it to allow them to get out of the water. They can be fed pieces of worm, grasshoppers, mealworms, or grubs, and will live in captivity as long as they are fed and not handled too much.

Many shops carry frog harnesses, but I find them to be a nuisance to use. I hook frogs in two different ways. When fishing them on the surface, I hook them through both lips with the point of the hook facing upward to keep it from getting snagged. For subsurface fishing I hook them through the thigh.

Whether fished on the surface or the bottom, frogs must be cast gently. I enjoy lobbing a frog into weeds or lily pads and slowly moving it across the pads. If there are bass, pickerel, or pike in the vicinity it won't be long before the frog disappears into a swirl of moving water. There is no need to let a fish run with a frog and I set the hook immediately. When fishing a frog on the bottom it must be brought to the surface every three or four minutes or it will drown. I have never taken a fish on a dead frog, although some catfish anglers use dead frogs fished on the bottom at night.

One of the fringe benefits of gathering your own frogs for bait is having an occasional meal of frogs' legs. Keep a few of those real big bullfrogs, the ones that stretch out to fourteen or fifteen inches, for your own enjoyment. The legs should be removed, skinned, and fried in butter with a pinch of fresh parsley and a touch of garlic if you are so inclined. They are a real dining treat.

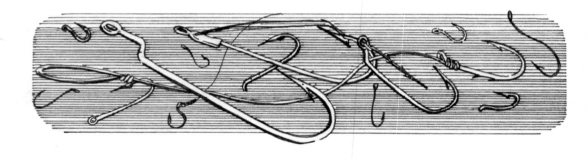

14

Hooks

Fish-hooks have come a long way since the days of Izaak Walton. At that time each angler had to make his own hooks. The common method was to use a sewing needle that was heated red hot in a candle flame and slowly and meticulously shaped by hand. The results left much to be desired. The hooks were very brittle from the heating and cooling, and many of them broke the instant a fish clamped down on them.

Today's hooks are good and inexpensive. They are the result of advances in metallurgy, and more recently of the benefits of computer design. The many hundreds of different brands, patterns, finishes and other variations can be confusing. Companies such as Wright & McGill, Mustad, Gill, Sealy, Partridge, and VMC are quality hook makers and sell their products under a wide variety of names. Unfortunately, there are also many bargain-basement specials that are of poor quality. I find it remarkable that some anglers will spend hundreds of dollars on first-quality rods, reels, and lines and then buy the cheapest hooks they can find. The difference between a hook that sells for one cent and a hook that sells for five cents can be significant in terms of strength, design, and the ability to take and hold a sharp point.

I learned the need for using quality hooks the hard way. A few years ago I was fishing for bass in a large southern impoundment. In my haste to get on the water I left my box of quality stainless-steel worm hooks in the car and was forced to borrow hooks from my fishing companion, who was using an off brand. He told me that he had plenty of hooks and not to worry about losing some because he bought them in large packages and paid less than a penny each for them. That morning I hooked a really big bass on a blue plastic worm —one of those lunkers that is so big it refuses to jump. My spinning outfit was a bit light for the job and when the fish would go deep and sulk I couldn't budge him (or, more likely, her.) But the water was free of obstructions and I was convinced that if I didn't lose patience, I would eventually land the fish. After a long fight I got the fish near the surface and got a good look at it. It was huge, one of the largest bass I have ever had on the end of my line, and I have to admit that I got a little shaky. The fish made a deep run and I let her go, knowing that my eight-pound-test line was not strong enough to stop her . . . then, my line went slack. I was heartsick and couldn't understand why, after all my caution, the fish had escaped. When I reeled in my line the reason was all too obvious. The hook had broken in half at the bend. I can assure you that I have never again left behind my own box of quality hooks.

A hook is more than just a bent piece of wire with a point at one end and an eye at the other. Most anglers think about size, but many disregard other qualities of the hook that can make a difference in their fishing results.

There are many different points and barbs on today's hooks, but the same principles apply to all. A long slender point will penetrate faster and easier, but it is also weak. Except when fishing with small flies and a light leader—a situation in which light but constant tension eventually tires the fish—short-pointed hooks are better than those with long thin points.

Curved- and hollow-point hooks will penetrate better than those with straight points, but they must be kept sharp and the angler has to set them with authority. The best of the hollow- and curved-point hooks are those in which the whole hook is designed to take advantage of the point. I have found that the Limerick and O'Shaughnessy designs are the best curved- and hollow-point hooks.

Many hooks have an offset point that bends to one side of the shank. Hooks with these bent points are called kirbed, or reversed, hooks, and are best for thin-mouthed, fast-hitting fish. Hooks with points that align with the shank are better for hard-mouthed, slow-biting species. They are also best for trolling because they do not spin when moved through the water, as do hooks with offset points.

The barbs on a good hook are small. Hooks with large barbs are difficult to set and make a large hole that may allow the fish to throw the hook when it jumps or during an instant of slack line. Barbless hooks hold well as long as the line is kept tight, but aren't as secure as hooks with barbs. They should, however, be used in all catch-and-release situations because they do slightly less damage to the fish than barbed hooks, and are much easier to unhook.

The gap and bite of a hook are also important. The gap is the distance between the point of the hook and the shank. The bite is the distance from the point of the hook to the bend. A hook with a wide gap holds well once it is set past the barb, and is best for hooking fish with long snouts such as pike and pickerel. If the gap is too wide, the hook will be weak; I have had wide-gapped hooks straightened out by big bass and pike. If a wide-gapped hook is to be used for big fish, the hook should be thick and very substantial.

It is the bend of the hook that gives it a name or style, and there are far too many names and styles to mention. What is important is that the bend determines the penetrating ability of the hook and its strength. A sharp bend is very difficult to spread open, but will break under extreme pressure. A hook with a round bend won't break easily but can be sprung open under extreme pressure.

A so-called "regular" hook has a perfectly round shank and bend. These hooks are best for fish with delicate mouths, such as crappie and shad. Forged hooks have an oblong shank and bend and are best for the biggest and hardest-fighting species.

Hook shanks can be long, short, straight, or curved. I prefer hooks with shorter shanks for most of my fishing because long-shanked hooks can more easily spring open at the bend. If you have two hooks the same size, and one has a long shank, the short-shanked hook will be almost 50 percent stronger. Light, long-shanked hooks are good when fishing for small fish where there are many obstructions. With hard and steady pulling on the line, these hooks can be straightened out and freed from an obstruction when they get hung up. They can then be bent back into shape and used again.

A bent or twisted shank changes the penetration and setting ability of a hook. Hooks with bent shanks are easier to use for some kinds of bait, and there are many designed for use with plastic worms hooked Texas-style. The plastic-worm angler should experiment with these bent-shank hooks until he finds one that he likes. My preferred plastic worm hook is the southern Sproat style, which can be purchased in stainless steel. Stainless steel has the advantages of taking a sharp point and not rusting when it gets water on it while sitting in the tackle box.

Hook eyes are available in everything from a simple ring to loops, needle-eyes, and flattened eyes both with and without holes. Hooks without holes are attached to the leader in the same manner as the leader is attached to a snelled hook. Hooks with eyes that are brazed shut are the strongest. Eyes that are turned up or down are designed for snelled hooks. They are also used by fly-tyers, most of whom prefer a turned-up eye for dry flies and a turned-down eye for bucktails and streamers.

There is also a wide range of hooks that have various designs to help hold bait more securely. Hooks with slices in the shank, popularly called bait-holders, are preferred by many worm fishermen. Hooks with tiny wire coils on the shank are preferred by anglers using doughballs and other soft baits for carp or catfish.

Many hooks come with weed guards made of wire, plastic, rubber, or nylon fibers. They are designed to enable a lure or bait to be fished through brush or weeds without becoming snagged. There is no such thing as a totally weedless hook. Hooks with weed guards should not be used unless necessary, because the guards will occasionally result in missed strikes.

Most spoons and crankbaits come with treble hooks. These hooks are excellent for relatively open water without a lot of debris; under weedy conditions they can be replaced with weedless hooks. When catch-and-release fishing I replace treble hooks with single barbless hooks. I find I hook almost as many fish and am able to quickly and gently remove these hooks from a fish with a minimum of fuss and damage.

No matter which hooks you use, they should be of good quality and kept sharp and free of rust. Most hooks are not very sharp when they come out of the box, and a few seconds of sharpening with a whetstone or tiny file will make a difference in the number of fish hooked. The smart angler also takes the few seconds required to touch up the point on his hook several times during the fishing day.

15

Weights

I have seen all sorts of objects used as fishing sinkers: old tire weights, strips cut from toothpaste tubes, pieces of lead-tin solder, and even small stones when nothing else was available.

Some anglers think of weights as being anything heavy enough to cast easily. They are making a mistake. A weight that is too heavy will prevent light strikes from being felt, and the fish will strip the bait without the angler's knowing he had a bite. Also, too much weight will often provide so much resistance that a fish will drop the bait before taking it completely into its mouth. The basic rule for sinkers is to use the very lightest that meets your needs, and no more.

For still-fishing in lakes and ponds the design of the sinker isn't too important, but where it is placed on the line can be very important. For some reason I've never understood, most freshwater anglers place their sinkers on the line above the hook. This means that the fish must move the sinker before the angler feels anything. For bottom fishing I prefer to tie a dipsy sinker (shaped like a teardrop with a brass eyelet) directly to the end of my line. I place my bait on a dropper about eighteen inches above the weight with the aid of a small, three-way swivel. This rig allows me to feel the faintest nibbles, and lets the fish swim short distances with the bait in its mouth without dragging the sinker along the bottom. A similar effect can be achieved by using an egg sinker (shaped like an egg) with a hole in the middle. Egg sinkers can be strung on the line above the hook, and when a fish takes the bait the line will run through the sinker with little or no resistance. When using an egg sinker, I string it on my line, add a snap swivel, and attach a snelled hook to the swivel.

When bottom fishing in very brushy water, a spoon-type sinker is best. The advantage of these flat, spoon-shaped disks is that the instant you start to retrieve your line, the sinker planes through the water and rises almost straight up from the bottom. These spoon sinkers are often called walking sinkers and are excellent for drift fishing as well as bottom fishing with bait.

Bullet, or helmet, sinkers are tapered egg sinkers with a hole through the middle. They are used almost exclusively by plastic-worm fishermen, and allow a fish to pick up the worm and move off with it without feeling much resistance. Some worm fishermen, myself included, don't like these slip-type sinkers. I have found that a bass will often pick up the worm and move off at an angle to the sinker; then, when I set the hook, there is often too much slack line to solidly hook the fish. When using plastic worms, I prefer to use a splitshot that I attach to my line right at the head of the worm. However, the tapered shape of the bullet sinker does allow it to be drawn slowly through weeds and brush with a minimum of hang-ups. For this reason, many worm fishermen peg these sinkers by sticking a toothpick or small piece of wood firmly enough into the hole so that the sinker won't slide up the line.

Sinker design is more important in rivers and streams than in lakes. In a river or stream round sinkers or splitshot are easily rolled along the bottom by the current, and so should be used when you want your bait to bounce along the bottom. Many stream fishermen prefer long, thin pencil sinkers. They are my favorite when bottom-bouncing the rock-filled steelhead streams of the West. I find that these sinkers catch bottom less frequently than any other kind. Pencil sinkers can be tied directly to the line, but I prefer to fish them on a short dropper of lighter line tied about eighteen inches to two feet above the lure or bait with the aid of a three-way swivel. The sinkers are easily made by cutting sections of lead wire, flattening one end with a hammer, and punching a hole in the flat surface with an ice pick.

There are times when the river angler will want his bait to sit in one place on the bottom. This is the case when fishing for big catfish or when using a big minnow for lunker brown trout. To hold bottom in a current, the sinker must be flat-sided, and for this kind of fishing a three- or four-sided pyramid sinker is excellent. For holding bottom in very fast water, open-centered triangle sinkers are best.

For trolling, weights serve a dual purpose. In addition to carrying the rig to the desired depth, they stabilize it and make sure that it runs straight. In the

West, round "cannon balls," banana-shaped crescents, and weighted trolling planes called stingrays are the favorite weights. In the East, trollers tend to stick with weights that have lead rudders or keels. For very deep trolling, many anglers use lead-core line, which eliminates the need for any additional weight. The disadvantage in using lead-core line is that it requires very heavy equipment, and for this reason many deep trollers have switched to down-riggers. Downriggers are discussed in Chapter 42, "Trolling."

For most light freshwater fishing, I believe the splitshot is the best all-around weight. Splitshot come in sizes from barely larger than a BB shot to over a quarter of an ounce. Just a few years ago splitshot were a bother to use. They had to be clamped on the line with pliers and once affixed were impossible to remove without cutting the line. Today's splitshot have notched openings that hold well on slick monofilament line and tiny "ears" that can be pressed between the fingers for opening or closing the shot. These removable splitshot are easy to put on or remove from the line, and can be reused many times. Sometimes using two or more small splitshot will result in a better drift in a stream than using a single large shot. You should experiment with combinations of splitshot until you find the one that works best for you.

Other sinkers that go on and off the line with a minimum of fuss are pinch-on clasp sinkers and those with rubber cores. The problem with clasp sinkers is that it is difficult to press the clasps tight enough to hold the sinker firmly on a monofilament line. Rubber-core sinkers hold well on the line, but both clasp and rubber-core sinkers hang up on the bottom very easily. Thus, while these weights can be used for bottom fishing, knowledgeable anglers use them for trolling or in locations where the bottom is free of obstructions.

No single sinker can be used under all conditions. You must consider your tackle, the conditions under which you're fishing, the habits of the fish you're seeking, and the design of the sinker. Just remember that in every situation it is important to use only as much weight as you need, and no more.

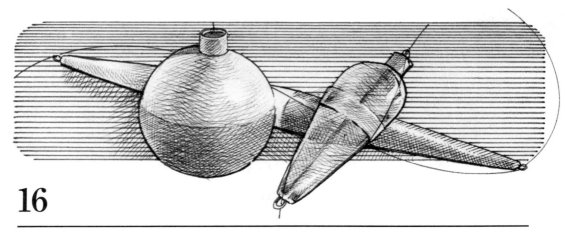

16

Bobbers

Bobbers and floats allow the angler to suspend baits at various depths, and have the added advantage of signaling when a fish has taken the bait. There are many types of floats available, and selecting the one that best suits your needs will make for easier and more productive fishing.

The buoyancy and sensitivity of a bobber are determined by its construction and shape. Bobbers were formerly made of cork or balsa, but today most are made of closed-cell foam or hollow, hard plastic. The best bobbers should be just large enough to support the bait but small enough to be pulled beneath the surface of the water with a minimum of resistance; long slender bobbers can be pulled under the water with less resistance than round hollow ones, and I prefer such bobbers for most of my fishing. When used without any weight beneath them, slender bobbers will stand up in the water when a fish takes the bait, making them very visible in rough water. When enough weight is added to the line to make the float stand vertically in the water, it will disappear beneath the surface with little resistance when a fish takes the bait.

British anglers have made a real science out of bobber fishing. The British Carbonyte system, recently imported in North America, has the advantage of allowing the angler to balance his float, hook, and sinker through a series of interchangeable float bodies. Each body is marked with a size and number that corresponds to the number and sizes of splitshot that will keep the float barely above the surface. The result is that when a fish takes the bait, it feels a minimum of resistance and is less likely to strip the bait or drop it.

Most North American anglers use the round, hollow, red-and-white bobbers that come in sizes from barely bigger than a fingernail to larger than a baseball. Some of these bobbers are red on top and white on the bottom while others have the reverse scheme, and color does make a difference: the red-topped bobbers are most visible on bright or windy days; the white-topped bobbers are very difficult to see on a bright day and are most visible on dull days and at dusk and dawn.

Sliding floats are used to suspend a bait off the bottom, and have the advantage of allowing the angler to reel in the line and float all the way to the rod tip for easy casting. These floats allow the line to slip through the body of the float until they strike a peg that holds them at the desired depth. Unfortunately, the peg or tiny splitshot that determines the depth at which the sliding float is to be fished can become a problem by catching on the rod guides during casting. I have yet to find a sliding float that eliminates this problem, and the basement inventor who comes up with a device that will enable a float to be used in deep water while still being cast easily will have his fortune assured.

Floats are attached to the line with all sorts of devices. Some, such as the pressure clips found on most round plastic models, are very convenient for quick changes; however, these clips have the tendency to kink and weaken the line. This is not a problem when using a float for panfish, but when using a large minnow for big pike or bass, the clip can create a weak spot that can cause the line to break when fighting a large fish. When using a float for large fish, I attach it to my line with a dropper to eliminate the problem of weak spots.

Popping corks are used by a few knowledgeable freshwater anglers. They were developed for saltwater fishing for sea-trout, but can be very effective for bass. A popping cork is simply a float with a concave top that pops when it is pulled sharply through the water. It is similar to a surface popper without any hooks. I know one bass fisherman who uses a popping cork tied about eighteen inches above a large streamer fly. He fishes this rig as if he were using a topwater lure and claims that to the fish, it appears to be a struggling surface creature with a large minnow in hot pursuit. He uses the rig when the bass are showing some interest in topwater lures but not striking them solidly, and he takes some very big bass this way.

There are also a number of subsurface floats designed for specialized kinds of fishing. These floats are placed on the line between the weight and the hook. Their advantage is that they allow a lure or bait to be suspended off the bottom in deep water. Their disadvantage is that they are cumbersome to cast and difficult to keep from getting tangled in the line. Recently, floating jig-heads have been developed that serve the same function and are much easier to use. I am still experimenting with these floating jig-heads and I believe that they are going to improve my deep-water fishing.

Spinning bubbles are being used by many anglers in lieu of traditional floats and bobbers. These bubbles are made of clear plastic and have chambers that can be filled with water to add weight for casting. They allow the spinfisherman to cast flies and very light baits long distances without having to add additional weight to the line. If enough water is added, they can be suspended at various depths in the water. When partially filled with water, they offer the advantage of sitting lower in the water than traditional bobbers, and do not blow all over the lake on a windy day. Their disadvantage is that they are difficult to see in the water, and for this reason are used most often when a bait or fly is to be cast and retrieved slowly, rather than for still-fishing. Some anglers daub red or yellow paint on their bubbles to make them more visible.

Spinning bubbles are excellent for fly-fishing ponds and lakes that are surrounded by trees that make the use of a fly rod difficult or impossible. I thread the bubble about three feet up the line and add a bucktail, wet fly, or nymph. I fill the bubble with just enough water for easy casting. For some reason, the transparent bubble does not seem to scare the fish, and I have dropped the rig almost on top of feeding trout and had one immediately take the fly. It is important to thread the bubble on the line through the holes on the top and bottom. If the line is tied directly to the bubble, a good-sized fish can break the fragile plastic.

The same axiom applies to floats, bobbers, and bubbles as to weights: use just enough to meet your needs, and no more, and you will catch more fish.

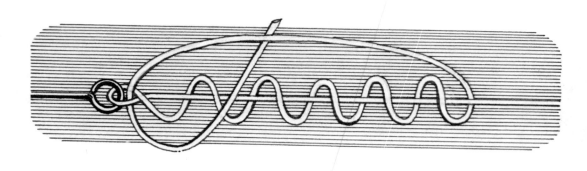

17

Knots

Your fishing line is no stronger than the knots you use. There are many different knots, some so exotic and difficult that I am sure a person would need four hands to tie them properly. I use only three basic knots for almost all of my fishing. These are reliable and well-tested, and while you can learn dozens more, these three are the only ones you will need for all but very specialized freshwater fishing situations.

IMPROVED CLINCH KNOT

The improved clinch (see the illustration at the opening of this chapter) is the most basic of all the fishing knots. It is used to tie any object having an eye to the line, including lures, flies, hooks, sinkers, and swivels. The knot is easy to tie and retains almost 100 percent of the line strength.

To tie the improved clinch, run the end of the line through the eye of the object and then double it back and twist it around the line. Make five twists around the line and, leaving a loop, push the end of the line through the space where the line joins the eye. Then pass the line back through the large loop.

Five turns around the line are best for assuring maximum line strength. If you use more than seven turns you will have trouble pulling the knot tight. Fewer than five turns and the knot might slip. When using heavy monofilament, over about ten-pound test, I like to touch the flame of a match or lighter to the end of the line that protrudes from the knot after it is trimmed. The melting action of the flame makes a tiny ball at the end of the line that assures that it will not slip under extreme pressure.

BLOOD KNOT

The blood knot is the best for joining two lengths of monofilament line of different diameters. Probably all fly fishermen use it when building tapered leaders, and it is also the best method I have found for making a dropper without using a three-way swivel. Some anglers have trouble tying the blood knot, but this is easy if it is treated as two clinch knots.

Start the blood knot by overlapping the two pieces to be joined by at least ten inches, or more if you are building a dropper. Hold the overlapping lines between the thumb and forefinger. Take the end of one of the lines, run it around the other strand five times, and then run it back through the loop that is created where the lines overlap. This is exactly the same first step in tying an improved clinch knot. Then transfer the knot carefully to the other thumb and forefinger and wind the end of the second line around the first line in the opposite direction for five full turns. Pass the line through the loop holding the other line-end, but in the opposite direction. The knot can then be released, and a gentle, even pull will gather it together. Be careful not to pull the ends out of the loop as the knot tightens. After this the ends can be clipped from the knot unless you are making a dropper, in which case you should clip off only one of the ends. Five twists in each direction will ensure a knot with almost 100 percent line strength. Four twists will make a knot with about 85 percent line

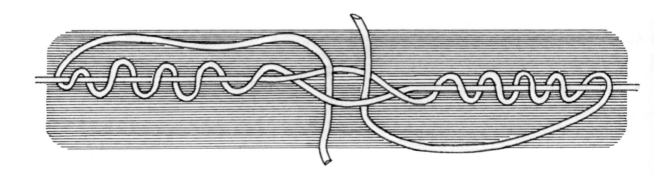

strength, and three twists with about 75 percent. When joining very light lines, such as when adding a tippet to the end of a leader, it is best to wet the knot before pulling it tight; this decreases friction and results in a stronger knot.

NAIL KNOT

The nail knot is the best I've found for joining a leader to the end of a fly line, or for joining a fly line to its backing. It has the advantage of being strong but not leaving a large bump on the line, which can be a problem in casting or when playing a large fish at the end of its fight, when it is often necessary to give line quickly and smoothly in those final frantic rushes at the boatside. Without a smooth transition from fly line to leader, the hook can pull from the fish, the leader can break, or the rod guides can be damaged. To make the knot, many anglers use a small plastic tube rather than a nail, but any straight object will do and I have used a piece of twig and a needle when I had nothing else with me.

To tie the nail knot, pull out a convenient length of line and lay the nail against it, leaving about four inches of line to work with. Lay the end of the leader next to the nail so that it points in the opposite direction from the line, and leave about a foot of leader material to work with. Hold the line, leader, and nail between the thumb and forefinger. Take the protruding short end of the leader and wind it in tight coils over itself toward the end of the line. Between five and seven coils are enough; too many coils will make it difficult to draw the knot tight. Holding the coils tightly so they won't overlap, pass the end of the leader back in the opposite direction, between the nail and the coils. Then, still holding the coils tightly so they won't overlap, carefully draw the nail out of the knot. The coils will feel soft but don't let go of them. Carefully pull the leader from one end at a time to tighten the coils around the line. When the leader is snug against the line, check to be sure that none of the coils

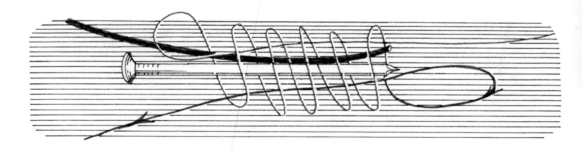

are overlapping. If there is any overlapping, adjust the coils with your fingernail so they lie flat against the line. Then pull hard on both ends of the leader
to make the coils bite into the line. Pliers can be used to pull on the short end
of the leader because that end will be discarded. When you are satisfied that
the coils are tight and cut well into the line, pull gradually and then hard on
the line and leader. If the coils have bitten well into the line it won't slip, and
additional pulling will make the knot even tighter. If you choose, you can then
make a few applications of Pliobond cement to the knot to smooth it. Once
properly tied, a nail knot will last almost indefinitely; I usually replace the ones
on my fly lines only every two or three years, for the sake of insurance.

18

Equipment Maintenance

There is always a day on some winter weekend when I get bored. The temperature is well below zero and I don't feel like ice fishing or cross-country skiing. The driveway is shoveled, there isn't a good game on the tube, and I don't have a new book to get into. That's the day I clean up my fishing tackle.

I find the best way to approach the mess in my tackle boxes is to pour everything onto a table. Every year I am amazed at what I find. There are always snips of line, candy wrappers, soaked matches, crushed potato chips and beer nuts, boat receipts, loose change, mummified nightcrawlers, many pieces of plastic worm, and the inevitable few items that will forever defy definition.

My first move is to sort the mess into piles. Hooks that aren't rusty, swivels, and sinkers can go back into the plastic containers where they started the season. Lures go into two piles, those that need cleaning and those that need repair.

Ordinary kitchen detergent is fine for most tackle-cleaning jobs. Lures that have dried weeds on them may need something a little stronger. I don't use abrasive cleaners on any lure with a glossy finish because it will dull the finish. I like silver polish for cleaning spinners, spoons, and the blades of spinnerbaits.

Rubber skirts on spinnerbaits and poppers should be replaced if necessary. I now use vinyl skirts on my lures. When exposed to sunlight, rubber skirts tend to decompose and stick together, while vinyl is unaffected by sunlight. Artificial flies and lures with feathers can be brought back to life by holding them in long-nosed pliers for just a few moments in the steam from a teakettle.

Be sure to check the hooks on all your lures. If they are not sharp and rust-free, they must either be sharpened with a small file or sharpening stone or replaced. Your local sporting-goods store will have new treble hooks and the split rings needed to attach them. I always take the old hooks and split rings with me to the store to be sure I get the right sizes.

For touching up the paint on crankbaits and spoons I like to use nail polish. In addition to leaving a lustrous finish that dries quickly, nail polish comes in a fine assortment of colors and each little bottle comes with its own brush. I have yet to find a good frog-green nail polish, but while the looks I get from cosmetic clerks are discouraging when I ask for this, I know that I'll eventually find the right color if I keep looking.

Rods should be washed with soap and water. When needed, new ferrules are easily installed by following the directions on the package of ferrule cement. New guides can be taped in place, but it's easy to wrap them with thread to match the other guides. Most good sporting-goods stores will have inexpensive booklets describing how to wrap guides. The tip guide should be carefully checked and replaced if it has tiny grooves cut into it from dirt on the line. If the guide is not replaced, the grooves will quickly weaken new line.

Before you put new line on your reels, they should be cleaned and lubricated. If they have broken parts, now is the time to replace them, not in the spring when fishing fever strikes. How far you tear down your reels depends on your mechanical ability. If you don't have the owner's manual for the reel, keep the process orderly and you should have little trouble.

It's a good idea not to take apart the drag on baitcasting reels. The drag is composed of a series of washers, and if you get them out of order it will not function properly. The drag mechanism rarely needs cleaning, but the pawl, a tiny ridged disk that fits into the grooved worm gear of the level-wind mechanism, should be checked and replaced if it is worn. Some modern baitcasting reels are put together as precisely as a watch, and unless you have dropped the reel and can hear sand in the gears, a total takedown is not necessary. Baitcasting reels have small oil ports, usually on both palm plates. Putting a few drops of oil in these holes at the end of the season, and occasionally during the season, is all the maintenance that is normally required.

Spinning reels have a gear box that is well sealed. If the seals have not been broken to the point at which water gets in, leave the reel alone. If water has gotten into the gear box, clean the box with gasoline and repack it with the lightweight grease that is sold for reels or power tools. Fill the gear box about one-third full of grease, being sure to cover all of the moving parts. The spool is easily removed from most spinning reels, and the area behind the spool, which has a tendency to collect dirt, should be cleaned and oiled. One potential trouble spot in many spinning reels is the bail and bail spring. If the bail does not close crisply, the spring should be replaced.

Fly reels are simple to disassemble and clean. Ordinarily, they require only a seasonal cleaning and oiling.

It is important to use the correct size screwdriver when removing or tightening the screws on your reels. The heads of the tiny screws are easily damaged, making it impossible to remove or tighten them properly.

Fishing lines need little maintenance. Fly lines should be cleaned at the end of the season, and there are many commercial line cleaners that will remove a buildup of slime or algae from them. Dishwashing detergent works just as well. A sinking line sinks better, a floating line floats better, and they both cast better when clean.

Monofilament lines should be changed at the beginning of each season if they have had a lot of wear. If the amount of line on the reel is enough for good casting, I usually try and get two seasons out of my lines. The way you can determine if your mono lines need changing is if they break easily when knotted or stay in coils after about twenty minutes of fishing. Monofilament line is not very expensive, and most good sports shops will refill your reels from bulk spools at a reasonable price. New line is your best form of fishing insurance.

It's a good idea to carry your rods in a case, especially if they are fragile graphite or boron. You can make your own rod cases from three-inch PVC plastic water pipe. Connecting sleeves are easily glued to the pipe with PVC cement, and a threaded adapter with a threaded plug can be added at each end for easy rod removal. A three-inch plastic rod case will safely hold several rods, is almost indestructible, and will cost under ten dollars to assemble.

If you don't already do so, it's a good idea to carry a couple of extra tip guides of different sizes and a package of ferrule cement in your tackle box. Rod tips are easily broken by car doors, by being sat upon, or if you take a fall. If you have only one rod with you, a broken tip means the end of your fishing day. By adding a new tip where the rod broke, you will at least be able to keep fishing. It won't look very good or cast as well as the original, but it will be functional.

When that first warm spring day arrives and you grab your equipment and head for pond or stream, open your tackle box and take a good look. If you're like me, it won't look that clean and orderly for another year.

19

Freezing Fish

The problem with frozen fish is that it just won't keep long unless special care is taken. Simply wrapping it in plastic or aluminum foil does not protect it, and in about three months it will have lost so much moisture and flavor that it will barely be worth eating. The drying results from freezer burn, or sublimation, a condition that occurs when ice turns to vapor without first becoming water. The low vapor pressure of ice in a cold freezer adds to the problem by removing most of the remaining water vapor as automatic defrosting occurs.

The process for keeping frozen fish from freezer burn is easy. The following method will safely keep fish frozen for two years without any drying or appreciable loss of flavor.

For all fish, clean, fillet, or skin them as you would normally. The heads and tails should be removed along with any dried blood at the top of the body cavity. An old toothbrush will easily remove this dried blood.

The sooner the fish is frozen the better it will taste when thawed. If your fish can't be frozen the day it's caught, it should be cleaned and put on ice as soon as possible. As long as it is kept cool, it can be stored for about three days without flavor loss.

I use well-rinsed milk cartons as freezer containers, but you can purchase plastic containers specifically designed for frozen foods. Place the cleaned and rinsed fish in the container and add water to within about an inch of the top. Cover the fish completely but be sure to leave space at the top of the container because the water will expand as it freezes. Tap the sides of the container to remove all air bubbles and place it in your freezer. That's all there is to it.

The success of this method is due to the fact that the fish is frozen inside a solid block of ice, thereby eliminating moisture loss. Once the fish is frozen, each container should be labeled with its contents and the date. In this way you can select your older containers for first cooking and ensure rotation of your stock.

To thaw the fish, remove the frozen block of ice and fish from its container, put it in a strainer or colander, and leave it at room temperature. This allows the melting water to drain away from the fish and keeps it from becoming soft or mushy. If you're in a hurry, run cold water over the block of frozen fish. Don't use warm water because it will soften the fish.

Once the fish is completely thawed, pat it dry with a paper towel and prepare it with your favorite recipe. If you enjoy eating fish as much as I do, you'll find this little extra work well worth the effort.

PART TWO

THE FISH
and
HOW TO
CATCH THEM

20

Largemouth Bass

If all of the approximately 100 million anglers in North America got together and designed a fish that had the best characteristics of a fine aquatic adversary, they would undoubtedly come up with the largemouth bass. This fish is by far the most popular and sought-after game fish in North America.

Largemouths are called by many names, including black bass, green trout, and old bucketmouth, but nobody calls them pretty. When young, bass might be called handsome and trim in their quasi-formal attire, but when they get big (over about six pounds) they change into something resembling a middleweight prizefighter who has spent too many years in the ring. Big bass look nasty. Their mouths and heads grow large and out of proportion to their bodies; their stomachs drop and they get thick around the middle. Many have scars around their mouths and heads from run-ins with something they tried to eat that had a serious objection. I am reminded that when I dove on Australia's Great Barrier Reef, I was warned that the big groupers, which resemble largemouths, were to be treated with respect and were as dangerous as sharks. If bass grew as big as grouper, no one would ever go diving—or for that matter, swimming—in fresh water.

The black basses are members of the sunfish family. There are six species and five subspecies, but the most widely distributed and popular of the group are the largemouth bass (*Micropterus salmoides*) and the Florida largemouth bass (*Micropterus salmoides floridanus*). The Florida bass differs from the northern form only in scale count and size. For example, the northern largemouth has from fifty-nine to sixty-eight scales in the lateral line. The Florida largemouth has sixty-nine to seventy-three scales in the lateral line. The Florida subspecies, however, grows larger than its northern cousin regardless of environment.

Contrary to popular belief, bass are not a very "smart" fish. Many anglers believe that bass can learn the difference between natural baits and artificial lures, and that this is why a lure that was good one year will not be good the next. In very small ponds or controlled test tanks the fish may learn to differentiate between bait and lures, but my experience is that bass in the wild don't learn from their experiences with lures. I have taken the same fish from the same location year after year on the same artificial lure, and there is no doubt that they are the same fish because I have tagged them.

Bass have a huge mouth and a high ratio of fin surface to body size, giving them great maneuverability. They can swim quickly in short bursts in any direction, even backward. Their design makes them efficient aquatic predators.

The fish have extremely sensitive taste buds inside their mouths and on the outside of their lips. Their nostrils are so sensitive that they can smell minute traces, in parts per million, of substances in the water. For this reason I wash my hands before starting to fish and again during the day to remove traces of gasoline, insect repellent, or suntan lotion. I would like to be able to state with certainty that washing my hands makes a difference in the number of strikes I get, but I really can't. However, I do believe that some lures, such as plastic worms, pick up and transmit scents, and I feel that when using these soft lures washing my hands is a form of insurance. Besides, I like the ritual aspects of the handwashing process.

Largemouths have an excellent sense of hearing. Their ears are deep inside their head and consist of a series of connecting bones and an air bladder that acts as an amplifier. They also pick up sounds and vibrations through their lateral lines, which contain highly sensitive nerve endings and run—one on either side of their body—from their gills to the base of their tail. Conversation between anglers in a boat apparently does not disturb them, but dropping something on the deck will send a largemouth scurrying for cover. A piece of carpet on the deck of the boat reduces the amount of noise and scares fewer fish. The noise of electric or outboard motors apparently does not upset fish that are in water deeper than about six feet.

Bass do become accustomed to sounds and recognize familiar forage by their vibrations. Also, injured forage fish give off vibrations that attract and excite the bass. For this reason it pays to experiment with different "sonic" lures. These lures are designed to give off underwater vibrations, and when you find one that emits a sound familiar to the bass in a particular body of water, you will catch more fish. The secret to sonic lures is to experiment until you find the one that sounds like the common available forage. Some anglers who use large minnows for bass have discovered that they can frequently trigger a feeding reaction by clipping a bit of the tail fin off the baitfish, prompting it to give off distress vibrations.

Bass are nearsighted. Their eyes contain no lids and the iris of each eye is fixed, which is why the fish prefer locations where the light is subdued. But while they are nearsighted, bass can see above the surface of the water on a calm day. This above-water vision is very restricted, but an angler fishing from an elevated seat or standing in a boat will scare more fish than an angler sitting lower in the boat.

The eyes of the bass contain rods and cones similar to those present in our own eyes. Under low light conditions and at night the fish cannot distinguish between colors, but during the day color can be important in lure selection. Some studies have suggested that when bass are in an aggressive state gold and yellow repel them while blue and green attract them. I can't testify to the veracity of these findings. I have taken bass on lures of almost every imaginable color, but on some days the fish do display a preference for a specific hue. Again it pays to experiment, and if your chosen lure is not producing, a change to another color may make all the difference.

Young bass will feed on almost anything they can catch, but the older fish tend to become specialized in their feeding habits. Big bass are sedentary loners and prefer such high-protein forage as golden shiners, shad, crawfish, and salamanders. Fishermen who specialize in big bass know the common types of forage available in the body of water they are fishing, and seldom carry tackle boxes loaded with scores of lures. The lunker hunter usually concentrates on properly presenting three or four kinds of offerings that represent the common available forage.

The metabolism of bass is determined by their internal enzyme activity. Water temperatures between 68 and 72°F produce peak enzyme activity. However, because bass are cold-blooded and their bodies are always at the same temperature as the surrounding water, water temperatures above or below this preferred range mean less enzyme activity and reduced feeding by the fish. Therefore, at water temperatures above or below the preferred range, knowledgeable bass fishermen use live bait or lures that can be retrieved slowly. Some bass anglers have taken to using commercial temperature indicators that can read water temperatures at depths of up to a hundred feet. But while temperature indicators may be helpful in determining the activity of bass, most bass fishermen realize that the comfort zone for these fish is comparatively warm and that in most bodies of water they will be in water from six to fifteen feet deep. I've found that a good indicator of proper water temperature is the presence of bluegills, which are close relatives of bass. Wherever large concentrations of bluegills are found the bass usually won't be far away, because bluegills prefer approximately the same water temperature and frequently make up a substantial part of the forage for the larger bass.

Largemouths spawn under a wide variety of water conditions. Most spawning takes place in the spring when water temperatures are between 63 and 65°F, but spawning can occur at any temperature between about 60 and 70°F. A sudden change in water temperature will interrupt spawning, and the fish can wait until conditions are once again to their liking, for as long as two months, before spawning again. Largemouths usually build their nests within ten feet from shore, at least twenty feet apart, and near some sort of cover that will offer protection from predators for their young. The nests may be built in a wide variety of bottom conditions from sand to mud. The loose debris is swept away with broad strokes of the tail until hard clay, rock, or gravel is reached. I have found bass nests in water as shallow as eight inches and as deep as about twenty feet. In bodies of water that are discolored or muddy the nests are usually shallow, while in clear lakes the nests are ordinarily deeper.

A healthy female bass may produce more than thirty thousand eggs. After she has deposited them into the nest, the male moves over the area and releases his milt, which he spreads over the spawning site with sweeps of his lowered tail. Occasionally two or three pairs of bass will spawn in the same nest, but only the dominant pair will remain to guard the young.

After spawning, the male remains on the nest and drives away any intruders that enter the area. The female usually moves to deeper water near the nest for about two to five days and repels intruders that would enter the area from deep water. The longer the female stays near the nest, the better the chances for a successful spawn.

Bluegills and salamanders are notorious nest raiders. If a lake contains a very large bluegill population, the male bass may have a difficult job keeping them away from the eggs. I have seen bass nests that were literally surrounded by a wall of bluegills waiting for the opportunity to rush in to grab a quick meal of bass eggs. Even when spawning is successful, the exertion required by the male bass in guarding the nest may cause him to die from exhaustion. The presence of large numbers of bluegills may also put so much stress on the spawning female that she may lay her eggs prematurely, thereby reducing successful spawning.

When the female eventually moves away from the deep side of the nest she drifts into deeper water, or, in very shallow lakes, into open pockets in the weeds. The fish suspend themselves between the surface and the bottom and barely move while recuperating from the spawning effort. A few females die after spawning, but most fish that are in good physical condition recover quickly.

Bass do not feed while recuperating from spawning. The reason that they can be caught throughout the spring is that not all are recuperating at the same time. Spawning takes place over several months and involves many different groups of fish.

After the young emerge from the eggs the male bass guards them for a few days. He then goes to deeper water where he suspends and enters a recuperation period of a week or longer. The bass fry remain on the nest until their yolk sacs are absorbed and then school in shallow water near cover. They feed on microscopic plankton until they reach a length of about two inches, when they seek increasingly larger food items such as insects and smaller fishes. Bass fry are a transparent yellow color with a distinctive black stripe down each side, and are a favorite forage for other predator species.

Most bass live out their lives within a few hundred yards of where they were hatched. They do change position during each day, and general location as the seasons progress, but do not roam throughout the lake or other water body in which they live.

STRUCTURE

Largemouths inhabit an amazing variety of waters. I've taken fish over eight pounds from tiny farm ponds of just a few acres that are no deeper than five feet. In summer these ponds look and feel like a hot chocolate milkshake, and I'm amazed that the fish are able to survive the heat and turbidity. I've also taken big bass from crystal-clear impoundments, and many of those fish were hooked at depths exceeding fifty feet. It would be impossible to describe every type of water in which bass are found. Thankfully that isn't necessary, because throughout their range bass have one thing in common: they are rarely found far from some kind of "structure."

A structure is nothing more than any underwater feature that is noticeably different from the surrounding area. Brush piles, logs, stumps, dropoffs, old creek beds, ledges, submerged islands, deep points, and bridge pilings or abutments are all forms of structure. In some lakes a change in the composition of the bottom, say from mud to rock or sand, is enough structure to attract and hold the fish. Naturally not every structure in each lake will attract and hold bass, but as professional guides are so fond of saying: "You may find structure without bass, but you will never find bass without structure."

One good way to get a feeling for structure is to drive around the countryside looking at various types of landscapes and then imagine them submerged under water. You will notice that hills become points projecting out from your imaginary shoreline, elongated mounds running across fields become underwater humps, small rolling hills become submerged islands, and depressions become holes. Once you have identified the structures in your "lake," pick out the following areas: the deepest part of the lake, the shallows where bass might spawn, areas where the bottom would be rocky or soft and muddy, and areas where there would be underwater steps of ledge or bedrock. This part is easy, but the next one is harder and more important: try and pick out locations where the structure would extend from the imaginary shoreline to the very deepest water in that area. A long sloping ridgeline would be a good example. In a real lake these are potential hot-spots for bass. Other hot-spots are the most irregular structure in a particular area. For example, if there are brush piles and downed trees in one area of your imaginary lake, look for the biggest pile or the largest tree, the ones that stand out from the rest. These features are the ones most likely to hold large concentrations of fish in an actual body of water. Remember, *structure* simply means *object*, and the more irregular the object, the better the chances it will attract and hold bass.

ELECTRONIC EQUIPMENT

A lot of electronic equipment is available to the bass angler. Depthfinders are the most popular, but there are also temperature indicators, oxygen meters, and pH meters. I don't own any of them. I'm sure that these instruments can improve one's fishing productivity, but having spent time fishing with friends who own electronic devices, I've decided to do without them for the time being. My experience is that I spend almost all my time watching the electronic gear. Even when the depthfinder is turned off, I still keep glancing at the little green box. The use of electronic gear is positively addictive, and I wish I had been as wise about my reaction to my first cigarette as I was about my first reaction to electronic gear. I don't want to spend most of my fishing time looking over my shoulder at gauges and dials. I like being able to look around at my surroundings while I'm fishing, and I enjoy mentally charting the bottom of the body of water I'm fishing by feeling what is happening at the end of my line. Whether or not to use electronic equipment is something each angler has to decide for himself. If you are very limited in your fishing time, and if catching a lot of fish is of primary importance to you, then you should consider purchasing a depthfinder. With a depthfinder the bass angler can easily find the necessary structure, and once you learn to use it your fishing will improve if your techniques for presenting bait and lures are good. Depthfinders can make deep trolling easier and more productive, and I discuss their use in the sections dealing with the individual species of fish and in Chapter 42, "Trolling."

SPRING FISHING TECHNIQUES

Spring bass fishing, before the fish spawn, is some of the best fishing of the year. However, the fish are very vulnerable at this time and a greedy fisherman can do real damage to the bass population. A few states don't open their bass season until after much of the spawning is complete. Unfortunately, many states have no closed season at all. Studies have shown that in smaller lakes, particularly those in the northern half of the country where the growing season is short and the bass population limited, the killing of too many bass can do irreparable harm to the breeding population. Fish hooked at this time of the year should be brought quickly to boatside, held partially out of the water by the lower lip as the hooks are gently removed, and then released. (See Chapter 44, "Catch-and-Release Fishing," for a discussion of how to do this properly.) There is plenty of time—the whole summer, fall, and winter—to take all the bass any civilized person could possibly eat.

In the spring, more than any other time of the year, the weather directly influences bass fishing. A temperature change of just a few degrees can determine whether the fish are feeding aggressively or lying quietly beyond a cold-water dropoff. Until the water temperature reaches about 55°F there isn't much feeding. The bass tend to be logy and immobile in cold water. But some areas of a lake will warm faster than others, and you would be wise to concentrate your early spring efforts on the western shoreline of the lake, the area that receives the first sun in the morning. Shallow bays warm faster than the main body of the lake and may be as much as five degrees warmer than surrounding waters, especially if they have a dark-colored bottom that absorbs the sun's heat.

In that brief period just prior to spawning the bass are very aggressive and can be taken on a variety of lures. I use standard baitcasting equipment: a medium-weight rod about six feet long and an Ambassadeur 5000C reel spooled with twelve-pound-test line. One of my favorite spring lures is a quarter-ounce spinnerbait. Color doesn't seem important, although I find that I instinctively reach for a lure that is chartreuse. At this time of the year it isn't necessary to impart any special action to the spinnerbait, and I use a slow, steady retrieve. I drift in deeper water and cast into the shallows. The fish can be at very shallow depths, and I sometimes do best by tossing my lure right on the bank and dragging it off into the water. I've taken big fish in water so shallow that their backs were literally out of the water when they hit the spinnerbait. If I'm not getting strikes in the shallows, I let the lure flutter down to the bottom on the edge of deeper water. Sometimes the shallows will contain only small male bass and the larger females will be found just off the deep edges of the dropoffs.

Plastic worms, rigged Texas-style, are also excellent in the early spring. The bass often hit the worm when it is sinking and immediately swim toward the nearest deep water. If I fish straight in toward the bank I frequently have trouble hooking a fish, because it swims directly toward me with the worm in its mouth and it is difficult to take up slack line quickly enough to set the hook. I do better by making long casts parallel to shore. In this way, when a fish heads for deep water, he is swimming away from me or to one side, and I can maintain enough tension on the line to solidly set the hook.

When the fish are feeding actively and can be seen chasing forage in the shallows, a floating-diving lure such as a Rapala or Bang-O-Lure will often trigger explosive strikes. I like to toss these lures into pockets in the brush and let them sit quietly with occasional twitches. I have a couple of topwater lures that I have rigged for early spring fishing. I have removed the treble hooks from these lures and replaced each with a single No. 2/0 long-shanked hook. I seem to hook as many fish with these singles as with trebles, and besides not hanging up in the brush as often, the single hooks allow for quick, easy release of the fish.

In the spring I cover a lot of water until I find the fish. I concentrate on bays, channels into bays, and sloughs. As mentioned earlier, shallow areas with a dark bottom warm fastest, and I have found that small depressions in a dark-bottomed flat will frequently hold large numbers of fish. You should fish these shallow depressions in dark-bottomed bays with real care.

When the waters warm to the low sixties the female bass become less aggressive and extremely wary. The males, on the other hand, remain aggressive, and although not feeding will strike almost anything that passes near the nest. I stop all bass fishing when the fish are actually spawning; while male fish can be taken easily at this time, the moment they are removed from the nest site bluegills will rush in and decimate the nest. Even if the male bass is quickly and carefully returned to the water his fight has robbed him of much of his strength and he may be unable to successfully defend the nest.

SUMMER TECHNIQUES

Summer is my favorite time of the year for intensive bassing. The lakes, and the fish as well, have established their warm-water patterns, and while some anglers claim that the actual summer conditions last only a few weeks, I believe they last from about two to six months, depending upon the location.

During the summer period the aquatic ecosystem reaches its growing peak. Spawning is complete, the waters have warmed, weed growth has matured, and abundant prey is available in the form of rapidly multiplying plankton and schools of recently hatched fry. At this time of the year it isn't difficult to determine the general location of the bass. The deep, open water basins will contain few forage fish and consequently few bass. For the balance of the summer the bass will inhabit areas from just off the deep side of weedbeds into the weeds themselves where the water is about four to twenty feet deep. These areas are commonly called "flats," and the best are those with a widely varying bottom composition, ranging from rock to mud, as well as surrounding areas of thick aquatic growth that offer shade and protection. The best weedy areas are those with openings and pockets where the bass can hunt.

Submerged humps and ridgelines are also excellent for summer bassing. During the day I like to fish a Texas-rigged eight-inch blue or grape-colored plastic worm on a No. 4/0 stainless-steel southern Sproat worm hook. I add a single #5 splitshot just above the hook and work the worm in rapid hops along the deep side of the structure. If the water is very clear I crawl the worm very slowly. I usually start by fishing a lot of water rather quickly until I find the fish, then I slow down and start fishing methodically. I wear polarized sun glasses, which allow me to see the outer edge of submerged weedbeds. Because weedbeds have many dips and bends and the location of the shade will change throughout the day, I have found it important to note the location of the summer sun when fishing these areas. I concentrate on casting into areas where the sun is shining directly into my face. That means that the weedbed is throwing a shadow over its outer edge in my direction, and these shady areas will frequently attract and hold large numbers of light-sensitive bass.

In some bodies of water the weedbeds are dense mats or carpets of surface growth that do not reach to the bottom. It is shady and cool under these mats, often as much as ten degrees cooler than the surrounding open water. The best way I've found to fish these large floating mats is to hook a six- or eight-inch golden shiner near the base of the tail and try to get it to swim under the mat. Sometimes it takes some doing to get a minnow to swim under the vegetation; some minnows won't get anywhere near it, whereas others will eagerly strike out for the center of the mat. Sometimes adding a small splitshot at the head of the hook will cause a hesitant minnow to change direction and swim under the weeds. When a bass hits one of these big minnows it often looks as if there is an explosion under the weeds. I have taken some of my biggest bass using this technique.

Another way I like to fish heavy vegetation with a minnow is to use a bobber. The bobber should be placed far enough above the minnow to allow it to almost reach bottom. I add just enough weight to let the minnow come to the surface and then drift back down. I believe the continual surfacing and drifting back down of the minnow is the natural action of a wounded baitfish, and more than once I have had my minnow jump over the bobber followed closely by a big bass. I prefer to hook the minnow lightly under the back fin, and I fish the rig on the outside edges or in pockets in the weeds.

A friend of mine discovered another productive way to use minnows for bass. He and his son were fishing a lake in southern New York State. They were using large minnows fished under a bobber and were catching some big bass. The problem was that small pickerel were killing their pond shiners at an alarming rate, and there was no chance that they would make it through the afternoon without running out of live bait. They began to throw dead shiners back into the bucket for emergency use. When the live shiners were gone they began to experiment with the dead ones and came up with a method that was even more successful than the bobber and live-shiner technique.

They fished the dead shiners in conjunction with northern spinnerbaits. The most effective of these lures proved to be a three-quarter-ounce purple Rooster Tail with a large dead shiner hooked through both lips on one of the treble hooks. The small pickerel were intimidated by the total size of the lure, but casting it parallel to the outside edge of the weedbeds proved excellent for big bass. I've found this rig also to be excellent on hot summer afternoons when trolled about three feet off the bottom in water about twenty feet deep. I wouldn't go out and kill a whole bucketful of minnows to try this method; it's smarter to just save the dead minnows from the morning hours and put them to use with a Rooster Tail during the "dog" hours of midday.

One mistake many anglers make is to continue to fish topwater lures in holes or pockets in the weeds through the heat of the summer day. This is an excellent spring or fall technique, but during the summer heat the bass are closer to the bottom and ordinarily feed near the surface only on windy days or under the low light conditions at dawn and dusk. Fishing the bottoms of pockets and hole areas with a plastic worm, jig-and-minnow combination, or slow-moving spinnerbait will be much more productive than tossing topwater lures.

Bass strike different lures in different ways. A big bass can inhale a large crankbait, even one fitted with three sets of treble hooks, move along with the lure in his mouth, and then expel it without the angler's ever knowing that he had a strike. It is essential that you become familiar with the action of the lure you're using so that you can recognize any unnatural interruption in that action. For instance, every bass fisherman has had the experience of moving a crankbait through underwater obstructions such as limbs or stumps. On the retrieve there will be a second or two when the lure doesn't seem to run properly, its vibrations stop, and for an instant the line goes slack. Many anglers assume that the lure has caught on a branch for a second, and as they keep reeling in the action of the lure returns. What may have happened is that a big bass that was following the lure has flared his gills and taken the lure completely into his mouth. In that instant of slack line the fish has "tasted" the lure and expelled it. It is essential that you learn to recognize these unnatural actions of your lure and react by instantly setting the hook. Sometimes you will find yourself attached to some underwater obstruction, but when you set the hook you will as often as not find yourself attached to a big angry bass.

I've also found that deep-running crankbaits with large lips or bills will often bounce off an underwater object without becoming snagged. Many times a bass will strike just after the lure bounces off the object. These strikes are difficult to detect and often feel like a faint "click" on the line. As mentioned earlier, it is essential that you become familiar with the action of the lure you're using so that you will recognize the unnatural actions that signify a strike.

When fishing shorelines we all occasionally toss our lure into the branches of a tree that is hanging over the water. When this happens don't be in too much of a hurry to yank the lure out of the tree. Often, bass that are in the area will move under the lure and look up at it, and if you can free the lure with gentle twitches and allow it to fall into the water beneath the tree you'll get an immediate strike. If the lure drops from the tree and you don't get a strike, don't be in too big a hurry to retrieve it. Let it sit for a moment and give it occasional twitches. Even sinking crankbaits, spinnerbaits, jigs, and worms that have been pulled out of a tree should be allowed to sit under the tree before being retrieved.

One additional word about crankbaits. Although I have found that in clear water those crankbaits that have shot-filled rattle chambers that create underwater sounds when retrieved will frequently scare the bass, when the water is very dingy or muddy, these lures will often produce. The reason for this is that in muddy water the fish feed more by sound than sight, and as a general rule I would suggest that you use these rattle lures primarily when the water is discolored.

I have sometimes had trouble hooking bass on spinnerbaits. In such cases I have found that it helps to add a trailer hook, called a stinger, to the lure. It is a simple matter to slip a No. 2/0 or larger hook with a large eye over the point and barb of the hook on the lure, and it will make a difference in the number of fish you hook. I have also found that bass often hit a spinnerbait from the side, in which case the strike is not a distinct pull on the line. When using spinnerbaits, any movement to the side should be answered with an immediate setting of the hook.

Bass strike plastic worms differently under different water conditions. I've found that when the water is discolored the fish will often take the worm when it is falling toward the bottom. This is an indication that you should work the worm in active hops along the bottom. There is little doubt when a fast-moving worm is taken by a bass. The worm will stop suddenly, and if the fish is a big one, there will be an arm-wrenching yank on the line as it heads for the nearest cover. It is very difficult to stop a big bass bent on burying himself in the nearest brush pile. Some of my bassing buddies kidded me when I put seventeen-pound-test line on one of my baitcasting reels, but after losing a few really big bass in obstruction-filled waters they have done the same.

Fishing a plastic worm in clear water is another story. Many anglers work the worm too quickly. In clear water I've watched bass rush to a worm, assume a head-down position a few inches from the worm, and study it. The instant it moves, even slightly, the bass rush away. In clear water a plastic worm should be almost still-fished, and when it is moved it should not be hopped, but dragged very slowly over the bottom barely an inch at a time. This kind of fishing takes real patience, and recognizing a strike can be difficult. I describe these strikes as feeling as if someone has gently closed a door at the other end of the line, which I believe best describes the slight change in pressure on the line that often signals such a strike. Sometimes there will be a few gentle taps or twitches of the line when the bass engulfs and mouths the worm. After enough experience with fishing plastic worms you will learn to strike as much from instinct as from feel.

One additional word about fishing plastic worms. When I first started using them I was sold on using bullet-type slip sinkers, my feeling being that a slip sinker would allow the bass to be able to pick up the worm and swim away with it without feeling the weight of the sinker. The slip sinker did work that way, but when the fish moved off at an angle to the sinker there would be too much slack in the line to solidly set the hook. These days I use a weighted jig head in water without many obstructions, and where I'm using a Texas rig I clip a splitshot to the line right at the head of the worm. It has become obvious to me that the bass takes the whole worm and weight into its mouth with no hesitation, and the fixed sinker allows me to hook many more bass.

Like most bass fishermen I prefer to catch the fish on topwater lures. I like to be able to see the strike, and the topwaters are easy to fish. You can work them fast or slow or toss them into pockets in the weeds and give them an occasional twitch. Most of the big flashy strikes on surface lures are from small bass, but I have taken some of my biggest bass on such lures. When a big bass takes a surface lure he usually comes up under the lure, flares his gills, and the lure simply disappears from the surface of the water in a tiny whirlpool. This kind of a strike can make you cross-eyed, and if you aren't ready you'll miss a lot of big bass. All of the really big bass I have taken on surface lures have hit the lure when it was not moving at all, and many of these fish have taken the lure after it was lying motionless on the water for more than two minutes. It takes a lot of patience to let a lure sit motionless on the water, but the longer you let it sit the better your chances of hooking a really big bass.

DEEP-WATER BASS

Most bass are taken in water less than twenty feet deep, the exception being in the deep impoundments of the South and Southwest and in southern California. The California lakes were stocked with northern largemouths in the 1940s, but during the late 1950s many of the lakes received additional stockings of the Florida subspecies. A number of bass over twenty pounds have been taken from these lakes and I believe the next world record will be a California bass. The current record is twenty-two pounds four ounces, taken from Montgomery Lake, Georgia.

In the spring and fall some big bass are taken from the shallows of the California lakes, but most of the real lunkers are taken deep. In fact, they are taken so deep that many experienced bass anglers are wondering if traditional bassing methods are literally touching only the tip of the bass population. My feeling is that bass are going to seek out the kinds of structure they prefer, and in very deep lakes the reefs, dropoffs, and submerged islands and humps that bass tend to populate are also very deep.

The deep-water bass were discovered by fishermen trolling for rainbow trout. With a few adaptations, bass anglers are now bottom-scratching and picking up lots of huge fish. The most popular equipment consists of large reels like the Garcia Ambassadeur 7000 and the Penn 500. A heavy baitcasting or trolling rod and lead-core line testing up to thirty pounds are used to troll large, deep-diving crankbaits such as Rebels, Cisco Kids, and CD-18 Rapalas. The lures are trolled over structures in depths up to and exceeding eighty feet, and the use of a depthfinder is essential for locating these structures. Many anglers believe that lures representing small rainbow trout are most effective, and small rainbows may indeed be the major bass forage in these deep impoundments.

I prefer to stand while trolling and hold the rod in my hands. When there are more than 100 yards of line between the rod and the lure, the line stretch is considerable even with lead-core line, and you must be able to feel the strike and react quickly. If you put your rod in a holder you'll miss many strikes.

Deep trolling can get expensive. The big lures tend to hang up easily, and at a minimum of about five dollars each you don't have to lose too many to put a dent in your wallet. This kind of deep trolling isn't for every bass angler, especially if you like to cast, but if you're looking for a new world's record it's probably your best bet.

NIGHT FISHING

During the summer, anyplace where bass are found, some of the best bassing is at night; but some lakes are better than others. I've found that bodies of water that are naturally discolored or muddy produce better during the day. Lakes with ultra-clear water, especially those that are busy during the daylight hours with swimmers and water skiers, come alive with feeding fish after the sun goes down and their waters become quiet.

The best night fishing takes place when it is pitch black and there is no moon. Bass are very light-sensitive, and on these dark nights you must be careful not to shine a light on the surface of the water, an action that will instantly spook the fish. When I use a light to change lures or to unravel a tangle in my line I keep it very low in the boat. It helps to wrap your flashlight in red cellophane or to use one of the so-called Moon-Glo softlights that cast a gentle circle of light over a very small area.

At night the bass enter the shallows to feed, and I've had my best results along shorelines with downed trees, sandy beach areas, and off rocky points. I've also had excellent fishing around boat docks and swimming floats. One of my favorite night bassing locations is a large lake where there are three summer camps. During the day the lake is literally full of kids swimming, boating, canoeing, and doing a variety of other water activities. At night, when things quiet down, I have taken some real lunker bass by casting surface lures to the boat docks and swimming floats that dot the lake. If the kids ever saw the size of some of these fish they would probably be afraid to dangle their feet off those docks.

Surface lures are my favorite night lures and I fish them on spinning tackle. I find spinning tackle to be best because there is less possibility of line tangles and backlashes, and at night even a minor backlash turns into a major headache. I use traditional surface lures such as Jitterbugs and Crazy-crawlers; buzzing a spinnerbait can also be effective. It is important to use a steady retrieve, regardless of the lure you're using, because at night the fish find the lure by its sound. If you vary your retrieve you'll hear splashes in the vicinity of the lure but feel nothing. The splashes are fish that have homed in on the lure but missed it when the retrieve was stopped or varied.

COLD-WATER BASSING

When the water gets cold it is difficult to find and catch bass. A few fish are taken by northern ice fishermen, but when water temperatures get below about 48°F the bass don't feed actively and tend to bunch into very tight schools as if attempting to keep warm. As the water gets colder, even the bass in southern lakes that never freeze over drift into deep water near some sort of structure such as a stand of timber, brush, or a rock pile. In many lakes the bass suspend themselves in cover that is well off the bottom, such as submerged tree tops, making it even more difficult to find and catch them.

When fishing open lakes in winter, I concentrate on steep shorelines where cliffs drop off into very deep water near the shore and where I know there is submerged timber on or near the bottom. Vertical jigging with spoons is the most productive method under these conditions, and my favorite lures are the Hopkins Shorty and the Little Cleo. I drop the spoon to the depth at which I think the fish will be found and simply jig it up and down. I believe the reason that vertical jigging with spoons is so effective, especially in southern lakes, is that the bass have been conditioned by their last big feed. The first real cold weather to hit the lake usually results in a tremendous winter kill of shad. The shad sink slowly to the bottom with a fluttering and twitching movement. The spoon probably looks like a dying shad and the bass often hit it as it is sinking, or on the downward jigging motion. Remarkably, for reasons that I don't understand, this same technique also works in lakes containing no shad population.

When vertical jigging you must remain alert to any slight hesitation as the spoon sinks, and you must set the hook quickly. Spinnerbaits can also be jigged vertically, or if you must cast, they can be retrieved with a very slight pumping action.

It is important that you mentally mark the depth at which you take your first winter bass. By fishing at that depth you may discover a large concentration of fish clustered into a very small area. When a school of cold-weather bass can be located they can be caught, but the lure must always be fished very slowly.

In winter some huge bass are taken from lakes in the Deep South. The fish feed actively in the comparatively cool waters and can frequently be found in the sun-warmed shallows during the day, often in water less than a foot deep. Casting the shoreline with a plastic worm or spinnerbait can be very productive, especially around the edges of reedy flats.

Small farm ponds are also excellent for winter fishing. When I was an Arkansas resident I would travel around the state looking for tiny farm ponds. When I saw a likely looking one I would stop and ask permission to fish, and I was rarely refused. The biggest bass I ever caught was taken from a pond of less than three acres in Palarm, Arkansas. It was New Year's Day and cold, but I had the day off from work and was determined to fish. I knew the farmer who owned the pond and we had an agreement that I could fish whenever I wished, but that all the bass I caught had to be released. I was casting an eight-inch black plastic worm with a small splitshot just above the hook, just enough weight to let me feel bottom. The deepest part of the pond was less than six feet deep and I would let the worm sink to the bottom and crawl it slowly back in to me. On this particular cast I felt a faint tap when the worm was in very shallow water almost at my feet. I lifted the rod tip and a huge bass immediately came to the surface and lay on her side, my worm in the corner of her mouth. The fish didn't fight at all in the cold water but just lay there, gills pumping. I lipped the fish and slid her gently onto the bank. I quickly cut a piece of line the length of the fish and then slid her back into the pond. I wish I had thought to cut another piece of line that measured the fish's girth, but at the time I didn't. Back at the house the piece of line I had cut to measure the fish came out to be 28½ inches long. I don't even want to venture a guess at the weight of that bass, but it was by far the largest one I have ever taken, even if the fight was something short of spectacular. You can be sure I fished that pond very hard the next spring, but my best fish after that went only a shade over eight pounds, twenty-two inches. If you have small farm ponds in your area it is definitely worth giving them a try, and leave your ultra-light gear at home.

MEXICAN BASS

I would be remiss here if I didn't mention bass fishing south of the border. Many lakes in Mexico and other Central American countries have been stocked with Florida bass, and winter fishing there is phenomenal and a great excuse for leaving cold weather behind. My favorite lake is Vicente Guerrero on Mexico's east coast, not far from the beautiful Ciudad Victoria. Guerrero has the reputation of being a lake where an angler can catch over a hundred bass a day, and that is not an exaggeration. In fact, an experienced angler can catch twice that many fish in a day's outing if he sets out to do so. My only complaint with Guerrero is the size of the fish. The biggest bass I have ever taken there was a shade over five pounds, and while I have seen a few fish from that lake that weighed over seven pounds, they were the exception. Most of the bass are in the two- to three-pound class, and while it is great fun to catch them easily on almost any lure, I would look to the lakes of southern California and those of our own southeastern states if I were hunting for a trophy fish. In a few years, however, Guerrero should be producing lots of very big bass.

I have a lot of respect for largemouth bass, so much that I find it difficult to kill even a few for the frying pan. There is a popular view that holds that it is impossible for anglers using conventional fishing equipment to do damage to the bass population in any body of water. I don't believe this. Our increasing knowledge of the habits of these fine fish, and advances in equipment and electronic gear, have made it possible to take so many fish that many bodies of water are suffering from angling pressure.

I don't mean to suggest that there is anything wrong with the angler who keeps fish for his own table or who decides to have a real trophy bass mounted for his wall. But more than once I have been disgusted to find that the person holding the stringer full of bass doesn't like to eat fish and gives them to neighbors or throws them away after showing them off. Many of today's bass anglers have developed a new ethic. Instead of getting their kicks from killing a lot of fish, they get their satisfaction from putting to use the skills required to find and catch bass, and they know they don't have to kill the source of their enjoyment to satisfy their egos. Once he has found and caught the fish, the modern angler carefully releases most of them with the certain knowledge that by so doing he is assuring the future of his sport.

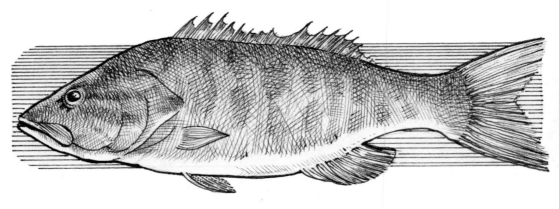

21

Smallmouth Bass

The smallmouth bass (*Micropterus dolomieui*) is one of the most sought-after game fish in North America. It is excellent table fare, but the quality that most endears it to the angler is its fighting ability. When hooked near the surface a smallmouth will ordinarily jump high into the air and can often shake the hook or lure from its mouth. When hooked in deep water the fish is a determined, powerful fighter, and even after it has been landed it flares its fins, clamps its jaw, and continues to look and act belligerent. The smallmouth bass is a fish that just won't quit.

The original range of the smallmouth was through the Great Lakes and St. Lawrence and Ohio River drainage systems, but when the railroad cars of the United States Fish Commission began to roll in the late 1800s, smallmouth bass fry were among the early passengers. Today, as a result of extensive stocking, the fish is found throughout southern Canada, south to Alabama, and west to Oklahoma.

Smallies thrive in clear rocky lakes and streams. They prefer lakes that have depths of at least thirty feet and summer water temperatures between 50° and 80°F. In rivers the fish prefer fairly fast, clear water that flows over gravel, boulders, or ledges. For a river or stream to maintain a good smallmouth population it should have a pitch or drop of not less than four feet per mile and not more than twenty feet per mile.

Smallmouths feed very little at water temperatures below 50°F. They spend most of the winter months lying on the bottom in water from about thirty to thirty-five feet deep. When the water temperatures rise to about 55°F the fish congregate in large schools in water from about ten to fourteen feet deep, not far from their shallow spawning areas. Spawning itself takes place when the water temperatures reach the low sixties, which may occur from April to June, depending upon the weather and location.

Prior to spawning, the male smallmouth scrapes a nest about thirty inches in diameter in gravel or coarse stone at a depth of from four to twenty feet. When the nest is finished, the male leads a female to it. After she has deposited her eggs he drives her from the nest and selects another ripe female. As many as half a dozen females may deposit their eggs in a single nest. A female smallmouth may produce up to five thousand eggs per pound of body weight, but many of the eggs are not fertile. The average nest, regardless of how many females have deposited their eggs, contains about two thousand fertile eggs, which hatch in from three to ten days, depending upon the water temperature. The male guards the nest until the eggs hatch. Smallmouth fry are coal black with bright golden eyes.

After the female has deposited her eggs she swims to the bottom in about twenty feet of water and lies on her side. During this time many females develop a white, mucuslike covering over their whole body. A few of the old or weak fish die from the spawning effort, but most survive after a recuperation period of about one week. After the eggs hatch, the males also rest for a week or more. The fish do not feed during the recuperation period.

The growth of the fry depends on the fertility of the body of water. In some lakes it may take up to four years for the fry to reach a mature length of about nine inches. In very fertile lakes maturity may be reached in only two years, but it takes almost ten years for a smallmouth to reach a length of about twenty inches and a weight of about five pounds. Throughout their range smallmouths average between one and three pounds; the largest ever recorded weighed almost twelve pounds and was taken in 1955 from Dale Hollow Lake on the Kentucky–Tennessee border.

After the fish have recovered from spawning they break into two groups. One group, made up of fish that are long and slender in appearance, roams throughout the lake following schools of forage fish. The other group, composed of shorter, stockier fish, immediately takes up residence in deeper water off the spawning grounds and spends the balance of the year in a very small area. These resident fish, in addition to being short and stocky, often have round black spots on their bodies, a result of rubbing on rocks and debris. After about a month the roving fish take up semipermanent residence in water from fifteen to twenty-five feet deep with distinctive bottom features such as rock piles and deep shoals, but they continue to occasionally roam the open-water areas of the lake, individually or in schools. Some fisheries biologists theorize that there may be two subspecies of smallmouth bass, those that roam and those that take up permanent residence, but the existence of any distinct subspecies has not been confirmed.

In the fall the smallmouths move into water about fifteen or twenty feet deep, following schools of forage fish. Many separate schools will band together as the water cools, and divers in Lake Erie report that some schools of fall smallmouths contain many thousands of fish. When the water temperatures once again drop below 50°F the fish move into deep water and become inactive.

Most large bodies of water contain many rocky points and dropoffs that look as if they would hold smallmouths. In fact, the requirements of these fish are so exacting that only a few areas of the lake will attract and hold large numbers of them. To maintain a good population of smallies, an area must contain shallows with a sand-and-rock bottom for spawning. It must also contain large areas of rocky bottom that attract crawfish, weak lake currents that attract baitfish, and a mix of mid-depth and deep areas that meet the temperature requirements demanded by the fish during seasonal changes.

The following are what I believe to be the necessary requirements for prime smallmouth territory. In other words, these features are what I look for when I'm trying to find smallmouths in an unfamiliar body of water. I look first for a flat, shallow point, about eight to ten feet deep, that extends well into deeper water. The point must contain large areas of sand, rock, and gravel, and in the shallows there must be reeds or other aquatic growth. The shoreline itself must contain lots of debris such as stumps and fallen trees. As the point extends into the lake it must drop quickly from about fifteen to forty feet or more in a series of steps that are covered with sand, rocks, and gravel. The very best areas will also contain submerged islands or humps in deep water off the point. These humps should come to within about fifteen feet of the surface and must be flat on top with lots of fist-sized rocks, which provide cover for crawfish. The humps must also go in steps or taper quickly into deep water, and the bottom composition in the twenty- to forty-foot areas must contain a mixture of sand and gravel. That, in a nutshell, is prime, first-rate, four-star smallmouth territory.

SPRING FISHING TECHNIQUES

As mentioned earlier, when water temperatures reach the low fifties the smallmouths start to move. They enter shallows of between about two and eight feet deep and feed on crawfish that are spawning there. If I had to pick one time throughout the season when it is easiest to catch smallmouths, this would be it.

Fishing techniques for spring smallmouths are a matter of personal preference. In the shallows the fish feed actively around fallen trees, rocks, reeds, and even boat docks and floats. They can be taken on almost any small lure that is presented carefully. The only problem at this time of year is that the fish are extremely wary. For this reason, many anglers prefer to troll small crankbaits such as Rapalas, Rebels, Lindy Bait Fish, and Bagley Crawfish. These lures must be trolled on a line at least sixty yards long. As the boat passes overhead the smallmouths will retreat into deeper water, but by the time it is sixty yards away the fish will be returning to the shallows, just in time to intercept the lure. Trolling also has the advantage of covering large areas in a search for the fish, and once you find one you'll usually find a bunch, although they may be fairly well spread out over a large shallow area.

Once I've located some fish by trolling, I prefer to cast to them. When casting it is essential to drift or scull quietly into the area. An outboard motor will spook smallmouths in the shallows, and even an electric trolling motor will send them running into deep water. I like to drift through an area and cast with ultra-light spinning equipment that allows a long cast with light lures. I usually start off casting a small floating-diving crankbait; a small Bang-O-Lure would be an excellent choice. If that doesn't produce I switch to spinning lures such as a Mepps or a Panther Martin. I haven't found that lure presentation makes much difference when the fish are feeding in the shallows. Almost any small lure that passes near them, provided they aren't spooked, will usually produce a strike. By wearing polarized sun glasses I can often see individual fish and cast to them. Another of my favorite shallow-water methods is to use a fly rod and floating deer-hair bugs. I use a nine-and-a-half-foot or longer leader that is tapered down to a four-pound-test tippet and gently drop the bug right against the shore near fallen trees or stumps. The fish often hit the bug the instant it lands on the water. Deer-hair bugs or small poppers are particularly effective at dawn and dusk.

If I can't find the fish in the shallows, I look for them over the rocky fingers that extend into deeper water. For this kind of fishing, in water from six to twelve feet deep, I use ultra-light spinning tackle and a one-eighth-ounce yellow jig tipped with a piece of nightcrawler. I fish the jig by casting it over the rocky point and working it slowly along the bottom with little hops. My guess is that the jig represents a crawfish or a leech, and the smallies really eat it up.

Just before the fish begin spawning their feeding slows. The smaller males will stay in the shallows while preparing the nest. The larger females tend to school off the rocky points in about ten feet of water, where they can be taken on jigs and small crankbaits worked slowly. I release all the fish that I catch at this time; they are very vulnerable and the greedy angler can make a severe dent in the breeding population. Even after the females have spawned and are recuperating in deeper water, the males guarding the nest will attack anything that comes near them. I stop all my smallmouth fishing at this time. I see no reason to disturb the nest and tire out the male fish, thereby hurting the chances of a successful spawn. Without the male fish on guard, the eggs are quickly eaten by small fish, newts, and crawfish. If you have good smallmouth fishing available to you, enjoy it to the fullest, but during spawning treat the fish gently and return them to the water unharmed. There will be plenty of time during the summer and fall to bring home fish for the skillet.

SUMMER TECHNIQUES

In summer I look for smallmouths in water from fifteen to thirty feet deep over or near the humps and shoals I discussed earlier. During the summer the fish usually travel in loose schools and will change depth often. Many times I've caught fish in twenty feet of water over a rocky hump and then had them stop biting as suddenly as if someone had thrown a switch. This doesn't mean that they have left the area and stopped feeding; they may have moved into shallower water where they spread out over a flat to graze on crawfish, or they may have been attracted to deeper water off one edge of the hump by the appearance of a school of shiners. The smallmouths' change in depth may last a few minutes or many hours; and they may change their depth by more than ten feet and travel as much as fifty yards in any direction. The changes may also take place as often as a dozen times a day. When fishing for summer smallmouths you must be prepared to do a lot of moving many times during the day.

My favorite summer smallmouth bait is a small live crawfish or minnow. I use lightweight spinning gear with six-pound-test line and hook the minnow through both lips and the crawfish near the end of its tail with a No. 4 or No. 6 hook tied directly to the line. I don't use swivels except with lures that would otherwise twist my line. I add just enough splitshot to bring the bait to the bottom and retrieve the minnow slowly and the crawfish a bit faster with small hops. If you don't keep the crawfish moving it will immediately bury itself under the nearest rock. Hooking the crawfish near the end of the tail makes it easier to pull out from under a rock, but you will still lose lots of bait. I find that I need at least four-dozen crawfish for an afternoon of fishing.

Sometimes small split-tail plastic grubs or a four-inch plastic worm will be more attractive to summer smallmouths than live bait. I fish these lures with little hops right along the bottom and set the hook the instant I feel a strike. A smallmouth won't hold an artificial lure in its mouth for very long before he realizes it isn't edible. If you see fish following your lure and not striking, it usually means you should switch to live bait. Crawfish, minnows, hellgramites, or nightcrawlers should produce when the fish are following artificials but hesitant to strike them.

Anyplace you find summer smallmouths during the day will provide excellent topwater fishing at dawn or dusk. I like to use long, thin floater-divers like the Bang-O-Lures, and the larger sizes produce best for me. On some evenings I have had excellent fishing by casting off rocky points in over thirty feet of water. The smallmouths will often take the lure the instant it hits the water or after it has been lying motionless on the surface for a few seconds. Catching smallies on the surface is great sport. The fish make twisting jumps, and I have had one fish throw my lure and the minute it hits the water have another grab it and immediately go airborne with it.

FALL TECHNIQUES

When the water temperatures begin to drop, the smallmouths move into deeper areas of their home territory. The fish can be in water anywhere from fifteen to forty feet deep, but I consistently take more at the forty-foot depths than in the shallower areas. The fish tend to move down the steps off the shallow flats, where they can feed on minnows and crawfish that are also deeper at this time of year. In the cooling water the schools of smallmouths may be tremendous, often numbering hundreds of fish, but they bunch into small, select areas and can be difficult to find.

The best fall locations for smallmouths are sharp dropoffs into deep water, over a deep food shelf, or off the end of a point that is surrounded by deep water. I cover a lot of water trying different depths until I find a school, and then I like to back-troll (see Chapter 37, "Walleyes," for the back-trolling technique) using a gray or green quarter-ounce jig with a plastic grub. The fish can also be taken by jigging bait or small spoons.

When jigging in cool water it is important that the rod be moved slowly and deliberately, and sometimes the fish will strike only when the jig or bait sits motionless a few inches off the bottom. Jigging at depths of thirty to forty feet requires patience and good line control. I find that light baitcasting equipment, a graphite or boron rod, and an eight-pound-test line give me the best control and feel when a fish gently mouths a minnow over thirty feet down.

RIVER SMALLMOUTHS

Smallmouth bass are easier to find in rivers than in lakes. In large rivers I consistently find them below dams on the edges between fast water and an eddy. Below power-generating stations I like to fish right along the side of the dam when power is being generated. Schools of smallies will often trap schools of minnows right against the dam, where the baitfish can be seen leaping from the water. A small spoon or crankbait tossed into the melee will usually result in a strike. Often, letting a jig sink below the surface action will produce much larger fish than those feeding on the surface.

In smaller rivers and when power is not being generated at power stations on larger rivers, the smallmouths tend to drift downstream. I have had consistently good fishing off the underwater points of islands or ledges just where the flow of the current comes around the point. I sometimes find a big school of small fish off the point. When that happens I move downstream below the island or ledge, where there is ordinarily a deep pool with slick water. These deep, slick areas usually hold bigger fish. I like to fish these areas with small orange or brown jigs tipped with a piece of nightcrawler or a crawfish tail. Light spinning tackle and about six-pound-test line are ideal for this kind of fishing.

In summer, river smallmouths tend to congregate at the mouths of cool tributary streams or at the edges of center-stream channels. I like to fish these areas slowly by back-trolling with a jig-and-minnow combination. If you're having trouble finding the fish in a large river in summer, try trolling a small crankbait upstream along the edges of the center channel. Once you hook a fish you can switch to jigs and minnows.

In the fall, smallmouths congregate in large numbers along rock shelves that drop into deeper water or near brush piles or fallen trees on the edge of deep water. A live crawfish or minnow dragged slowly through these areas is my fall choice.

A few years ago I discovered, by accident, a tactic for taking smallmouths that has rarely let me down regardless of the season. I was fishing from shore below a small hydroelectric dam when power was not being generated. It was a relatively small river, and when the flow was down as it was that day there were huge, slippery piles of rock below the dam, with the water isolated into a number of swift runs between the rock piles. It was a very windy day and on one cast the wind took my small spoon directly upstream and threw a few turns of line around my spinning reel. When I finally got the line untangled the spoon had drifted to the bottom, and I anticipated that it would be wedged in the rocks. As I tightened my line I felt a pulsing resistance and set the hook. The fish turned out to be a scrappy two-pound smallmouth. I made another cast directly upstream and allowed the spoon to settle to the bottom, once again expecting it to become entangled in the rocks. Instead, I took another smallmouth, of about two and a half pounds. Using this upstream technique I took a fish on almost every cast for over two hours before rising water forced me from below the dam. I hadn't lost a single lure and had learned that these fast runs had very smooth bottoms with no rocks, obviously a result of the fast current when the water was high. The smallies had been lying right on the smooth bottom. Now, whenever I find a fast, deep run through bedrock or a ledge, I fish it directly upstream with a small spoon that I allow to settle right to the bottom. This particular tactic has proven successful from Arkansas to Maine, and on many occasions my catch has been a mixed bag of smallmouths and walleyes.

Smallmouths are also found in smaller rivers and streams, and frequently share the same waters with trout. In small streams I've taken my best fish around big rocks, in riffles, in the heads of pools, and under undercut banks and ledges.

I like to fish small streams with a fly rod and a weighted Muddler Minnow or small streamer or bucktail. Spinning lures such as the Mepps and Rooster Tail are also excellent, and should be fished slowly and allowed to hang in the current around big rocks and ledges at the edge of the fastest water.

Bait is also excellent for small-stream smallmouths. Crawfish and minnows work well, but I have had my best results with a live hellgramite fished right on the bottom below a riffle at the head of the deepest pools. Light spinning tackle, a No. 6 hook, and a small splitshot are the best gear for this kind of small-stream fishing. If there are trout in the stream you can never be sure which fish you're going to take, and I have had many days when my catch has included both trout and smallmouths taken from the same locations.

Smallmouth bass are a great game fish, and I wish they could be protected by law during their spawning season. I realize, of course, that this would be impossible because spawning times differ widely from year to year depending on temperature and water conditions. Perhaps the answer is to make the fish a catch-and-release species until, say, the first of July. That would assure a future supply of fish and would leave the balance of the summer and fall for fine meals of smallmouth fillets.

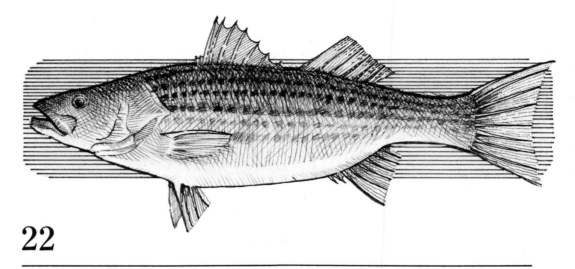

22

Striped Bass

The striped bass (*Morone saxatilis*) is a popular marine fish native to the Atlantic coast of North America. In 1879, striper fry were carried by Fish Car—special railroad cars of the U.S. Fish Commission—to the West Coast. The tiny fish were carried in milk cans that were cooled with ice and aerated by hand, an arduous round-the-clock process. This early experiment proved successful and as a result a new fish species was established on the West Coast. Today, marine striped bass are among the most popular saltwater game fish along almost the full length of both the Atlantic and Pacific coasts.

The striped bass would probably have remained a marine game fish had it not been for the building of the Wilson Dam and the Pinopolis Lock on the Santee and Cooper rivers in South Carolina in 1941. At that time a large number of stripers that had entered the rivers to spawn were trapped in the lakes that were forming behind the huge Santee-Cooper complex. The fish lived and reproduced, and within five years stripers over fifteen pounds were being taken with regularity, many by accident by anglers seeking largemouth bass. By 1960 an estimated half-million stripers had been taken from the two large lakes, Marion and Moultrie, and some of these fish weighed over fifty pounds.

Striped bass grow large; the largest recorded fish weighed 125 pounds and was taken by commercial fishermen off Edenton, North Carolina, in 1891. Fish over fifty pounds are taken with regularity from some bodies of freshwater, and many anglers feel that stripers approaching 100 pounds will eventually be taken in freshwater impoundments.

Word of the excellent landlocked striper fishery at Santee-Cooper spread quickly, and other states were soon experimenting by placing striper fry in their own large impoundments. A hatchery was built on the Cooper River and the fish have proven to be comparatively easy to propagate under artificial conditions. As a result of extensive stocking, stripers are now thriving in large lakes and rivers from the East Coast, across the South, and all the way to California. They are doing so well that a major sport fishery has developed in many impoundments that had been considered fished-out.

The problem with large impoundments is that when they are built, most of the trees, brush and other cover necessary to provide habitat for native species is removed. When the lakes are filled the only cover is directly along the shoreline, and there simply isn't enough of it. In many lakes threadfin and gizzard shad were introduced to provide forage for the hoped-for populations of native game fish, but this didn't work. Shad are open-water fish, and even though they thrived, they did nothing to help the native game fish populations.

Fisheries biologists envisioned that the introduction of the striper, also a pelagic, or open-water, fish, would control the growing population of threadfin and gizzard shad in freshwater impoundments. It is interesting to note that to date, there has been no documented evidence that the shad populations in these bodies of water are declining, but it is obvious that the striped bass populations are growing like wildfire. Even largemouth bass anglers, who initially feared that the introduction of stripers would eliminate their favorite fish, have been forced to admit that the stripers have not harmed their fishing. Many of these anglers have all but given up on the spotty populations of largemouths in the big impoundments and are now concentrating on stripers.

The spawning requirements of stripers are stringent. In the spring the fish ascend rivers when the water temperatures reach about 55°F. Actual spawning takes place at water temperatures between 60° and 67°F. During the spawning act each large female is accompanied by a number of smaller males, and as the eggs and milt are released, the males splash furiously in what anglers call "rock fights." No nest is constructed, and the eggs are fertilized as they float in the water. A four-year-old female striper weighing about five pounds may produce over sixty thousand eggs. A twelve-year-old fish weighing between forty and fifty pounds may produce over 5 million eggs.

The eggs, which are semibuoyant, must be released into moving water with enough flow to keep them floating for from thirty to seventy hours depending on the water temperature. If they sink to the bottom they smother and die.

With such rigid spawning requirements, it is obvious that only a limited number of tributaries are suitable for successful reproduction, and most of the freshwater striper population is the result of extensive and continual stocking programs.

There has been limited natural striper propagation in freshwater. The Santee-Cooper complex has proven self-sustaining, as have sections of the Arkansas, Missouri, and Washita rivers, and the Colorado River below the Davis Dam, which forms Lake Mohave.

RIVER TECHNIQUES

One of the easiest times to catch river stripers is in the spring when they move upstream to spawn. On the larger rivers the fish congregate in huge schools below dams. When the river flow is light, and where it is legal, anglers tie their boats directly to the dam. You won't have to look hard to determine where to fish because there will be boats full of anglers all along the face of the dam at the hot-spots. For this kind of fishing I use my medium baitcasting outfit with my reel filled with twenty-pound-test line—the identical outfit I use when casting for largemouth bass in obstruction-filled waters. I hook a large shiner, shad, or herring under the back fin with a No. 3/0 hook, add enough weight to keep it down, and lower it over the side of the boat. Ordinarily, that is all that is required, and you will have no problem determining when you have a strike. Stripers take a live bait with authority and usually hook themselves.

In rivers with fast currents I like to cast from shore when possible. I enjoy wrestling with big fish in fast water when I'm standing on the bank, quite a different experience from taking them from a boat. I use a twelve-foot surf rod and a spinning reel spooled with twenty-pound-test line. My favorite lures are yellow or white leadhead jigs weighing between one and two ounces. Sometimes I add a yellow plastic grub or six-inch plastic worm to the jig. If the fish aren't hitting jigs I switch to large silver spoons. It is essential to attach these spoons to the line with a good-quality ball-bearing swivel because in the fast water the spoons will quickly twist the line so badly that it will be impossible to cast.

The best spots in fast rivers are ordinarily just below power-generating stations. When the generators are running, small fish are sucked through the generator tubes. The stripers congregate in the tailrace below the discharge tubes, where they have easy pickings. I like to cast as close as possible to the tubes and allow the jig or spoon to sink. I reel in just fast enough to keep from hanging up on the bottom, not an easy feat, and I lose my share of lures. I set the hook firmly every time the jig stops moving or when I feel a change in pressure on the line. In the fast water the stripers simply open their mouths and let the lure drift in; there is rarely a solid strike.

Some rivers are too big to be fished easily from the bank, and fishing fast tailraces from a boat can be dangerous. When fishing from a boat, it's safest to keep the motor running and take a position at the edge of the fast water, not in it where a sudden surge can easily overturn the boat. It is also unsafe to anchor the boat if the dam is operating. I fish fast tailraces by lowering a jig or large minnow over the side and drifting downstream slowly with the motor running at low speed. After I reach the end of the tailrace I motor back upstream and begin another drift.

I prefer a live shad or minnow for drift fishing, and it is essential to hook the bait through both lips when doing this kind of fishing in fast water. If hooked under the back fin the bait will inevitably be torn off by the fast current, and if hooked through the tail it will drown. I use my medium baitcasting equipment when drift fishing. I hold the rod in my hands and leave the reel in the free-spool position, keeping my thumb on the spool. When a striper takes the minnow, I let him run for a few seconds before engaging the reel and setting the hook.

In some rivers it is possible to safely anchor a boat just off the main current. I find it much more enjoyable to fish from an anchored boat than drifting with a continually running motor. A good spot to anchor is about thirty feet above a "boil" that indicates a current-breaking structure on the river bottom. Water churning over the structure will have scoured a hole in the bottom, and stripers tend to congregate in these potholes. The holes can be fished with live bait or jigs, but I find a deep-running crankbait easiest to use when anchored in fast water. My favorites are Bombers or Magnum Hellbenders, whose action takes them right into the pothole. You should experiment with lures until you find one that will tic the bottom when you make a sweep with the rod. With the right lure it is an easy matter to keep it fluttering in the pothole and to vary its speed and action by raising or lowering the rod tip.

When power is not being generated and the water flow is down, I have consistently found stripers in the first large pool below the dam. Under low-water conditions the fish will sometimes take a surface lure or a floater-diver, and I like to start my fishing day casting a big silver Bang-O-Lure or a Rapala.

If I can't tempt a fish on the surface, I like to drift through below-dam pools using a large yellow jig garnished with a four-inch yellow plastic fliptail worm. I let the jig-worm combination sink to the bottom, reel it up about eighteen inches from the bottom, and let it hang there with occasional lifting and dropping of the rod tip. If the water is deeper than about twelve or fifteen feet I'll try different depths.

Some really big stripers are also taken from smaller rivers and streams that flow into large impoundments. Many of these streams are too small for successful spawning, but the stripers' instincts force them to try. When water temperatures reach the mid-fifties, the fish move into the streams and school in the deepest holes, protected eddies, and in the pools just below any spot where the river narrows.

In the early spring I've had my best results using cut bait. My favorite is a piece of cut shad about four inches long and in the shape of a triangle. I run a No. 2/0 hook through the bait and add just enough weight to keep the rig bouncing along the bottom. I cast slightly upstream and allow the bait to bounce naturally along the bottom with the current. It is important to keep slight tension on the line because strikes can be very gentle. I set the hook when I feel any unnatural hesitation in the drift.

LAKE TECHNIQUES

Most of the time, stripers are hard to find in big impoundments. The fish swim continually and a boat equipped with a good depthfinder is essential. There is, however, one time when big stripers can be taken with some consistency by casting from shore. In the late spring, after the stripers have returned to the lake from the feeder streams, the gizzard and threadfin shad move into the shallow bays to spawn. The stripers are feeding actively at this time, and while they won't follow the shad into the very shallow water they will hold in deep areas close to shore, where they can ambush the passing schools. Shad spawning takes place at night, and there are few more exciting fishing experiences than playing a big striper from shore on a warm spring night.

I use heavy spinning equipment, twenty-pound-test line, and deep-running crankbaits when shore-fishing for stripers that are feeding on spawning shad. I like to fish steep rocky banks with a dropoff of ten to twenty feet near the shore, and I cast parallel to the shore and work the lure just fast enough to keep it running at its maximum depth. Crankbaits with rattle chambers filled with splitshot work well at night, and sometimes, while you won't find the stripers, you will find some really big largemouths.

As mentioned earlier, a depthfinder is almost essential for finding stripers in big impoundments in the summer, and many anglers also use temperature indicators. What they are searching for is the layer of water called the thermocline. Most large lakes stratify into three distinct layers during the summer. The layer at the surface is called the epilimnion and is warm and low in oxygen. The layer at the bottom is called the hypolimnion and is cold and low in oxygen. In the middle layer, the thermocline, the water cools as it gets deeper, and this cool water is rich in oxygen. The cool temperatures and high oxygen levels attract both shad and stripers.

Most anglers troll a crankbait or drift a live shad in the thermocline layer. Sometimes stripers can be spotted on the depthfinder, but the fish keep swimming, and a school that is directly under the boat could be a quarter-mile down the lake a few minutes later. For this reason you should concentrate on fishing the depths and locations of water that are likely to hold the fish, rather than trying to follow the fast-moving schools.

Stripers seem to prefer the lower half of the lake during summer. If the lake has a dam, the fish will consistently be found near or right against the dam at a depth from about twenty to forty feet. Where it is legal to fish right against the dam I like to drop a live shad or minnow against the face of the dam and let it sit about thirty feet down. Casting a jig parallel to the dam and letting it drop into the thermocline is also effective. Other likely summer locations for stripers are the lower half of an impoundment along old river channels, off the ends of points that have a sharp dropoff into deep water, and over submerged islands and ridges whose tops are in the thermocline area.

EARLY FALL TECHNIQUES

At the end of summer, when the water in a lake is still warm, the feeder streams can be more than ten degrees cooler than the lake surface as a result of cooler night temperatures. Schools of shad often move into the streams to feed early in the morning or late in the afternoon, and the stripers follow. I like to fish these feeder streams in late summer after a good rain when there is a brisk current flowing into the lake. I fish areas where there is a stone riprap bank on either side of a bridge, and I limit my fishing to early morning or late afternoon unless it is a very cloudy, dark day.

My preferred bait for this kind of fishing is a live shad or shiner hooked through both lips with a No. 2/0 hook and enough weight, about eighteen inches up the line, to keep the bait on the bottom. It is easiest to fish the downstream side of the bridge, and I cast across and slightly downstream and allow the bait to settle to the bottom. I find it best to let the bait sit and wait for a striper to find it, although I have taken a few fish by dragging it slowly over the bottom. When a fish takes the bait I slip the reel into free-spool position if I'm using baitcasting equipment or open the bail if I'm using spinning equipment, and let him take about ten feet of line before setting the hook. This kind of fishing can be slow, and many anglers like to cast out and prop their rod in a forked stick. A few years ago I lost an expensive baitcasting outfit by doing this; one minute the rig was sitting in the forked stick and the next minute it was gone. If you aren't going to hold your rod in your hands I suggest that you don't stray far and that you tie it to something.

COLD-WEATHER TECHNIQUES

Some of the best striper fishing in large lakes is in the late fall and winter, when the fish feed on shad they trap against the surface of the water. This vigorous surface feeding can be seen and heard from a considerable distance and is often accompanied by flocks of diving gulls enjoying an easy meal of fresh shad.

The stripers usually don't remain on the surface for long, and when a school is sighted, all boats in the area will rush to the spot, an action that inevitably puts the fish down. The chasing of surfacing stripers is called "jump fishing" in many areas of the country, and some anglers who practice it keep a half-dozen rods rigged and ready in the boat. When a fish is boated they don't bother to unhook it; the striper is dropped into the boat and the angler grabs another outfit and casts into the school of feeding fish. When they're feeding on top, stripers are not selective and will take almost any plug, spoon, or jig. Sometimes after the surface activity is over I can pick up a straggler or two by jigging a large white or yellow jig at a depth of about thirty feet, but most of the time the fast-moving fish have gone off following another school of shad.

Early in the fall the schools of surface-feeding stripers tend to run small, and may average only four or five pounds. By December the weight average is up to eight or nine pounds, and by January some schools will contain fish averaging over fifteen pounds. When the surface feeding is in cover-free areas of the lake, I like to try for these big fish with a fly rod and large streamers. I haven't landed many fish on my fly rod, and I usually end up chasing a hooked fish all over the lake until the hook pulls out or the fish breaks off, but it's great fun.

Striped bass are now found in large impoundments in about half the states. Contacting your state fish and game department is the best way to locate striper waters in your area. In each lake the fish have their own quirks and areas where they tend to concentrate, and other anglers are your best source of information concerning techniques and locations. Naturally some anglers will be very tight-lipped about their favorite baits and locations, but others will be happy to help the newcomer to the sport.

There are many striper clubs forming all across the country and the beginning striper fisherman will find it helpful to join one of them. Club members will teach the local variations of the striper theme, and in a club you can always find someone who wants to go fishing. The success of the freshwater striper fishery has been nothing short of phenomenal, and the future for the sport looks fine indeed.

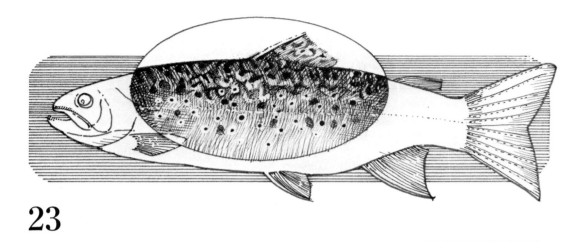

23

Brook Trout

The brook trout is not a trout. Its scientific name, *Salvelinus fontinalis*, classifies it as a salmonid, and it is actually a member of the char group. Other fish included in the char group are the Arctic char, the Dolly Varden, the lake trout, the blueback trout, and the Sunapee trout. Brook and lake trout are the most popular of the chars owing to their relatively wide geographic distribution; the remaining members of the group are limited to isolated areas or the very northernmost reaches of North America.

The brook trout is a native of northeastern North America. Its range extends from the Arctic Circle south to Georgia, but it has been introduced into suitable waters all over the United States and as far away as South America and Europe.

The brookie is still considered the principal game fish in many areas of New England despite the fact that the habitat needed for a healthy population of the fish is quickly dwindling. Brook trout like water of almost pristine quality, and that kind of water is becoming as endangered as the fish living in it. Good brook trout water is cold, 55 to 60°F, and is clean and free of pollutants.

In the United States only Maine still provides fairly good brook trout fishing, but even there the days of brookies reaching five pounds are about over. An

133

occasional lunker is still taken, but these days any fish over two or three pounds is considered exceptional.

The biggest brookies are found in Canada's Hudson Bay region and in Labrador, where five- and six-pounders are still relatively common. The farther south one goes the smaller the fish become, and for most of the United States a two-pound brookie is considered a large fish. There is some fine brook trout fishing to be found in the Rocky Mountain region, but most western anglers prefer to concentrate their efforts on the native cutthroats and rainbow trout. Occasional five-pound brookies are taken from waters in Idaho and Montana, but they are the exception rather than the rule.

Brook trout spawn from mid-September in their northern range until mid-December in their southernmost regions. Like salmon, they construct a shallow depository called a redd in coarse gravel and, depending on the size of the fish, deposit from a few hundred to many thousand eggs. The incubation period depends on the water temperature. At 40°F, hatching requires about 135 days. At 55°F the eggs hatch in about 35 days. Hatching does not occur all at once, and may take place over a period of many weeks.

Brook trout are among my favorite fish, perhaps because my very first trout was a ten-inch brookie unceremoniously yanked from a tiny stream not far from my boyhood home in rural New England. I don't remember my first fish of every species, but this brookie had become a personal challenge to me. I had spent weeks lying on my stomach, my face concealed by brush, watching the fish go about his business. By the standards of that tiny stream, that ten-incher was a real monster, and I will always remember the mixture of elation and sadness I felt when I finally dragged him up the bank. The time I spent studying that fish was invaluable, for I had learned that if I was very careful, these extremely wary fish could be caught.

The fact of the matter is that brook trout are not very difficult to catch. If not disturbed, they will strike almost any lure or bait that is presented in a natural manner. It is the ease with which they can be caught and their demanding water-quality requirements that have so drastically reduced their size and numbers throughout their range. In addition, brook trout are relatively short-lived fish, four years being about their maximum life span. Biologists are currently attempting to develop a long-lived strain of brook trout and have succeeded in keeping one new strain of the fish alive for up to nine years. It will be interesting to see how this new strain holds up outside hatchery conditions.

TECHNIQUES FOR BROOK TROUT

In the big brook trout waters of northern Canada I use three- or four-inch spoons in red and white, silver, or gold. The big brookies tend to hold in pocket water behind boulders and in deep pools. I cast my spoon above the area to be fished, let it sink for a moment, and begin a slow retrieve.

The strike of these large fish is fast and hard, and while they don't exhibit the aerial antics of the other trout, a big brookie is a determined, powerful fighter. There are occasional days when these wild northern brookies will refuse to strike anything, and I have been frustrated watching fish in the five-pound class follow a variety of lures without striking. But these Canadian waters can quickly spoil the brook trout fisherman, and under most conditions a full day of casting will yield a half-dozen trophy-sized fish.

My preferred equipment for these big Canadian rivers is a medium-weight spinning outfit with eight-pound-test line. This outfit allows me to make long casts and cover a lot of water without having to continually move my casting position. The fish can also be taken on ultra-light gear and with a fly rod, a red-and-white bucktail being my preferred fly.

Canada has the market for big brook trout all locked up. The Canadian government has wisely reduced the bag limit on these fine fish, and my last Canadian trip was to an area where the angler was allowed to keep only one fish per day. Many anglers keep a single trophy fish for mounting and one each day to eat, and there are few tastier fish. Brookies inhabit waters rich in small crustaceans and do much of their feeding on freshwater shrimp (scuds). The pink flesh of these shrimp-fed trout is a gourmet's delight.

In the United States most brookies are found in small streams, and fishing these is a real challenge. A surprising number of brook trout streams are relatively near urban areas and the reason that they contain good populations of brookies is that they are surrounded by dense growth of willows or alders. Just reaching the banks of these streams can be a challenge, and there is usually no casting room whatsoever.

The small-stream fisherman will usually use bait and will often have to resort to ingenious methods for presenting it. I have spent hours floating a night-crawler down a tiny stream on a piece of wood in an attempt to get the bait in front of a school of nice brook trout. When the bait reaches the area I want to fish, I gently pull it from the floating piece of wood. When the method works I'll almost always catch a fish, but more often than not I'll scatter the fish with this attempt at a natural presentation.

Under these brushy conditions I use my fly rod and a level, four-pound-test leader about four feet long. I hang a worm on a No. 8 or No. 10 hook and cautiously push the bait through the brush surrounding the stream. Grasshoppers, crickets, small dead minnows, and caddis worms taken from the stream bottom are also excellent baits. Again, the bait is not nearly as important as the presentation.

While I prefer to use a fly rod in brushy streams, a spinning rod can be easier where there is enough room for a short cast. With ultra-light spinning equipment it is easy to use an underhand flip of the rod tip to drop the bait under the brush that overhangs the water. I can't overemphasize the necessity of using a quiet approach in a small stream. Once a brookie has been spooked he will not strike no matter how skillfully the bait or lure is presented. Many times it will be necessary to literally crawl to streamside to keep from scaring the fish.

One frequently overlooked method for taking brook trout from small brushy streams is to fish while walking upstream in the middle of the brook. In some streams this is the only way to get to the water. This kind of wading must be done with extreme caution. When I reach the tail of a tiny pool I kneel and make a gentle underhand flip or cast to the head of the pool with ultra-light spinning equipment. I try to drop my bait on a rock or log and then pull it gently into the water. The brookies will be facing upstream, and if my stalk and cast are successful I usually have no trouble taking a fish from each pool.

In large streams throughout the country the brook trout is frequently overlooked. The reason for this is that most fishermen concentrate their efforts on the deeper runs and pools, and in a large stream the brook trout know better than to venture into this deep water where they become a quick snack for a large brown or cutthroat trout. In larger streams the brookies will be in shallower water than the other trout, in runs and riffles and along the shore by undercut banks.

Brook trout in small ponds and lakes are easier to catch than those in small streams, but are still very wary. I have fished beaver ponds swarming with schools of nice-sized brookies only to have them spook at my first cast. Under these conditions a fly fished on a long, light leader or ultra-light spinning equipment is essential. Ultra-light outfits allow for long casts with tiny spinners and spoons as well as a fly or bait, and lures work particularly well when the water is slightly discolored after a rain. Many brook trout anglers fail to catch fish because they use lures that are too large. It is best to use the smallest lures that can be cast a reasonable distance.

As mentioned earlier, brook trout spawn in the fall. At this time they collect in large numbers in the mouths of cool tributary streams and are very vulnerable because they lose much of their natural wariness. Fall fishing for brookies is very easy, and the angler who cares about the future of his sport will gently release the drably colored females and keep only a few of the bright-red males.

In areas of the country where cool streams enter the ocean, brook trout that have taken up residence in the brackish areas where the stream and the ocean mix will enter the stream in the fall for spawning. Known as "salters," these fish look more like silvery rainbow trout than brookies. Salters run considerably larger than their stream-living brethren, and many anglers are unaware of their presence. The brook trout fisherman living near the ocean should inquire about these fish at his state fish and game department. Where they are found, they offer fine sport.

The future for the brook trout is questionable. In the United States the only populations of native fish are in tiny underfished streams and remote rural areas. Elsewhere the fish are stocked and quickly caught. These days I fish for brookies only a few times each season. I enjoy stalking them in clear, cold, brushy brooks, and I keep just enough fish for one good meal. It doesn't matter to me that these fish aren't whoppers. They are a real challenge, and as table fare they are unsurpassed.

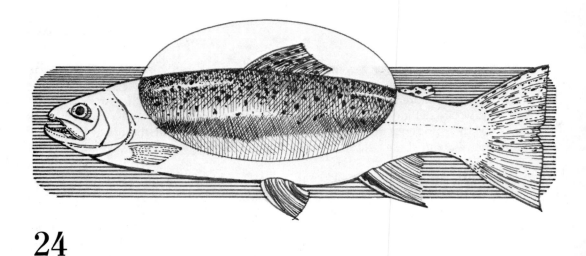

24

Rainbow Trout

The rainbow trout (*Salmo gairdneri*) is a native of North America. There are two distinct strains of the fish. The most common is the steelhead strain, which carries a migratory instinct to return to the sea. Tales abound of the traveling abilities of steelheads. Tagged rainbows of the steelhead strain stocked in small streams along the East Coast have been recovered from the nets of commercial fishermen in the Gulf of Mexico. Fish tagged by Japanese research vessels near Kiska Island in the Aleutians have been recovered in the rivers of Washington State.

The other strain of rainbow trout, called the shasta, is nonmigratory. Some biologists believe that if inland stocking programs were limited to this strain, a resident population of rainbows could be established in freshwater rivers. Unfortunately, the steelhead and the shasta strains have been mixed, and the migratory instincts of the former are dominant. It is a fact that most stocked rainbows end up in the sea, if they can get there, and while state fish and game departments publicly assert that over 70 percent of stocked rainbows are taken by fishermen, many admit privately that the figure may be substantially lower, perhaps as low as 20 percent.

The natural range of the rainbow is from northern Mexico to the Aleutian

Islands, and the fish has been stocked in suitable waters all over the world.

The rainbow is a fast-water fish tolerating temperatures from near 32°F to over 80°F. This ability to withstand extreme fluctuations in water temperature, and the fact that the fish gain more weight with less food than any other trout have made the rainbow a favorite of hatchery operators.

The life span of the rainbow is approximately six to ten years. Landlocked rainbows spawn from January to July, but selective breeding in hatcheries has created strains of the fish that can spawn at all months of the year.

STEELHEAD

It might be in any river from California to Alaska, or any river that flows into the Great Lakes. You see an angler running along the river bank, his rod held high over his head as far downstream a long silver fish takes to the air. When it comes to steelies, bent rods and screaming reels are not clichés; steelheads are fish to reckon with. Fresh from the sea or the Great Lakes, the fish have spawning and not feeding on their mind, but they are ready and willing to strike flashing, colorful objects that drift by on the current.

In the Pacific Northwest, steelhead spend most of their lives at sea, returning to their natal rivers only to spawn. These spawning runs take place in summer, fall, and winter and are largely determined by river conditions, the turbidity and flow of the water. If the water flow is too low, the fish do not enter the rivers. If the rivers are high and muddy, the fish will move upsteam—but the conditions make the water unfishable. Therefore, a knowledge of individual rivers is essential, because in some of them the water clears faster than in others, and in the space of a few hours a river can go from worthless to ideal.

SUMMER STEELHEAD

Summer steelies tend to run smaller than their winter cousins, but they are full of energy. The fish usually enter the rivers in May, and the run can continue into early October. These slightly smaller fish seem to take a fly more readily than winter steelhead, and it is in the summer that the fly fisherman has his best sport.

The rivers are lower in summer and the fish tend to hold in water a minimum of at least eight feet deep. In summer the angler can forget about shallow stretches, even favored winter locations where large boulders can clearly be seen. In summer I do all my steelhead fishing in the pools just downstream from a white-water riffle.

Fly-fishing techniques for steelhead are substantially the same in summer as the rest of the year, the only difference being that the fish are in deeper water. My steelhead fly rod is a nine-footer, and I use a weight-forward sinking line that enables me to easily cast weighted flies long distances. There are so many steelhead fly patterns that it would be impossible to discuss them. I check with the local sports shops to find which are popular during each season. I always purchase some from display cards that have only a few flies left.

In summer, the presentation is more important than the fly pattern for catching steelhead. I start at the head of the pool and carefully move downstream, fishing the waters closest to me and then lengthening my casts to cover runs against the far shore. I make repeated casts to likely areas, and have had strikes after thirty or more casts to the very same spot. It isn't necessary or desirable to give the fly any action; I simply toss it across and slightly upstream and let it drift on a tight line. Sometimes when I'm getting tired of casting, I will occasionally twitch the line and impart a darting action to the fly. I have hooked a few fish in this way, but most of the time I find that a dead drift produces best.

Fly-fishing for steelhead has its disadvantages regardless of the season. The required casts are comparatively short, and it is necessary to ease into casting position with care to avoid spooking the fish. Splashy casting, and occasionally too many false casts, will also scatter the fish.

Summer steelhead can be very finicky and will often follow a fly or lure without striking. When that happens I change my fly or lure to the next smaller size, which often brings an immediate strike.

WINTER STEELHEAD

Winter steelheading can be a cold sport and the weather conditions can be just plain nasty. The fishing techniques are substantially the same as in summer except that the higher waters are better suited for spinning or baitcasting equipment than for a fly rod.

The season starts after the first fall rains hit the Pacific Northwest coast, and a hush seems to descend on the river valleys as anglers wait for the first fish to arrive. These fall and winter fish are bright silver, muscular fighting machines, a worthy test of any angler.

Winter steelies lie practically on the bottom, behind large boulders in water from about four to eight feet deep that is flowing at about the same speed as that of a brisk walk. The cold water somewhat reduces the activity of the fish and they won't move far to take a bait or lure. For this reason I prefer to use bait rather than lures or flies when fishing for winter steelhead.

My winter equipment is a medium-weight baitcasting rod that has two handles, a light, sensitive tip, and is about seven and a half feet long. My reel holds 200 yards of ten-pound-test line. Many anglers like to use spinning equipment, but I believe that with baitcasting equipment I have a better sense of what is happening at the end of my line.

The most popular baits for winter steelhead are canned or fresh roe, single eggs, and in some rivers, nightcrawlers. My favorites are Egg-drifter Balls or Okie Drifters, both of which resemble clusters of spawn, and which I rig in the traditional manner. I tie a three-way swivel to the end of my line. To one eyelet of the swivel I tie about eighteen to twenty-four inches of line with the hook at the end. To the lower eyelet of the swivel I tie a four-inch piece of four-pound-test monofilament and add a pencil sinker, a short, straight piece of lead that doesn't get hung up as often as conventional sinkers do. When I do get hung up, which happens often, I give the rod a sharp jerk and the light leader attached to the weight breaks easily. I always carry lots of weights, lures, and hooks because I leave more than my share on the stream bottom.

I identify what I feel is a good lie for the fish and assume a position almost directly downstream. I then cast the bait about thirty feet above the suspected lie and allow it to settle with the current. The bait should be bumping bottom as it passes through the lie, and I reel in just fast enough to keep control of my line. By keeping the rod tip low I can feel the bait bumping the bottom and I set the hook the instant the bouncing of the sinker stops. Because steelhead take a bait very softly and hold it for just a few seconds, the slightest unusual feeling at the end of the line must be answered with a strike. Sometimes I feel foolish setting the hook too often—that is, until I lift the rod tip and find myself fast to a big angry steelie that seems determined to reach the ocean as soon as possible.

At times lures will produce better than bait. Steelhead lures come in a multitude of sizes, shapes, and colors, and it is best to check with local tackle shops to see which ones are producing. During some years the fish will show a marked preference for one lure over all others, while a lure that is hot one year may fail to produce the next. Wobblers such as the Lil Jaspar and the Fat Max are consistent producers, as are cherry bobbers and the Luhr Jensen Fireplug and Prism-Glo. With lures no weight should be used because it will interfere with the lure action. One of the nicest aspects of fishing a spoon or spinner is that there is no doubt when a fish takes it; the steelhead really smack them. My general rule of thumb for lures is that I use smaller ones in clear, low water and larger bright ones in darker, heavier water.

A lure fished for steelhead must be allowed to bounce along the bottom at a speed just fast enough so that the action or vibrations of the spinner blade can be felt. It takes some practice and a thorough knowledge of your equipment and the action of your lure to get it to tumble along the bottom without being snagged. When I'm fishing a particularly obstruction-filled run I often take the treble hook off the lure and replace it with a single hook. I don't get hung up quite so much with the single hook, and I seem to catch just as many fish.

Many times steelhead will take a lure at the end of a drift. For this reason you should let your lure hang in the current at the end of the drift for a few seconds. Do not add any action to the lure, simply let it hang with its own natural action.

It is important when steelhead fishing to get to know very well one area of the river you're fishing. Your chances of catching fish are much better if you get to know the bottoms of a few runs like the back of your hand. In that way you can present your bait or lure right along the bottom without continually getting snagged. If you keep on moving to new spots you will spend much of your time learning how to drift-fish each of them rather than being able to concentrate on the proper action of your lure or bait over a run that you know well.

Steelhead runs were once restricted to the Pacific Northwest, but today there are excellent runs in streams entering the Great Lakes and in rivers entering large impoundments in the Northeast and as far south as North Carolina. The fishing techniques for steelhead in the East are substantially the same as those used in the Northwest, although Great Lakes anglers do well trolling silver spoons off the river mouths, and many eastern river fishermen prefer night-crawlers over spawnlike baits or lures.

The steelhead runs in the East are shorter than those in the West, with October through December being the peak months. The major difference in the eastern steelhead fishery is that the fish tend to lay offshore in the mouths of the rivers until their eggs and milt mature and only then begin their run up the rivers, which are much shorter than those of the Northwest. Great Lakes and eastern steelhead are primarily stocked fish; natural reproduction in these areas has not been very successful. There is also a spring run in the Great Lakes, and in both the spring and fall fishing is at its peak when the water temperature in the rivers is around the 45°F mark.

To the newcomer to steelheading I must say that this is an avocation in which you have to pay your dues. You will lose tackle, can be miserably cold, and will often go for days without a fish. But if you have the determination and are willing to put in the time needed to learn your equipment and the waters you are fishing, you will eventually have some of the finest freshwater sportfishing imaginable; and some excellent table fare. Steelhead meat is firm and moist; I prefer the fish charcoal-broiled because they contain just enough natural oil to be self-basting. As with all fish, the sooner you clean your steelhead and the cooler you keep it while in transit, the better it will taste.

Most of the rainbows taken from inland lakes and streams are stocked fish, but that is not a criticism. The fish adapt quickly to their environment, are fine fighting and eating, and were it not for stocking programs much of North America's waters would contain few trout.

LAKE TECHNIQUES

In the early spring all across the country, the banks of many lakes are lined with trout fishermen. Most are fishing for, and catching, stocked rainbows, and the techniques for catching these fish are very similar wherever they are found. In lakes and ponds most anglers use spinning gear, a light or medium rod, and reels spooled with six- or eight-pound-test line. The rig is a simple one. A splitshot or light weight is attached about eighteen inches above a small hook, on which the bait is impaled. Worms and nightcrawlers are universal favorites, but salmon eggs, corn, small marshmallows, and pieces of cheese are used successfully by spring trout fishermen. In western lakes cheese baits are the favorite, and special hooks have been designed to help keep the bait on the hook.

Regardless of which bait is used, it is cast into water about six to ten feet deep and is allowed to sit on the bottom. The same rig can be fished three or four feet deep under a bobber, and the fish will sometimes prefer a bait that is suspended. Most anglers prop their rod in a forked stick and wait for a school of rainbows to enter the area. When the trout arrive the fishing is fast and furious.

Some anglers who disdain the use of bait prefer to walk or wade the shoreline casting spinning lures. There are literally hundreds of spinning lures available, but each area seems to have its favorites. I have done consistently well casting a small Al's Goldfish, a small gold Castmaster, or a yellow Rooster Tail. Sometimes adding a piece of nightcrawler to one of the treble hooks on the lure can trigger otherwise hesitant fish into striking. Spring rainbow fishermen also troll spinning lures, small spoons, bucktails, and streamer flies just under the surface. Ordinarily, when you can find fresh-stocked trout, you can catch them with relative ease.

When the surface waters of the lakes and ponds in which they live warm to over 65°F., the rainbows go deep, seeking the cooler, oxygen-rich water. If they do any surface feeding it is usually very early in the morning, when the surface waters are the coolest of the day. Sometimes on a cloudy, windy, rainy day in the middle of summer the rainbows will feed actively on the surface throughout the day.

In large lakes, once the fish go deep, trolling with the help of a depthfinder and downrigger is usually required to take rainbows. For the balance of the

warm weather the fish will stay deep, in water with temperatures between 55°
and 60°F, and it won't be until fall, when the surface waters cool, that they
can once again be taken near the surface or in the shallows.

In small lakes and ponds a nightcrawler fished right on the bottom in the
deepest water you can find is a good way to take summer rainbows.

STREAM TECHNIQUES

In lakes and ponds rainbows occupy the same water as brook and brown trout,
but in streams they prefer faster water than these other species. Even in early
spring the best rainbows will be found in fast water that is considered unfishable by many anglers. A fast current bordering fallen trees, large rocks,
or undercut banks are my favorite areas.

Baitfishing a stream for rainbows is an art at least as difficult as learning to
fish an artificial fly. It is similar to steelheading and requires the same sensitive
touch as the bait bounces over the bottom. The low metabolic rate of these
cold-water trout demands that the bait be presented within a few inches of the
fish; they won't chase a bait or lure as they will in warmer waters.

The stream trout outfit is similar to the one used by lake fishermen, a light-
or medium-weight spinning rod, a small hook, and just enough weight to keep
the bait bouncing along the bottom. Worms, nightcrawlers, salmon eggs, corn,
and small dead minnows are all excellent baits. Many experienced bait fishermen use a light spinning reel on a fly rod, and claim that the longer rod gives
them better sensitivity and control.

Many spring anglers like to use live nymphs that they gather under rocks in
the shallow areas of the river they're fishing. On some large western rivers
there are huge hatches of salmon flies, which are over two inches long in their
mature nymph stage. The live nymphs, fished along the bottom with light
spinning tackle, will take large rainbows as well as other trout, and should be
given a try when they are available.

Early stream rainbows are also taken by die-hard fly fishermen using
weighted nymphs, bucktails, and streamers, but it is later in the season when
the waters warm that the fly fisherman will do best. It is unfortunate that so
many bait fishermen are hesitant to try fly-fishing. It is not nearly as difficult as
many of them seem to believe, and as the waters warm and aquatic insects
begin to hatch, fly-fishing for rainbows can be truly exceptional.

Rainbows become more selective in their feeding habits as the amount and
variety of food available to them increase, but when aquatic insects first begin
to appear in large numbers, almost any wet fly will produce. When fishing a
wet fly, I stand above the area I'm going to fish, cast my fly across the current,
and simply let it drift downstream. The fly can be easily steered into pockets

and riffles, and the rainbows will frequently dash almost across the stream to take it. There is, of course, much more to fly-fishing than this, and anglers interested in more detail are referred to Chapter 5, "Fly-fishing," in Part One.

Small spinning lures are also very effective for late-spring rainbows, especially in waters containing varieties of small minnows. I fish spinning lures much like wet flies, casting them across the current and steering them through the runs and riffles and around underwater obstructions.

In summer, when the streams are low and clear, the rainbows are found almost exclusively in fast water, except at the first light of morning, when they will cruise the pools looking for minnows. At daybreak they can be taken from these pools on carefully presented bucktail and streamer flies and small spinning lures. During daylight hours, summer stream fishing can be difficult. The rainbows will feed throughout the day, but even though the streams are full of aquatic insect life the fish become very selective and often pick one insect to feed on to the exclusion of all others. The fly fisherman who can select the right fly, and present it gently, can take rainbows from the fast water; however, determining which fly will work is a process of trial and error.

The only bait I've found effective for rainbows in low summer waters is grasshoppers. Nightcrawlers and worms don't work for me except right after a summer rain, when a wide variety of food is washed into the stream and the rainbows feed on almost anything that drifts past them. After a summer rain, when the water rises and becomes slightly discolored, spring baitfishing techniques and spinning lures will work, but as soon as the streams clear and return to normal summer flow the fish once again return to selective feeding on insects.

In the fall, when the water cools, I go after rainbows with spinning lures or bucktails and streamer flies. At this time the streams contain the entire summer crop of minnows, and the trout feed on them voraciously, as if in preparation for the cold winter months. In the fall I've found large concentrations of fish where smaller tributary streams enter a main river; these fish will often be in very shallow water and spook easily. I sometimes stand twenty feet away from the river to cast to these wary fish.

In the rapidly cooling waters of fall I've often had rainbows bump a fly or lure as if attempting to stun it. When this happens I continue to let the fly or lure drift with no additional action after the apparent miss. The fish will frequently follow the lure and take it as the line straightens at the end of the drift. If the fish hang in the current directly behind the fly or lure I apply a gentle pumping action and allow it to drop back. This will often trigger a strike from a hesitant fish.

There are some techniques for rainbows that many anglers overlook. Everywhere in their range, these fish inhabit waters that contain many species of small fishes, and every year some real lunkers are taken by anglers using large crankbaits designed primarily for bass. Deep-water trollers know this and use these big baits with great success in large impoundments; but these lures can also produce some remarkable fish in small lakes and streams. When nothing else is working, pick a large minnow-type lure out of your tackle box and give it a try. You may be pleasantly surprised at the results.

Another mistake rainbow anglers frequently make is to stick with one technique that has produced in the past. For instance, the rivers that flow from beneath the dams of large impoundments maintain a temperature between 50° and 55°F the year around. Under these cold-water conditions most rainbows are taken on bait. One day when I was having no success using nightcrawlers on the White River in Arkansas I switched to my fly rod and a No. 18 Black Midge fly. I could see fish occasionally rising in the fast cold water, but no matter how hard I looked I couldn't determine what they were feeding on. My choice of fly was sheer guesswork. In less than two hours I landed four fish over three pounds each, and when I returned to the boat livery not a single fisherman would believe that I had taken the fish on a fly.

When fishing for rainbows it sometimes pays to pull the largest, smallest, or most bizarre fly or lure out of your tackle box and give it a try; these trout are proof positive of the fishing axiom that it pays to experiment.

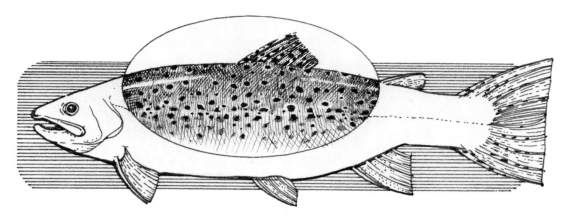

25

Brown Trout

The brown trout (*Salmo trutta*) has been around for some 70 million years. It is native to Europe and North Africa, first reaching North America in 1882 when William Gilbert of Plymouth, Massachusetts, imported about five thousand brown trout eggs. Most of the eggs proved to be infertile and failed to hatch, and only three of the fry grew to maturity and spawned, but those three fish were the basis of the American brown trout fishery.

In the early days of brown trout in North America, fishermen complained that when these fish were introduced to an area they ate the other trout. They called the fish, among other things, speckled carp. The charge of cannibalism is true. Browns are cannibals, as are all species of trout, but they are also the members of the trout family that will most readily take an artificial fly. The brown was the honored favorite of fifteenth-century angling author Dame Juliana Berners and the renowned seventeenth-century Izaak Walton, author of the classic *Compleat Angler*, and retains that honor today with dedicated fly fishermen.

Brown trout can tolerate water temperatures at least ten degrees warmer than can brook trout and five degrees warmer than can rainbows. The fish are also tolerant of limited water pollution and relatively low oxygen levels. Were it not for the brown, many semiurban streams would contain no trout.

The brown is a homebody who stakes out a particular stretch of water and guards it against all comers. He is so territorial that he will never leave his lair if it contains enough food and cover. The territorial nature of the fish is known by successful brown trout anglers. When they encounter an apparently barren stretch of river they assume that it is the home of a big brown that has driven away or eaten all of the other fish that have ventured into his area. The wise angler gives these apparently barren areas complete and careful attention.

Browns are light-sensitive, and the bigger they get the more they do their feeding after dark. It is the natural wariness and light-sensitivity of the fish that account for their preference for large brush piles or downed trees, a choice of habitat that adds to the angler's difficulties. It is often impossible to present a bait, lure, or fly close enough to the fish to generate a strike, and even when hooked a big brown is usually near enough to his den to wrap the line around an obstruction and break off. Even in relatively open water the fish has the habit of grabbing a submerged tree branch or other obstruction in his mouth and hanging on. Of course he can't stay that way for long because he is forced to open and close his mouth to breathe.

Ichthyologists generally agree that the brown is the "smartest" of the trouts. They base this finding on the fact that an artificial fly or lure must represent the brown's natural food before it will respond. Brook and rainbow trout react to brighter colors and seem unable to detect such an obvious counterfeit as, say, a red, white, and blue fly.

All trout have excellent senses of sight, smell, and hearing. They also have well-developed threshold vision, which enables them to see well in dim light, and the ability to focus on two objects at once: one near and one far away. Add to these the brown's choice of habitat and the angler finds himself faced by a most worthy opponent.

Brown trout spawn in the fall, between September and December, depending on weather and water conditions. The eggs are deposited and fertilized in a shallow depression dug in gravel on the stream bottom. The eggs slip between the spaces in the gravel and are incubated by the flow of the water. They hatch in three to five weeks, and both the eggs and newly hatched fry are very vulnerable. Biologists estimate that over 95 percent of brown trout eggs and fry are eaten by minnows, sculpins, crawfish, and other predators. When spawning in lakes, the fish broadcast the eggs over gravel bars near the shore, in water from eight to fifteen feet deep.

RIVER TECHNIQUES

In rivers and streams, trout are ordinarily found near obstructions or at the edges of the main current, where food will be carried to them and where the moving water contains enough oxygen for their needs. In such locations small browns are found in the company of brook and rainbow trout and should be fished in the same manner as these other trout. But the brown does have some characteristics that set him aside from brookies and rainbows. As he grows larger he seeks out a territory of his own, and the essential feature of that territory is the presence of cover. Brookies, rainbows, and small browns all seem to feel safe if the water is moving fast enough to make them invisible from above, but as mentioned earlier, the brown feels safe only when his cover is a veritable fortress.

When seeking big browns you must be aware of their territorial nature and read the waters accordingly. A large undercut rock, a brushpile, or a fallen tree in deep water are where the larger fish will be found. As mentioned earlier, browns are more tolerant than other trout of warmer water with less oxygen, and many anglers overlook the most likely locations for the fish, believing that the slow, deep pools of a river contain only suckers and minnows. But the brown is an exasperating fish, and even when you know his lair, catching him is another matter. Really big browns feed somewhat like largemouth bass; they will try and eat almost anything that moves, and the stomach contents of big browns have been known to contain such treats as baby muskrats, watersnakes, ten-inch brook trout, and even bluebirds.

Being light-sensitive, most big browns are taken at night or on dark, overcast days, but they will do limited feeding throughout the day if they are not disturbed. A three- or four-inch minnow, alive or dead, is probably the best all-around brown trout bait, and medium-weight spinning or baitcasting tackle is best suited for its presentation. Ordinarily, the bait must be presented within a few feet of the fish to produce a strike. I thread the minnow on a No. 4 hook that is tied directly to my line. I don't use snelled hooks or a snap swivel. I add just enough weight, about sixteen inches above the hook to bring the bait to the bottom, and I cast into the current well above the area I suspect holds a fish. As the current carries the bait toward the obstruction I keep gently lifting the tip of the rod to be sure the bait doesn't get hung up. Once the minnow has settled into deep water near the fish's lair, I let it sit as long as my patience will allow. The best big brown fisherman I know props his rod in a forked stick and does not touch it again until he has a strike or it is time to stop fishing. If your line becomes tangled in the obstruction you are fishing, and you have to break the line to free yourself, you can usually forget about catching a big brown from that particular spot for the balance of the day. The same techniques used to fish a minnow can also be used to fish other baits, such as crawfish and nightcrawlers.

Spinning lures and spoons can also tempt a big brown, but presenting the lure close enough to the fish to generate a strike is not easy. Lures with a gold finish consistently produce the largest fish for me, and in brushy streams I fish them downstream, very slowly, and allow them to flutter in the current as long and as close to a suspected trout-sheltering obstruction as possible. I have had big browns come out of their lairs and follow a spinner but not strike it. When this happens I rest the spot for about fifteen minutes and then try again, but with an added attraction—a streamer fly tied directly to the tail hook of the lure with about twelve inches of ten-pound-test monofilament. This tandem rig will often bring a savage strike from a large brown that is hesitant to strike the lure alone.

In large, open rivers without obvious obstructions, the big browns will usually be found in the very deepest water, behind rocks or other objects that disrupt the water's flow. If the river has undercut banks I fish them carefully because they provide the cover and shade preferred by browns.

I prefer medium-weight spinning equipment and eight-pound-test line for large rivers. I cast upstream and reel the lure downstream at a forty-five-degree angle to the current so that it will swing naturally downstream in the current and reach bottom when it is opposite my position. Lead-head jigs are excellent for this kind of fishing because they sink right to the bottom and can be worked much more slowly than a spinning lure or spoon. The slower the jig can be crawled over the bottom the better, and it should even be allowed to sit motionless for a few seconds at a time. It sometimes helps to add a minnow, nightcrawler, or crawfish tail to the jig.

The color of the jig can make a difference. I use black or brown jigs when the water is high and discolored after a rain, and I prefer white or yellow jigs in low, clear water.

Brown trout and fly-fishing go together naturally, and no member of the trout family is more susceptible to the artificial fly then the brown. Fishing a dry fly for browns in an obstruction-filled stream is very difficult because for a natural presentation, the fly must be fished upstream, and it is hard to present a dry fly in a big brush pile or downed tree. But when the fish are feeding actively on the surface, a big brown will often leave his lair to take a floating fly.

In open rivers the fly fisherman has more flexibility. At certain times of the year some large rivers have dramatic hatches of aquatic insects, the western salmon fly hatches being an example, and under these conditions even the largest browns can be taken on dry flies. It would be impossible for me to discuss all the varieties of aquatic insects that the fly fisherman attempts to copy. It is best to check with local fishermen and area sports shops on the size, color, and pattern of the flies that best match the local insect populations.

Unless there is obvious surface feeding I do most of my fly-fishing for browns with large weighted nymphs and streamers. If I had to pick one fly that has been consistently productive, I would pick the Muddler Minnow—and would use a plain brown one with a gold body. Muddlers can be dead-drifted, slowly retrieved along the bottom, or worked in minnowlike jerks around obstructions. I have taken more brown trout on a brown-and-gold Muddler than any other fly in my collection. Readers interested in more specific information on flies and fly-fishing are referred to Part One.

NIGHT TECHNIQUES

The brown trout changes its personality at night, and it is under cover of darkness that I have taken some of my best fish. At night the big browns lose much of their natural caution, and can often be heard thrashing around in the shallows chasing minnows or small trout. A likely pool deserves a half-hour of listening before you start casting. But night fishing is difficult and you must be very familiar with the stretch of river you are planning to fish. A tumble into a river on a dark night can result in more than a cold dunking and a loss of fishing equipment.

The equipment for night fishing can be substantial. I use a ten-pound-test tippet and big, bushy flies. Fly pattern or color doesn't seem important after dark, and when casting these big flies I keep a good grip on my rod. Night-feeding browns really smack a fly and can pull the rod from your hand if you aren't prepared.

Many night fishermen use baitcasting equipment and large bass plugs fished downstream in the big pools. A big, noisy topwater lure is particularly effective at night during the hot summer months, when the big browns spend the balance of the day in their lairs awaiting the cooler evening temperatures to feed. When night fishing you must take care not to let the beam of your flashlight strike the surface of the water; when using a light to change lures or flies, be sure to turn your back to the water and shield the light or you will scare the fish and put an end to your fishing.

LAKE TECHNIQUES

Many small lakes and ponds contain a few huge brown trout, and they are extremely difficult to catch. I have seen these huge fish cruising the shallows in spring and fall, but they are so wary that I have never been able to cast to one without spooking it. Your best chances of taking one of these big fish is at night in the summer with a bass plug, or during the day by dropping a live minnow to the bottom in the deepest water you can find, and letting it sit there.

When it comes to lake fishing for big browns, the Great Lakes are the best brown trout fishery in North America and perhaps in the world. In the 1970s, when the water quality in the lakes began to improve and the lamprey problem was brought under control, there were extensive stockings of browns. The fish flourished, but not many were taken because the trolling tactics used for salmon and lake trout were not effective for the browns. The noise of a boat motor will send these fish in another direction, and even the vibrations from a downrigger cable are enough to spook them. Finally, a few wise anglers figured out that these big, wary fish could be taken by trolling a lure at least 150 yards behind a boat, using light line testing six or eight pounds.

Throughout the hot summer months, the browns in the Great Lakes seek the cool, oxygen-rich thermocline, which is ordinarily between about thirty and sixty feet deep. Letting out about 150 yards before attaching the line to the downrigger ball made it an easy matter to keep a lure running at the desired depth without spooking the fish. Silver spoons or wobbling crankbaits such as the Flatfish are the preferred lures of most Great Lakes trollers for browns.

One aspect of fishing for big brown trout in the Great Lakes that I like best is that these big fish can be taken by casting in both the spring and fall. In April and May smelt and alewives, forage for the browns, run into the feeder streams to spawn throughout the Great Lakes watershed. Some of the best fishing of the year can be found by wading the shoreline adjacent to the mouths of the feeder streams. I've found that the best shoreline fishing is after a storm, when the water is discolored and the browns will often feed in shallows 3 feet deep or even shallower. I like to wade the shoreline casting small silver spoons with light spinning tackle. It is important to use a spinning reel that holds at least 250 yards or more of line because these fish run big, browns over ten pounds being common, and you have the real opportunity of hooking a fish that runs over thirty pounds. If you don't have enough line to let these lunkers run, you will lose most of the fish you hook.

During these cold-water periods the browns can often be seen rolling in the shallows. It is easy to mistake these fish for spawning carp, although the latter will occasionally jump completely out of the water, while the trout rarely do this. When you see rolling fish, you should drift or wade very quietly into the area and make a long cast with a small silver spoon. If they're browns, and you haven't scared them, they will take the spoon with no hesitation and immediately head for deep water. Again, your reel must hold at least 250 yards of line to give you the opportunity to land these lunkers.

In the spring and fall the big browns in the Great Lakes can also be taken by trolling without the aid of a downrigger. In clear, cool water these fish will be found about ten to fifteen feet deep, and by slow trolling with at least 150 yards of line you can catch some. In large lakes even the biggest browns will feed throughout the day, provided they aren't disturbed.

On these clear sunny days I also like to cast to fish that are cruising the dropoffs near shore. Sometimes the fish will school in the shade of large rock piles on the dropoff, where they wait to ambush passing schools of smelt or alewives. For this kind of fishing I like to use ultra-light spinning tackle, four-pound-test line, and small blue or white lead-head jigs. By wearing polarized sunglasses I can often see the fish, and casting to individual fish under these clear-water conditions is a real challenge. Again, I cannot overemphasize the need to keep noise and commotion to an absolute minimum so as not to scare the fish. Casting to brown trout along the shore is also effective in the winter in the large impoundments in the South and Southwest that contain these fish.

In the fall, when the water once again begins to cool, the big browns of the Great Lakes enter tributaries to spawn. The biggest runs will be into the largest rivers, but I have seen fish as long as my arm in streams that I could almost step across. The techniques for this fall fishing are identical to those used in the spring.

The fall spawning runs are, of course, not limited to the Great Lakes. Any pond or lake that contains brown trout will have a spawning run into its tributary streams, and while the fish do lose some of their innate caution at this time, they must still be stalked carefully.

In waters where brown trout propagate naturally, I return all spawning fish, unharmed, to the locations from which they were taken. Killing the fish at this time will do irreparable harm to the brown trout population in areas where they depend upon natural reproduction. In the Great Lakes, however, there is very little natural propagation, and most of the fish are the result of extensive and continual stocking.

If you want to catch a real trophy brown trout, you don't have to leave North America and head to New Zealand or Chile. The brown trout fishing in the Great Lakes is some of the very best anywhere in the world. By contacting the various state fish and game departments you will get all the information you need about where to fish, accommodations, boat rentals, and the best time to plan your trip. The fishing potential for lunker brown trout in the Great Lakes is unlimited.

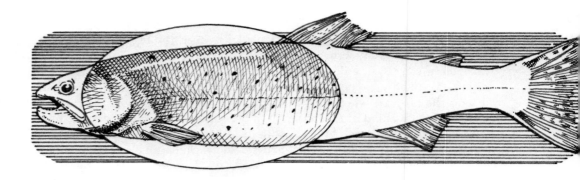

26

Cutthroat Trout

The cutthroat trout (*Salmo clarki*) is native to the western United States. Its range is from Prince William Sound, Alaska, to northern California, and inland to the Wyoming-Yellowstone-Idaho areas. The fish derives its name from the red slash of color on its lower jaw under the dentary bone.

Cutthroats hybridize easily with other trout, most notably the rainbow, which is a distant cousin, and in many areas of its range it does not exist in a pure state. The fish can be compared to the brook trout in that it does not compete well with other fish and does not withstand heavy fishing pressure. Like the brook trout also, the cutthroat is not known for its great fighting ability, and when its head can be pulled above the water it quickly tires. Moreover, the cutthroat, like the brookie, is top-rate table fare.

Coastal cutthroats spawn in February and March. Inland they spawn in April and May. The fish must be at least four years old before spawning, which occurs on alternate years. Their life span is from six to ten years.

Coastal cutthroats are anadromous (migratory), and go to the ocean in the second or third year of life. They spend two years in the ocean before returning to coastal rivers to spawn.

Young cutthroat feed almost exclusively on insect larvae and tiny freshwater shrimp, but as they mature their eating habits change drastically. As soon as they become large enough to compete with the other inhabitants of their ecosystem they become entirely piscivorous, a term biologists use to describe a fish that feeds almost exclusively on other fish.

Increasing angling pressure has hurt the cutthroat, and these days a fish over five pounds is notable. The most popular cutthroat fisheries are Yellowstone Lake and the Snake River in Wyoming, but the best fishing is restricted to smaller, spring-fed streams in wilderness areas where fishing pressure is the lightest. Even in these isolated western streams, however, the fish is struggling to maintain itself. Indiscriminate stocking of other species of trout may be responsible for the eventual demise of the cutthroat, due to the fact that other trout species tend to dominate and eventually wipe out native cutthroat populations.

In rivers, cutthroats are ordinarily found in the same faster waters preferred by rainbow trout. They are wary fish, but if not disturbed can be caught quite easily on a variety of baits and lures. Smaller cutthroats are taken easily on artificial nymphs of the stonefly and caddis variety, fished slowly near the bottom of a stream or pond. Bait fishermen usually use nightcrawlers or minnows where these are legal. One interesting characteristic of the cutthroat is that certain streams will be very productive when minnows alone are used for bait, while other streams just a few miles away will produce with nightcrawlers alone. As mentioned earlier, mature cutthroats are almost entirely piscivorous, and the reasons for the marked preference of these fish for nightcrawlers in some bodies of water are unknown. When streams are high and discolored in the spring or after a rain, the fish respond well to small silver spinners, especially those with red or orange bodies. Regardless of the bait or lure being used, it must be fished deep and slowly, since cutthroats are notorious bottom-feeders.

I have had my best lake fishing for cutthroats in early spring, at ice-out time. I walk the shoreline and cast into areas of open water surrounded by ice. But even under these early spring conditions it is essential that the lure or bait be worked just off the bottom. The technique I've found most effective is to cast a small silver spoon into the open-water areas and to let it sink to the bottom. I retrieve the spoon with a jerking motion and allow it to flutter back to the bottom. Most strikes occur when the lure is fluttering down, and I keep pressure on the line and set the hook at any unnatural line movement or change in pressure. Fishing a spoon in this manner will result in frequent hang-ups, and I make sure I'm well stocked with lures because I lose many.

When the waters warm the cutts go even deeper, and most are taken by deep trolling using cowbells, or Davis-rigs as they are called in the East. These are composed of a string of spinners and beads to which a spoon or bait is attached by a leader. In summer months shore fishermen do well bottom fishing off points and deep dropoffs, using traditional rainbow trout baits such as worms, cheese, marshmallows, and minnows where they are legal.

When the water cools in the fall, cutthroats may be taken near the surface, but the natural wariness of the fish makes it difficult to cast to them without putting them down. Even the longest casts with a fly rod will often spook the fish, and I have found that spinfishing with a small wet fly or midge and a spinning bubble is best. When using a spinning bubble, I tie a ten- or twelve-foot leader, testing only two or three pounds, below the bubble. The rig is extremely cumbersome and difficult to cast, but the long leader is necessary if the fish are not to be put down.

The future of the cutthroat is questionable. Some state fish and game departments have gone to great efforts to attempt to maintain pure strains of these fish in native waters. Size limits have been increased and daily bag limits have been lowered. Unfortunately, many cutthroat waters have been stocked with brown trout, and the young cutts become fodder for the hardier browns. The larger cutthroats are easily taken by anglers, and to add to the problem, fishermen using minnows not native to cutthroat waters have introduced species that dine on cutthroat eggs. Moreover, the channelization and building of dikes on many western rivers has eliminated protective shoals where cutts feed, and has also blocked access to feeder streams previously used for spawning. The cutthroat, like the brook trout, may soon be found only in a handful of large lakes and isolated small streams in the most remote wilderness areas of their range.

27

Lake Trout

The lake trout (*Salvelinus namaycush*) is a large member of the char group. It is called togue in the Northeast, mackinaw in the West, and gray trout throughout much of Canada. The natural range of the fish is throughout Canada southward through the Great Lakes, the Finger Lakes of New York State, and larger bodies of water in New England and the West. In recent years, experimental stockings have been attempted in some of the deep impoundments of the South. It is too early to tell if these pelagic (open-water) fish will take hold in southern impoundments, where some biologists feel they will compete with striped bass, also a pelagic fish.

Lake trout demand cold, well-oxygenated water ranging from 43° to 56°F, which limits the waters capable of sustaining them. Water temperatures exceeding 66°F for an extended period of time can be fatal to lakers.

Lake trout spawn in the fall over a gravel bottom at depths ranging from more than one hundred feet in Canada and the Great Lakes to shoalwater in shallower lakes. No redd or nest is used, as it is with other members of the char group. The spawning area is swept clean by strokes of the female's tail until all silt and debris are cleared from the site. Tiny eggs, less than one-fifth of an

157

inch in diameter, are scattered over the site, and many are eaten by small lakers, suckers, and other fish. The incubation period is from 50 to 150 days, depending upon the water temperature. After hatching, the fry remain in very deep water and develop cataracts if exposed to sunlight. For this reason the hatchery propagation of lake trout is extremely difficult.

The Canadian government has made extensive studies of the lake trout. One such study found that the lakes of northern Quebec contained, for the most part, only very small or very large lake trout. The reason for this is that young lakers, if not eaten by other fish, grow very quickly to maturity, and once mature may live for more than forty years. In many lakes the newborn fish were found to be the main food source for their elders. Biologists call this intraspecific density-dependent predation, which, simply stated, means cannibalism. The problem inherent in this type of food chain is that if too many adult fish are killed by anglers, too few young will be produced to support the remaining adults. This fragile balance is the reason why strict laws have been instituted for lake trout fishing in the lakes of Canada's far north. These Trophy Trout Regulations limit the angler's kill to only one lake trout per day of fishing. The regulations are no hardship to the fisherman, because in many lakes the average weight of the fish exceeds twenty pounds. Lakers weighing over one hundred pounds have been netted by commercial fishermen, but the all-tackle record has stood at about sixty-three pounds for many years.

TECHNIQUES FOR LAKE TROUT

In the fall, winter, and early spring, low water temperatures allow lake trout comfortable access to shallower water, but much of the time they prefer deep water, often at depths of one to two hundred feet. In the northern areas of their range, where surface waters remain cold throughout the summer, the fish may be found near the surface at any time, and even in rivers flowing into frigid lakes.

The equipment used to take lake trout varies according to their location. When they are near the surface the problem is more one of finding than of catching them. In most large, cold lakes anglers prefer to troll, although once the fish are found they can be taken by casting.

While lakers run substantially larger than the trout of warmer climates, this doesn't mean that very heavy tackle is necessary for taking them. Northern lakes tend to be open, with relatively few line-grabbing obstructions, and some anglers like to troll the surface with fly rods or ultra-light spinning tackle. Since large lakers feed on good-sized fish, the fly fisherman or ultra-light spinfisherman ordinarily favors large bucktails or streamer flies which can be trolled with such light tackle. Fly patterns aren't too important, although at times the fish can be very selective. I prefer long-bodied streamers with flashy Mylar bodies.

Most laker fishermen prefer baitcasting or spinning gear, which permits them to use large spoons, spinners, and crankbaits that would be impossible to use on lighter gear. Big spoons are best for large lakers and should, if possible, resemble the common baitfish of the waters being fished. But much of the time color seems to make little difference; I have taken lakers on homemade spoons that resemble nothing the fish have ever seen.

In the spring and fall, live bait fished in water as shallow as ten feet can also produce some big lakers. Where it is legal, fishing a live six-inch sucker on the edges of deep dropoffs is particularly effective. Live bait is used extensively in the Finger Lakes of New York State and in large New England lakes.

In the summer, the lakers in most big lakes are found in the middle, thermocline, layer, which is rich in oxygen and where the temperature drops rapidly. Pinpointing the preferred 50°F temperature ordinarily requires a temperature probe and depthfinder. In lakes in which the preferred temperature is at very deep levels, most anglers troll. Some deep trolling is done with wire or lead-core line, and more than four hundred feet of line may be necessary to bring the lure to the desired depth. Downriggers, on the other hand, are fished directly under the boat and give the angler the option of using much lighter equipment. The deep-trolling lures used for lake trout are the same as those used for surface trolling and casting, although at times the fish will respond better if an attractor spinner such as a Davis rig is used. In the Great Lakes, using a depthfinder to locate schools of smelt or alewives is a popular way of finding lakers; in fact, fishing near a school of forage fish regardless of depth is usually productive. Wherever there is a good supply of food, there will be lake trout.

Deep holes are also favorite locations of summer lake trout anglers, and the best are those with a distinctive rim or lip at the edge of a deep dropoff. In the early summer, lakers tend to congregate at the rim of a deep hole. As the water temperatures rise, the fish often drift deeper, to the sides of the hole. At the peak of summer they will be at the bottom of the hole.

Some real summer hot-spots for lakers are deep humps that stick up in the bottom of a deep hole; slots—narrow underwater chasms that run between deep water and shallow flats—are other hot-spots for the fish. These humps and slots are almost impossible to find without the aid of a depthfinder, and summer lake trout fishermen rely heavily on the use of electronic gear as the only sure way of finding the fish.

One of my favorite ways of taking summer lake trout is by jigging. I like the process because I can use medium-weight equipment. I don't like to use the heavy equipment necessary for trolling a big spoon, and I don't like a downrigger between me and the fish.

Vertical jigging is easy, just a matter of dropping a spoon or jig to the bottom, lifting it, and allowing it to fall back. If a wind is blowing I retrieve the jig all the way to the surface and then drop it back to the bottom. On a calmer day, when the wind isn't moving the boat too fast, I leave my line in the water and work the jig up or down at the desired depth.

I prefer spinning equipment for jigging because the open-faced reel allows for a quick drop and good line control. Sometimes the lakers will hit a lure only after it has struck bottom and starts back up. If the lure doesn't touch bottom it will be of no interest to the fish. At other times the fish will follow a lure right up through the thermocline almost to the surface. I've had them hit a lure only twenty feet below the boat after following it up from a depth of over sixty feet.

My experience is that most of the time lakers will hit a jigged lure on the way up, although they will sometimes take it only when it is falling—a situation that can be difficult for the angler. To let the jig fall I open the bail and let the line run through my fingers. I do not cast. If the jig stops dropping or suddenly picks up speed, I close the bail and immediately set the hook. When the fish are taking a falling jig you must watch your line carefully and be alert to any change in line tension.

The color of the jig can make a difference. I take many more fish on yellow or white jigs than I do on jigs of darker colors. I prefer heavy jigs, between three-quarters of an ounce and one and a half ounces. These are heavier than necessary, but the additional weight gives me better line control, especially at depths over fifty feet.

I've done best with jigging when the fish are just off the bottom, in from fifty to eighty feet of water, and I don't jig in water shallower than about forty feet. If the fish are much deeper than about eighty feet, I stop jigging because I don't like spending most of my time dropping and retrieving. I also find that line control becomes a problem at such depths.

One tip about jigging: Where it is legal, a six-inch strip cut from the belly of a sucker and added to the jig will more than double the number of strikes you get. Throughout their range, lake trout are suckers for suckers.

In large northern lakes it is almost always necessary to hire a guide to help find the fish. These large northern lakes resemble the ocean, and without professional help you can spend all of your time trying to locate lake trout. An experienced guide knows the areas where the fish tend to congregate, and if those spots don't produce he can lead you into brushy coves or spots that you would never have thought of trying.

It isn't necessary to travel to the northern reaches of Canada to find lake trout, although that is where the biggest fish are found. The Great Lakes and many large impoundments in the East have been stocked with lakers, and in many areas these trout are underfished. The various state fish and game departments can give you the location of the body of water nearest you that contains these big fish.

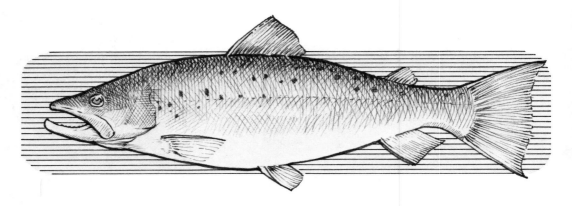

28

Atlantic Salmon

The Atlantic salmon (*Salmo salar*) is among the most highly prized game- and food fish in North America. Named by the early Romans, the "leaper" can be taken legally only with artificial flies, and once one is hooked there is a complete understanding of how the fish derived its name.

Not long ago the future of the Atlantic salmon was in doubt. Water pollution, dams that interrupted the spawning runs, and illegal netting and poaching had all but eliminated the fish from its native range in North America. But a concerted effort on the part of Canadian and New England wildlife officials, the building of fish ladders, and a gradual increase in water quality in northeastern rivers have combined to create a favorable outlook for the Atlantic salmon. The past few years have seen a dramatic increase in the numbers of fish returning to spawn, and extensive stocking has resulted in salmon runs in rivers once thought to be incapable of supporting these fine fish. Only in Iceland, where early and intelligent management has retained a healthy fishery, have Atlantic salmon escaped the ravages of our industrial world; however, the future for this fish is now as bright as the fish themselves.

The natural range of the Atlantic salmon is the northern Atlantic Ocean from Greenland to Cape Cod, and in Europe from Russia to Portugal. The species is anadromous except in some northeastern lakes, where resident populations of "landlocked" salmon—or *ouananiche*, as they are called in Canada—have established themselves.

All Atlantic salmon spawn at the same time, in the fall, in the upper reaches of rivers and streams that enter the Atlantic Ocean. The earliest fish to enter the rivers are called "bright" salmon and are those most sought by anglers. Fish entering the rivers later in the run are heavy with eggs and milt and don't have the high-powered energy or lustrous silver shine of the earlier fish.

Upon reaching the spawning grounds, the female salmon digs her nest, or redd, in a carefully selected gravel bar. After her eggs are deposited in the redd and fertilized by the male, she may immediately build another redd just downstream from the first one, and the spawning process will be duplicated.

Newborn salmon, called alevins, carry a yolk sac that nourishes them for about six weeks while they hide in the gravel near the redd. When the yolk sac has been absorbed, the young salmon leave the gravel beds and start to feed on plankton. They are now known as parr, and except for their widely forked tail they look very much like young brook or brown trout.

The parr don't all go to sea at the same time. Most remain in the rivers for two years and some for up to five years before finally migrating, usually during receding high water in the late spring and early summer. When the parr reach the estuaries that link their rivers with the ocean, they lose their troutlike markings and develop a silvery sheen, at which stage they are called smolts. Schools of smolts feed in the estuaries and eventually migrate to the sea, where they share a common feeding ground near Greenland with their European cousins.

Some smolts spend only one year at sea and return to the rivers of their origin weighing from about two to four pounds. These returning fish are called grilse. Although most rivers have grilse runs, some have runs consisting predominantly of grilse, while others have runs of both grilse and mature salmon. While most spawning fish are in the ten- to thirty-five-pound range, Atlantic salmon are known to reach weights approaching one hundred pounds. The world record rod-and-reel salmon, which was taken in Norway, weighed just over seventy-nine pounds.

Not all mature Atlantic salmon return to the sea after spawning. Some of the smaller fish stay throughout the winter, in the rivers in which they spawn, and these holdovers are called black salmon, or kelts. In the spring the kelts feed voraciously prior to their return to the ocean, and will take almost any artificial fly. While these fish are in excellent physical condition, they are not as good tasting as bright salmon because they contain no sea fat or luster. Fishing for kelts is legal only in New Brunswick Province, where the angler suffers the unique "problem" of trying to keep the three- and four-pound grilse from getting to his fly before the larger kelts, which may run over ten pounds.

The question of whether or not salmon feed while returning on their spawning run has been debated for years. Recent findings by biologists suggest that changes in the body chemistry of the spawning fish result in a condition in which they cannot eat because of the arrest of digestive juices in their stomachs. Nevertheless, the instinct to feed is still present, and the fish will strike brightly colored artificial flies. It takes but a single fish cartwheeling into the air, your fly embedded in the corner of its mouth, to make you an instant, lifelong convert to the sport of Atlantic salmon fishing.

Not many years ago fishing for Atlantic salmon was strictly a rich man's sport. Many of the top Canadian rivers were controlled by private clubs that restricted fishing to their own members. The only other salmon waters available to the angler charged extremely high prices for food, lodging, boats, and guide services. Today, the Canadian government is refusing to renew private leases, and once they expire the waters are classified as Open Crown Waters, making them available to anyone with a fishing license. The state of Maine has spent years on salmon restoration projects and has had great success. Some Maine rivers are now very productive, and all of that state's salmon fishery is open to the public.

TECHNIQUES FOR ATLANTIC SALMON

Considering the comparatively small geographic distribution of the Atlantic salmon, a remarkable amount of equipment has been designed specifically for this fish. There are long, double-handled fly rods, multiplying fly reels with sophisticated drags and capacities of over three hundred yards of backing, and fly patterns developed in England over one hundred years ago. If a fisherman were determined to do so, he could spend many thousands of dollars on a single, complete outfit. But that isn't necessary, and unless you are wealthy or deeply involved in the traditions of the sport, a strong trout rod with moderate backbone and power will be adequate for all but the very largest fish hooked in the biggest, fastest rivers. I use a medium-action 8½-foot rod and a reel with a 3¼-inch diameter spool which holds about one hundred and fifty yards of fifteen-pound-test backing. Under normal water conditions I use a 7½-foot leader tapered to a tippet of four pounds (2X). When conditions are low and clear I use a 9½-foot leader.

Atlantic salmon can be taken on wet or dry flies. Some of the traditional wet-fly patterns have wonderful names: the Jock Scott, Black Dose, Rusty Rat, and Green Highlander. Traditional dry-fly patterns include the Ratfaced Mc-Dougall and the Pink Lady. These flies, particularly the wet patterns, are complicated and difficult to tie for all but the most accomplished fly tyer. But while it is fun to use these traditional flies for this most traditional of fish, the fact is that the modern patterns are more productive. These modern flies are also easy to tie, in many cases consisting or little more than a body of fluorescent material and a brightly colored wing.

I prefer to use small flies for Atlantic salmon, and have had my best luck with the so-called "butt patterns," which have no tail. These are simple flies and I can tie my own. My favorite is the Red Butt, which has a black body with fine silver ribbing, a wing of red squirrel tail, and a sparse fluorescent red butt. I prefer No. 6 and No. 8 flies under most water conditions, but if the river is high and discolored I will use a fly as large as a No. 4. Under very low, clear water conditions I might use a fly as small as a No. 12. Salmon fishermen have a lot of fun arguing over fly size and pattern, but most agree that the darker flies are better on bright days and that bright flies are better on dull days or when the water is discolored.

A knowledge of trout fishing and the habits of the fish won't be of much help when it comes to salmon fishing. Trout fishermen are accustomed to presenting a fly to a feeding fish, but salmon are not feeding and it often takes many casts to arouse or anger them into striking. Trout also assume a somewhat permanent position in a stream, where the current will carry food to them. Salmon move around a river or stream, and since they are not looking for food drifting in the current they often lie in long, comparatively calm stretches of the kind the trout fisherman would bypass.

A knowledgeable guide is necessary for most salmon fishing unless you have spent time on the river or stream you're fishing and know the areas where the fish are likely to congregate. Under normal stream conditions—clear water at a temperature between about 65° and 70°F—I have found Atlantic salmon resting in areas with a moderate flow, often near obstructions close to the bank of the stream. I also like to cast to "edges," those areas in a pool where a slightly faster current meets a slightly slower one. When the water is high I have often found the fish over gravel bars that are too shallow to fish when the flow of the river is normal. Other potential hot-spots when the water is high are the long stretches of flat water below big pools.

One of the things I like best about fishing for Atlantic salmon is that when the water is clear I can often cast to fish I can see, which is much more exciting than blind-casting. If, when you're casting for salmon, a fish shows any interest whatsoever in the fly, it can probably be coaxed into striking. If a fish strikes short or follows the fly, or even moves ever so slightly in the direction of the fly, you have a hot fish. Sometimes all I have to do is change to a slightly smaller fly or a different pattern to generate an arm-wrenching strike.

Pools in large rivers are easiest to fish from a boat or canoe, and long casts are not necessary. One of my favorite methods for blind-casting a large pool is to anchor near the head of the pool and make casts of about forty feet in a semicircle around me. When I have covered this area with many casts I let the boat drift downstream just far enough to reach new water, where I repeat the casting process.

When casting from shore the same technique as in boat casting should be used to throughly cover as much water as you can reach. As mentioned earlier, if a salmon shows any interest in your fly it pays to keep casting to that fish. Some anglers like to rest an interested fish for a few minutes before making another cast. I've had my best results by making an immediate cast to an interested fish, but if it doesn't take the fly on that cast I'll wait a few minutes before trying again.

Fishing a dry fly for salmon is great fun and not as difficult as fishing a dry for trout. The large salmon flies are easy to see on the water, float very well, and you don't have to be concerned about the fly's dragging over the surface of the water, an action that will usually send trout running for cover. In fact, skittering a big dry fly on a tight line over an interested salmon will often result in a strike.

When fishing dry flies for salmon it is important that you don't strike too quickly. Salmon take a floating fly deliberately and usually hook themselves. The trout fisherman who is accustomed to striking instantly, before the trout realizes the fly is a phony, will take it right out of the salmon's mouth and spook the fish in the process.

Once a salmon is hooked it will usually run directly downstream and terminate the run with a series of majestic leaps. I drop the tip of my rod when the fish jumps to keep it from falling back on a tight line and breaking the tippet. If your salmon runs upstream, use the pressure of the water to help tire him. Once the fish begins to tire it can be led to the net or to a "tailer," a wire or rope noose that slips over the tail of the fish. You must be ready to give line when the fish is close. Often, at the sight of the fisherman, an apparently spent salmon will race downstream once again. Many fish are lost right at the angler's feet.

LANDLOCKED SALMON

Landlocked salmon are identical to Atlantic salmon with one notable difference: even when they have easy access to the ocean, they do not migrate.

The range of the landlock consists of approximately three hundred lakes in Maine, New Hampshire, and Vermont, and some lakes in Quebec, Labrador, Nova Scotia, New Brunswick, and Newfoundland. Landlocks, called *ouananiche* in Canada, were first discovered in Maine's Sebago Lake, where the rod-and-reel record fish of twenty-two and a half pounds was taken in 1907. Today the fish average between about three and five pounds, and any fish over seven pounds is a trophy.

Landlocked salmon feed primarily on small fish such as smelt and yellow perch, but they have been known to feed on insects and can occasionally be taken on a dry fly. Most fish are taken on live bait, smelt being the favorite. At ice-out in the spring, huge schools of smelt enter the tributary streams of the landlock lakes to spawn, and the salmon follow. In many lakes, anglers fish from bridges and jetties where these tributary streams enter the lakes.

Landlocks will take worms, plugs, spoons, and spinners, but most shore fishermen use a live smelt hooked lightly under the dorsal fin and allowed to swim free. Medium-weight spinning tackle is best suited to this kind of fishing, and it is important that the bait be alive and lively.

My favorite method for catching these fine fish is to troll a No. 6 or No. 8 streamer fly off the mouth of a tributary stream immediately after the ice has gone out. I use my sinking line, which brings the fly a bit deeper, and long-bodied streamers in a Grey or Green Ghost pattern.

When the smelt run is over and the landlocks have returned to the lake, I troll close to the shore, around islands, and over shallow bars and humps. The fish remain near the surface in the cool spring water, and it is not necessary to add any weight to the fly. Like their bigger brothers the Atlantic salmon, landlocks are great fighters and leapers, but their smaller size allows the luxury of using much lighter equipment when trolling for them. Any light- or medium-weight fly rod is adequate for such trolling, as long as the reel is large enough to hold at least one hundred yards of backing. Many anglers swear by ultra-light spinning tackle and four-pound-test line. Regardless of equipment, I get most of my strikes when trolling for landlocks by making long sweeps of my rod, which causes the fly to dart and pause. Most strikes come when the fly drops back and pauses.

Once the water warms, landlocks go deep and are difficult to locate. Anglers using lead-core line and Davis spinners do catch summer fish, but with heavy tackle used at great depths, the landlock has no opportunity to display its flashy aerial antics, and the fight is far from spectacular.

Occasionally in summer landlocks will feed on the surface at dawn and dusk. These summer surface-feeding sprees are usually very short-lived, but if you're lucky enough to be near the feeding fish almost any lure or fly that represents a minnow will generate a strike. I don't fish for landlocks in the summer, but have taken a few when I have seen smelt jumping out of the water while I was casting a deer-hair bug for smallmouths. In summer some die-hard landlock anglers troll at first light and pick up a few fish, but finding the fish under these conditions is largely a matter of luck.

In late fall the landlocks once again return to the surface and feed actively in preparation for fall spawning. I never seem to do as well in the fall as I do in the early spring, but the fish can be taken on top with streamers, spinning lures, or spoons such as the thin-bladed Mooselook Wobblers.

The populations of landlocked salmon in northeastern lakes have remained good due to extensive stocking programs. Fisheries biologists net the mature fish as they enter the rivers to spawn, "strip" them of their eggs and milt, and return them unharmed. The fertilized eggs are brought to hatcheries and the young fish are tended for two years, after which they are released into selected lakes. Thanks to this successful program of artificial propagation, the outlook for the landlocked salmon remains excellent.

29

Pacific Salmon

When I first started fishing on the West Coast, I was convinced that there were at least thirty different species of Pacific salmon. Everywhere I fished I saw salmon that looked alike but which were called by different names. There are, in fact, six different species of Pacific salmon, but there are literally dozens of local nicknames for the fish.

Among the names by which Pacific salmon are called are dog or chum salmon, blueback or sockeye salmon, kokanee salmon, chinook or king salmon, silver or coho salmon, and humpback or pink salmon. Among sportfishermen the coho and chinook are the most popular Pacific salmon, and I will discuss them in more detail later in this section.

Chum or dog salmon (*Oncorhynchus keta*) reach weights of over thirty pounds, although most run between ten and twenty pounds.

Chum salmon arrive in late fall at the mouths of northwestern streams that flow into the ocean. Very little angling is done specifically for these fish, although they are taken by anglers using fluorescent spoons and spinners while seeking other salmon, especially in the islands of British Columbia. The chum salmon spawn in November and December in the lower reaches of the rivers to which they come, where they are occasionally taken by anglers. This fish does not rate highly with most Pacific salmon fishermen.

Sockeye or blueback salmon (*Oncorhynchus nerka*) is the most commercially valuable of the Pacific salmons, and many of these fine-tasting fish are taken by commercial trawlers. The fish range all over the northern Pacific Ocean and as far south as the Columbia River.

Sockeyes are small members of the Pacific salmon family, with most fish averaging between four and eight pounds. The fish enter lake-fed rivers from late February through July and spawn in the feeder lakes from early August through December. Young sockeyes spend their first few years in the lakes where they were born, and migrate to the sea with the spring freshet. While some anglers fish for sockeyes, most are taken by fishermen seeking other salmon and steelhead.

Kokanee are sockeye salmon that have lost their anadromous instincts. These landlocked fish closely resemble trout and are popular with anglers who take them on small spoons and spinning lures. Kokanee run small, the record weight being about four pounds, and a three-pound fish is a big one.

Kokanee have been stocked in lakes all across the northern tier of the United States and southern Canada, and the size of the fish varies from one lake to another. They grow larger at the southern edge of their range, where slightly warmer water produces abundant zooplankton, their major food source. In lakes at the southern edge of their range kokanee may reach a length of over twenty inches and weigh over three pounds; in northern lakes they run considerably smaller. For instance, in northern British Columbia most of the kokanee average only about twelve inches, while in the southern waters of that province I have seen a few fish over twenty inches. Kokanee have been stocked in a few northeastern lakes, but only Lake Champlain on the Vermont–New York border produces fish over twenty inches in length. Kokanee stocked in some of Maine's lakes rarely exceed ten inches.

Humpback or pink salmon (*Oncorhynchus gorbuscha*) are also small members of the Pacific salmon family, reaching a maximum weight of about ten pounds. Most adult fish weigh between four and six pounds. The fish mature quickly, in about two years, and the male develops a pronounced hump on his back, from which the popular name is derived.

Humpback salmon spawn in the early fall in coastal rivers. Spawning occurs very near the sea and there is no consistency in the spawning runs; some years will see great numbers of humpbacks while in others there will be very few fish. Humpbacks are popular sportfish in Puget Sound, where they are taken on spoons and cut bait, but most are taken commercially. The majority of sportfishing for humpbacks is done in the waters around the Queen Charlotte Islands and a few rivers in British Columbia.

The coho or silver salmon (*Oncorhynchus kisutch*) are among the most popular game fish of the Pacific Northwest. These fish have been stocked in the Great Lakes, where since the mid-1960s they have become well established and the basis of an immense and growing sport fishery. In fact, the Great Lakes program has been so successful that the record coho (thirty-three pounds) was taken in 1970 from the Little Manistee River in Michigan. On the West Coast the cohos run considerably smaller, any fish over ten pounds being a good one.

Cohos leave the sea during the summer and spawn in the late fall and winter; they spawn on gravel bars throughout the length of the rivers in which they are found. The young fish migrate to the sea after about a year and reach maturity at between three and four years of age. The fry feed heavily on crab larvae until they grow large enough to forage on baitfish and squid.

Cohos are unique among the Pacific salmon because they don't travel far from the rivers where they are hatched. When mature they feed in the ocean just off the mouth of the parent river, and large concentrations of the fish can be found in a small area. While the range of the coho extends from California to Japan, each river contributes its own population, and fish tagged in one river have not been found to enter other rivers.

For the light-tackle fisherman the coho is a favorite. The fish often feed near the surface where they can be taken on trolled streamer flies and small spoons. When they are feeding on top the atmosphere is electric. Flocks of diving sea birds appear as if out of nowhere and scream as they dive into schools of baitfish trapped against the surface of the water by the salmon. As quickly as a school appears it is gone, and all eyes turn upward, looking for another flock of screaming birds. Cohos can be very wary when feeding on top, and it can be difficult to get close enough to cast to them without putting the school down. Under such conditions you will have your best luck by trolling the edges of a feeding school with a long line and a small silver spoon.

Trolling a streamer fly can also be very effective. I use a medium-weight fly rod and a reel that holds at least two hundred yards of ten-pound-test backing. My favorite flies are No. 6 long-bodied streamers in either silver or blue.

For casting into a school of cohos feeding on the surface I prefer light- or medium-weight spinning tackle. My reel holds two hundred and fifty yards of ten-pound-test line and I make sure to check that the drag mechanism on the reel is functioning smoothly before I begin fishing.

I once tried to land a coho on ultra-light spinning tackle. My tiny reel was filled with about three hundred yards of three-pound-test line. The captain of the boat, a good friend, grinned and shook his head at my choice of equipment. He carefully eased the boat near a school of wildly feeding fish and I tossed my small silver spoon in the mayhem. I never got the opportunity to even turn the reel handle. The tiny rod bowed and I watched as the line melted from the spool. Even with three hundred yards of line on the reel there was no way I could land that fish; I couldn't apply enough pressure to even slow him, and I watched as the last of my line peeled from the spool and parted at the knot. The whole process couldn't have lasted more than a minute, and the next time I use ultra-light tackle for cohos I'll try six-pound-test line.

Except when cohos are feeding on the surface, the tackle and techniques used for them are similar to those used for chinook or king salmon.

Chinook salmon (*Oncorhynchus tshawytscha*) are indeed the kings of the salmon, with fish over 125 pounds having been taken commercially. The rod-and-reel record is 93 pounds, but the fish average between 15 and 35 pounds.

Chinooks spawn from June to November in the main river systems that flow into the Pacific Ocean. They prefer large rivers, and the construction of dams on many of the larger Pacific coast rivers has eliminated some of the spawning waters of these fish and caused reductions in their populations.

After being hatched, most chinook fry go to the sea, where they travel distances of over two thousand miles and grow at the prodigious rate of three to six pounds per year. After about five years they return to the rivers of their birth to spawn. While at sea the chinooks feed on anchovies, herrings, crustaceans, and squid. They stop feeding upon entering fresh water, but will strike brightly colored lures and flies. Fishing is good as soon as the fish appear off the coast, and the largest concentrations of fish are in the estuaries, where they hold while acclimating themselves to the fresh water.

I will never forget my first chinook salmon. It was many years ago and I had a two-day layover in San Francisco before shipping out to the Far East. I couldn't interest any of my buddies in a fishing trip; they were turned on by the San Francisco night life. But I had heard on the radio that the salmon were hitting and nothing could have kept me on shore. I was up before dawn and got a space on one of the party boats that left from Fisherman's Wharf. The ocean was rough and I sat sipping coffee as we laboriously made our way through clashing tides and currents. Once outside the bay things quieted down to a gentle swell and we traveled north along the coast. When the sky turned pink and began to brighten, the captain slowed the boat and we began to troll.

We were using cut herring fished about twenty-five feet deep with the aid of large round balls of pig iron. Each "cannon ball" weighed about two pounds and was connected to the line with a spring-loaded swivel that would release the ball when a fish took the bait. These rigs were the precursors of today's modern downriggers. The rods were about eight feet long, soft and very heavy, and were placed in holders along the stern of the boat. It looked strange to me to see the rods bowed over from the weight of the iron balls, and I doubted that the large weights would drop free when a fish struck. I kept glancing at the huge landing net in a holder on the side of the boat and wondered if a net that large was really necessary. It didn't take long to find out. The rod on one side of mine bowed and jumped and line began to flow from the reel. The angler took the rod from the holder and began to fight his fish; then my rod bowed and the captain took it from the holder and thrust it into my hands. Another rod jumped and three of us were fighting fish. My chinook took so much line on its first run that I got worried and began to put a lot of pressure on the fish. The captain told me to "stop horsing him" and to take my time. I had never felt that much power at the end of my line, but I kept the rod tip up and the pressure steady, and eventually I could feel that the fish was tiring. A few times I had to dance around the deck with the other anglers who were fighting fish to keep our lines from getting tangled. There was a wild thrashing when one fish was netted, the second angler lost his fish, and finally mine was nearing the boat. The captain made a deft pass with the huge net and brought the salmon into the boat. My jaw dropped. A huge, bright silver chinook lay on the deck, its gills pumping. I had never seen a more beautiful fish and couldn't stop looking at it. The captain clapped me on the back and told me that it was a female that would go about twenty pounds, but I just kept staring at it. Prior to that time my biggest fish had been a three-pound trout, and while I had read about twenty-pound salmon, there is quite a difference between reading about a twenty-pounder and looking down at one you have just landed. At one point I lifted the fish and cradled it in my arms the way a person would hold a baby. I've since seen other fishermen do the same and I completely understand the emotion of that act. I have caught larger chinooks, but that first one remains etched in my memory.

The equipment and techniques used for offshore salmon vary, but there are a few things common to most methods. In the spring both the cohos and chinook tend to be deep and most deep trollers use downriggers or cannon balls. The fish move closer to the surface as the season progresses, and peak fishing is usually in August and September. When the fish are in the ten- to twenty-foot-deep range many anglers like to use plastic or metal diving planes, which will keep the bait or lure running at moderate depths without undue resistance when a fish is hooked. I have tried these; they require a bit of practice for best results, and the speed of the boat must be adjusted to suit the type of diving plane, which depends on water resistance to find its maximum depth.

Baits and lures for offshore salmon are matters of individual preference, with the same lure or bait being used regardless of the depth at which it is fished. I prefer to use a whole small herring or anchovy as a rigged bait. There are many different ways to rig a bait, but the important thing is that it not spin and twist the line. I run the eye of the hook through the anal vent, through the center of the body, and out the mouth; I then sew the mouth of the bait firmly to the hook. Other baits I've used with success are smelt, cut mackerel, and squid. Lures are usually silver or gold spoons, but a really shiny lure of any color may take the fish, and I've see coho taken on yellow and green spoons and even chartreuse ones with red dots. Streamer flies are particularly effective for surface-feeding fish; I prefer long-bodied models with shiny Mylar bodies and a white-and-blue wing.

If you're going to be fishing from a commercial party boat you will use heavy tackle. This is understandable because the crew cannot spend all its time replacing broken equipment. Standard party-boat equipment for offshore salmon fishing consists of two-handled boat rods about seven feet long and 3/0 star-drag reels loaded with three hundred yards of fifty-pound-test line. Some charter boats specialize in light-tackle fishing and will allow you to use your own light equipment such as a fly rod or light spinning gear, but you must check this out with the captain of the boat before you leave the docks.

"Mooching" is one technique popular with salmon fishermen everywhere the fish are found; it consists of little more than exaggerated jigging. I like to use an eight- or nine-foot boat rod with a fast tip and a good bit of backbone for this type of fishing. I use a medium-weight star-drag reel filled with at least two hundred yards of twenty- to thirty-pound-test line. Plug-cut baits or whole herring are my choice, but I have also taken fish using spoons. The boat is stopped over an area believed to hold fish or over a school located on a depthfinder. I add a little weight, usually less than an ounce, about eighteen inches above the bait, and lower it over the side to the preferred depth, usually between twenty and forty feet. I throw the reel into gear and lift the rod upward in long sweeps that start near the water and end with the rod above my head. The cut bait or spoon dances in the water, and if salmon are in the area they will often take it.

As good as salmon fishing can be on the West Coast it is at least as good in the Great Lakes. Extensive stocking of chinook and coho salmon started in the lakes in the early 1960s, and by the mid-1970s the fish were well established. Lake Michigan seems to produce the biggest fish, and many biologists believe that this is because Michigan is slightly warmer than the other lakes. But all the lakes have salmon, and fishing for them is becoming a year-round sport. As a result of extensive stocking programs, the big lakes now hold huge populations of coho, chinook, and Atlantic salmon, as well as brown and rainbow trout. Fish over fifteen pounds, of all species, are now common.

Locating salmon in the Great Lakes during the summer ordinarily requires depthfinders and possibly temperature probes. The depthfinders are used to spot schools of game or forage fish while the temperature probes find the desired water temperature of about 55°F. Once the fish are sighted, or when the fifty-five-degree mark is located, traditional trolling or mooching methods are used. Big crankbaits are more popular for salmon in the Great Lakes than on the West Coast; my favorites are six-inch Rapalas, Rebels, Tadpollies, and Headhunters.

As fall approaches, the Great Lakes salmon trollers work shallower depths at the mouths of streams and rivers. By early October the fish are starting to enter the rivers themselves. Fall fishing at the mouths of the rivers or in the rivers can be a mixed-bag affair. Trollers or river anglers using traditional steelhead techniques can take big salmon and real lunker brown trout.

If you're unfamiliar with Great Lakes fishing you'll have no trouble finding out where to fish and which lures or baits to use; all the states along the lakes have fishing information services. Accommodations are plentiful and there is a growing fleet of sportfishing boats available for hire.

One of the nicest aspects of fishing for Pacific salmon in the Great Lakes is that with a little planning and a little luck, these large, hard-fighting fish can be taken in incredible numbers. The habits of the fish are becoming well known, and downriggers and depthfinders have made it possible to catch them on all sizes and weights of fishing equipment. The populations of these fine fish are increasing, and as long as water quality doesn't deteriorate and stocking programs continue, the fishing can only get better.

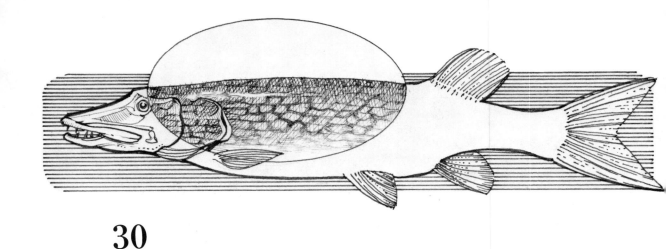

30

Chain Pickerel

Chain pickerel (*Esox niger*) are the smallest members of the pike family and are ordinarily not found in waters where the larger members of the family—the northern pike and muskellunge—are present. The range of the chain pickerel is from Maine to Arkansas and north to the Great Lakes, but they are most abundant in the Northeast where they are a popular game fish.

Pickerel grow quickly, and in fertile lakes reach a length of about sixteen inches in only two years. Their growth then slows and it takes another three or four years for the fish to reach a length of twenty inches. The life span of the pickerel is approximately ten years, by which time it may reach a length of over thirty inches and a weight of over six pounds. The largest recorded pickerel weighed almost ten pounds.

Chain pickerel feed extensively on small fish, which they ambush with a sudden rush from a weedy or brushy lair. They are rarely found far from aquatic growth, and share some of the preference for structure also common to largemouth bass. For this reason many pickerel are taken by bass anglers, some of whom are disappointed with their catch. But there are many anglers who pursue the pickerel; they know that a three- or four-pound pickerel on light tackle is a real challenge, and when prepared properly is excellent table fare.

TECHNIQUES FOR PICKEREL

At all times of the year a live minnow is the best pickerel bait. But fishing a live minnow in the areas preferred by pickerel—particularly larger pickerel—can be difficult. Pickerel are bottom-loving fish and the position of their eyes on the top of their head makes it easiest for them to look up. The biggest fish spend most of their time lying motionless near openings deep in weedbeds or under submerged logs. The smaller fish are found in shallower water, often on the edge of the weeds.

If you want to catch a bunch of sixteen-inch pickerel for the frying pan, fishing a three-inch minnow under a bobber around the weeds is your best bet. I tie a No. 4 hook to a piece of fifteen-pound-test monofilament about twelve inches long. The heavy leader doesn't scare the fish and is necessary to keep them from cutting the line with their razor-sharp teeth. I add a splitshot about a foot above the hook to keep the bait down, and place my bobber at a depth that will allow the minnow to hang over the weeds but not bury itself in them. I drop the rig into holes in the weeds or around the edges of dense weedbeds, and if the pickerel are present it won't be long before I start to catch them. If a particular weedbed doesn't produce in about fifteen minutes I try another one.

Pickerel take a live minnow with a solid tug that brings the bobber just under the surface of the water. They then pause and turn the minnow so that they can swallow it head first. Many anglers wait until the fish swallows the minnow and starts to swim off before setting the hook. I prefer to set the hook as soon as the bobber goes under. Pickerel usually grab a minnow right across the middle of its body, and if the bait is hooked lightly under the back fin an instant strike will see the fish well-hooked in the top or corner of its mouth. If you wait until the pickerel swims off with the minnow you will hook the fish, but the hook will lodge in the gills, deep in the throat, or in the stomach, making it impossible to remove without killing the fish. In pickerel ponds there will be many small fish, and when using minnows you will kill many of them if you give them time to swallow the bait.

I have consistently found the biggest pickerel on the bottoms of weedbeds in water from six to twelve feet deep. The only times I've found the bigger fish in shallower water are the spring and fall, when cool waters allow them comfortable access to the shallows.

Fishing a minnow over the top of a twelve-foot-deep weedbed is a difficult process. If the minnow is allowed to swim free it will bury itself in the weeds and inevitably be torn off the hook. That is why many big pickerel are taken by ice fishermen, who can set their tip-ups directly over a weedbed and carefully suspend their minnow barely over the top of the weeds until it entices a big pickerel that is lying in the weeds looking up for its next meal.

I prefer to use artificial lures for pickerel regardless of the season. My outfit is a light spinning rod about six and a half feet long and a spinning reel filled with eight-pound-test line. My all-around favorite pickerel lure is an eight-inch plastic worm hooked Texas-style (weedless). Pickerel prefer brightly colored lures, and I've done best with bright red or orange plastic worms that have a twisted tail that flutters as the worm drops to the bottom or is moved through the water.

In the summer, when the fish are deep, I cast the worm over deep weedbeds and retrieve it with active hops right over the tops of the weeds. Sometimes it may take between five and ten casts to the same spot to generate a strike. Remember, it takes at least six years for a pickerel to grow to a length of twenty inches or more, and when you're pursuing the thirty-inchers you're after wary old fish that didn't get that big by hitting the first thing that swam by them. The person who consistently brings in big pickerel is a careful, methodical angler who probably brings in big fish of many species.

One tip for fishing deep weedbeds is to retrieve your rubber worm right to the boat. Big pickerel will sometimes follow a lure a long distance before striking, and I've taken some that followed the lure from a deep weedbed and struck right at the boatside.

In the spring and fall, when the big pickerel are in shallower water, I cast my plastic worm into the densest brush or weeds and swim it quickly over the surface, with occasional stops and tantalizing twitches in openings in the brush. Pickerel strike a lure presented in this manner swiftly and violently, and you should set the hook quickly with a strong jerk of the rod. This method of fishing is actually a modern version of a classic pickerel technique called skittering, which is done with a long pole and a piece of heavy line the same length as the pole. A large weedless hook is tied to the line and a triangle of pork rind or a perch belly with the orange stomach fins intact is used for bait. The bait is dragged, or skittered, over the tops of weedbeds in the same manner I described for fishing a plastic worm. This traditional technique is still popular in some places in the Northeast, and is as effective today as it has ever been.

Pickerel will attack practically any lure that resembles an injured minnow as long as it is moving at a fairly rapid rate of speed. There are times when these fish will absolutely tear up surface plugs, and I have had big pickerel launch themselves like miniature submarines for fifteen feet through the weeds to grab a surface lure that I was tossing into open pockets of water. I like to use a large silver Bang-O-Lure or other floater-divers for this kind of fishing, working the lure quickly across the surface with occasional pauses. Even lures fitted with three sets of treble hooks can be worked through lily pads without becoming hung up very often, but it does take practice.

Once you find a particular weedbed or brushpile that produces pickerel you should fish it on every outing. While pickerel are not a school fish, a spot with good cover and forage will attract many fish, and most of my favorite spots produce year after year.

Pickerel are also found in rivers and streams, and one of the largest I ever caught took a Grey Ghost streamer while I was casting for trout. I was fishing a catch-and-release river in New Hampshire and had seen a big trout swirl behind my fly. The fish made its pass at the head of a long, deep pool, and after thoroughly working the head of the pool I decided to fish downstream. At the tail of the pool was a big brushpile in deep, quiet water near the bank. I let the streamer drift into the quiet area near the brushpile, and as I started my retrieve I had a terrific strike that almost took the rod from my hand. The fish fought hard and deep, and considering the slow, deep water where I had hooked the fish and the lack of aerial acrobatics I would have expected from a rainbow, I guessed it to be a big brown trout. I played the fish very carefully because I wanted to get a good look at it before I released it. When I finally got it to my feet I was surprised to see that it was a big pickerel. On my tiny pocket scale that fish went almost six pounds and was twenty-eight inches long, and its fight had been every bit as good as that of a trout of the same weight.

Many anglers don't pursue pickerel because they want to catch bigger fish. Many fishermen also believe that pickerel stop feeding when the weather gets hot. In fact, pickerel feed almost all the time, but finding the big fish—those over three pounds—is as difficult as finding and catching big fish of any species. Incidentally, it is a waste of time to fish for any member of the pike family at night; they are exclusively daylight feeders.

Pickerel are excellent eating, especially when taken from cold water, but they are a very bony fish. The smaller ones can be filleted and deep fried. The fillets will contain tiny Y-shaped bones, but they will dissolve during cooking. Big fish should be filleted and the fillets should be scored with a knife down to the Y-shaped bones. These big fillets can then be baked in an inch of milk at 250°F for about two hours and the bones will dissolve, leaving some top-rate table fare.

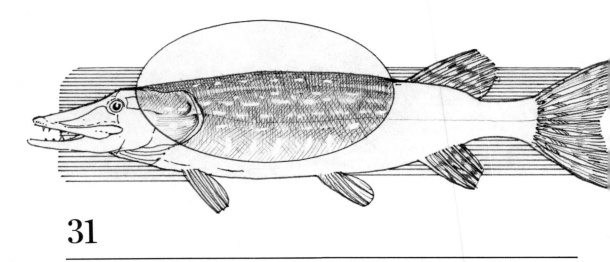

31

Northern Pike

The northern pike (*Esox lucius*) is found throughout most of North America but is most common from the Great Lakes north to central Manitoba. It is a very popular gamefish because it grows large and is a determined, tenacious fighter.

Pike spawn at the age of two years in the northern portions of their range. In their southern regions a few fish may spawn after one year. In the early spring the fish move into the shallows at night, but actual spawning takes place during the afternoon hours, when the sun warms the water to a temperature of approximately 50°F.

Northerns are extremely fast-growing fish. In the southern areas of their range they may reach a length of thirty inches or more in three years. In northern latitudes their rate of growth is slightly slower, but most fish reach a length of sixteen inches in their first year. Where conditions are right the fish grow large, and in some bodies of water they average between ten and fifteen pounds. The largest northern pike on record was taken in New York State in 1940 and weighed forty-six pounds.

TECHNIQUES FOR NORTHERNS

It isn't necessary to be up at first light to catch pike; these fish do all of their feeding during daylight hours, as do all members of the pike family. The cool waters of the spring, winter, and fall produce the most fish, but pike do not, as some anglers claim, stop feeding during the summer heat, and can be taken throughout the summer. Like many species of fish, they seek cool water when the waters warm, and for this reason are more difficult to find under such conditions, but when you can find them they can be caught.

Pike are not considered a school fish, but when conditions are to their liking they will group together. I found an example of this during a morning I spent looking for northerns in one of New York State's Finger Lakes. I had passed many hours tossing a spoon to the deep sides of weedbeds and letting it flutter down without getting a strike. Finally I tossed my spoon into one pocket and had a firm hit. I eventually landed a nice pike that went about eight pounds. I continued casting to that pocket in the weeds—an area about as big as a bathtub—and in less than two hours had landed four more fish ranging from six to fourteen pounds. The fish were clustered in that one area, and if my cast was off by even three feet I wouldn't get a strike. Pike may not be a school fish, but when you catch one it pays to fish the area with care.

Pike can be taken on almost any kind of equipment, but because they are primarily minnow eaters and also like yellow perch and suckers, large spoons and plugs ordinarily produce the biggest fish. Northerns are a big-lure, big-fish operation, and medium or heavy baitcasting equipment is my choice for tossing heavy lures.

Except when they are spawning, pike will be found in from five to about twenty feet of water. I've never taken one in very deep water. They like weedbeds, especially those along the edge of a sharp dropoff, and unlike their cousins the pickerel they are found on the edges of the weeds rather than in the dense growth.

Pike have voracious appetites and pugnacious temperaments, qualities that make them willing to attack almost anything that moves and looks like a potential meal. I've heard stories of anglers finding such things as a full-grown muskrat lodged in the throat of a dead pike, and it has been documented that Manitoba pike feed on ducklings.

I believe that Manitoba has the best pike fishing in North America, followed by areas in Minnesota, Wisconsin, Michigan, and the Thousand Islands area of New York State. I have found Winnipeg, Manitoba, to be the best jumping-off spot for pike and other fishing in the pristine waters of that northern province.

Where it is legal, using a large live sucker for bait will produce some big pike. My equipment for fishing these big baits is a heavy baitcasting outfit with twenty-pound-test line. I use an eight-inch sucker hooked lightly under the back fin with a 3/0 hook on a twelve-inch wire leader. I hang the sucker about five or six feet below a big round bobber and add just enough weight to keep the bait down. I lower the rig over the side of the boat and the sucker inevitably takes off for the weeds, towing the bobber behind. I let the sucker get near the weedline and hold it there. When a pike hits the sucker the bobber will stop moving, dip below the surface of the water, and sit motionless while the fish turns the bait to a head-first position in its mouth. Many anglers wait until the pike swims off before setting the hook. I prefer to strike the fish immediately, before it turns the bait in its mouth. In this way the pike is hooked in the front or side of the mouth, allowing me to release smaller fish unharmed. I rarely miss the big ones because the location of the hook under the back fin puts the bait well into the fish's mouth even before he swallows it.

As mentioned earlier, pike, although not a school fish, do cluster in small areas. I believe that water temperature is the reason for this cluster effect, at least in summer. Pike like cool water, and the summer angler will find it worth his while to spend the time necessary to find these cool-water areas. If you fish the same lakes year-round, the way most of us do, you don't need a temperature probe to find the locations and sources of cold water. For instance, when ice fishing on some of my favorite lakes I know areas where there is black ice—ice that never gets thick enough to be safe no matter how low the temperature gets. Most areas of black ice are due to springs that keep the water moving and too warm to freeze solidly. These areas, especially where the water is from six to twelve feet deep, are ideal locations for summer pike.

Other good summer areas are where cool rivers enter lakes and areas in shallow lakes that have been dredged or contain old river channels. These depressions in the lake bottom are deeper than the surrounding water, and the cooler water settles into them. Such cool-water depressions can be paved with pike. However, most cool-water depressions are small, usually not more than a few hundred square feet, and you must fish them slowly to get strikes. If you drag a lure quickly through a depression it may pass before a dozen big pike without generating a strike. For this reason, fishing a live bait right on the bottom or just off the bottom under a bobber is a very effective way of taking summer pike.

In most cases I prefer artificial lures to bait for pike fishing. For summer pike I like lures that can be worked slowly, such as the Mirrolures and Mepps Giant Killers. Lead-head jigs are also effective because they can be pulled slowly over the bottom, and it is best to drag and not hop them. Black or brown lead-head jigs have caught the most pike for me, particularly when fished in a cool-water depression in a sand or mud bottom.

Some of the best pike fishing is in the spring and fall, when the cool waters allow the fish comfortable access to the whole lake. At such times I look for the fish over flats of about six to twelve feet deep with submerged weedbeds or clumps of weeds scattered throughout the area. I use spoons and prefer to cast rather than troll. I start my fishing with a red-and-white spoon about three or four inches long, although in lakes where the primary forage fish are small yellow perch or walleyes I will use a red-and-yellow spoon. Bright silver or gold spoons are good on dark, overcast days.

My equipment for both casting and trolling consists of medium-weight bait-casting gear with a fifteen-pound-test line to which I add a wire leader about twelve inches long. Most of the time a wire leader won't scare the fish, but if I'm getting no strikes or if pike are following the lure refusing to strike I sometimes get better results by removing the wire leader. It is important to use high-quality ball-bearing swivels when casting or trolling a spoon. Cheap swivels kill the action of the spoon when it is worked slowly, and will result in a badly twisted line, especially with spinning equipment.

I use the count-down method for fishing a spoon over submerged weedbeds. A four-inch spoon falls at a rate of about one foot per second, and I count as the spoon sinks until I find the depth at which it is running just over the tops of the submerged weeds without getting hung up. Once I find the right level I retrieve the spoon quickly for a few feet and then stop my retrieve and allow the spoon to drop and flutter closer to the weeds. When I stop my quick retrieve I drop the rod tip a foot or two back toward the spoon. This causes the spoon to drop and actually move backward for a short distance. If a pike has been following it, as they often do, the change in direction of the lure back toward the fish will frequently result in a strike.

When casting over a mud or sand bottom I like to let the spoon settle right to the bottom, reel it in quickly for about three feet, then let it drop back to the bottom. Sometimes a short, rapid retrieve will excite the pike but they will take the spoon only when it is lying motionless on the bottom.

At other times pike will take a spoon only when it is falling. In this situation I use a jigging action, pointing my rod tip directly at the spoon and moving the rod quickly to a position directly overhead. I then immediately drop the rod back toward the spoon and reel in slowly, picking up slack line as the spoon drops. When the line comes tight I lift the rod back, with a quick jerk, to a position directly overhead. Most strikes occur when the spoon is dropping back, and the upward jerk of the rod will hook the fish. It is important to make this upward jerk a firm one. It is difficult to detect a strike on a falling spoon. Sometimes you may feel a slight "click" as you take up slack line, but most of the time you will feel nothing until you raise the rod.

If the waters you fish are very weedy, you may find it helpful to remove the treble hook from your spoon and replace it with a single large hook. The single hook will not hang up in the weeds as often as the treble one will, and can be dragged right through easy-to-tear varieties of aquatic growth. A single hook has the added advantage of being easier to remove from a tooth-filled mouth than a treble hook, and I don't believe I miss many strikes by using a single hook, especially from big pike that have the tendency to literally inhale the spoon.

Some of the best pike fishing of the year is in the fall, when the fish enter the flats and shallow bays of a lake just before the waters cool. The cool, windy days of early fall are a signal that the environment in the lake is about to change from one of stratified warm water to one of totally cold water. The pike must sense the coming change, and two or three days of cold, windy conditions really turns them on. I have found big concentrations of pike on flats where there are isolated clumps of weeds in five to ten feet of water. I troll about twenty-five feet behind the boat until I find the fish and then cast to them. When trolling I use a systematic pattern to be sure I cover the area completely. For some reason the pike will often select a single clump of weeds or other small area in a larger area that looks entirely the same to me, and large numbers of them may be concentrated in this small area.

Sometimes the fish will not be concentrated into a small area but will instead be widely scattered throughout a weedy flat. Trolling is the best way to take the pike when they are scattered in this way. At times I find that I get most of my strikes when making turns. This usually means that I'm trolling too fast and should slow my speed and allow the spoon to run a little deeper. It can also mean that the pike are following the spoon and striking when it slows and drops on the turn. Adding a jerky action to the spoon when trolling can also result in many more strikes. Be sure you make many passes over an area where you have a strike or see a fish following your lure.

The lures used in trolling for pike can be spoons, plugs, large spinners, and even streamer flies, but large spinnerbaits are my favorite fall trolling lures. I prefer those with a single, large silver Willow-Leaf blade and a black bucktail body, although under windy, rough conditions a yellow body will sometimes work better. If the water is discolored I stick with basic black.

Pike have the same habits throughout their range, and I use the same techniques when fishing for them in the Mississippi River as I do in Manitoba. By fishing the flats and weedbeds in the fall, winter, and spring, and cool-water areas and depressions in the summer, you can catch these fine, big fish throughout the year.

32

Muskellunge

There are many fishing experiences that set one's pulse racing, but for me there is nothing to compare with the excitement of watching a huge muskie following my lure. I find myself saying quietly under my breath, "Take it . . . take it," but more often than not the fish refuses to strike, and often a "follow" is the best I can expect from a day or many days of fishing. Muskies don't come easy, and one strike for every two or three days of fishing seems to be my average.

Why then all the hoopla, the "muskie fever," and the glazed eyes when anglers talk about this fish? You have only to hook one to find the answer. When a muskie takes a lure it is more than a strike—it's an event—a vicious slashing attack followed by a wild, seemingly berserk leap high into the air. And that is just the beginning. The power and strength of these fish are truly awe-inspiring, and any angler who lands a big muskie can feel duly proud of the feat.

A few years ago I was fishing in New York's St. Lawrence River with a ten-year-old friend who is a fine fisherman. His dad was fishing for smallmouth bass, but the boy had never fished for muskies, so we set aside all other fishing (not an easy thing to do on the St. Lawrence) to concentrate on finding him a fish. Muskie fishing is hard work and we spent a full day throwing big jerk plugs without a strike. Then, on the afternoon of the second day, it happened. One minute the boy was working his big jerk plug along a deep weedy dropoff and the next minute he was fast to a muskie, and a big one. I heard his sudden intake of breath and turned to see the fish thrashing wildly across the surface of the water. His eyes wide, the boy tried to hand me the rod. I refused, telling him it was his fish, and I sat back to watch. I've got to give the young man credit, he set his jaw and went to work; and work he did. At one point the fish dove so fast and with so much power that I had to grab the back of the boy's belt to keep him from losing his balance and tumbling overboard. A minute later, it was over. The fish made a rush toward the boat, got some slack line, and with a mighty jump tossed the lure right over the boat. The boy stood there close to tears and kept saying, "What a fish . . . what a fish!" While he complained of "limp line depression" for over a month, he did eventually land a thirty-three-pound nine-ounce muskie from that same spot. I'm sorry I wasn't there to witness the happening, but I do have a picture of the boy holding that fish. It is almost as long as he is and almost as wide as the grin on the boy's face.

There are three subspecies of muskellunge. The Great Lakes muskie (*Esox m. masquinongy*) is found in the Great Lakes basin. The Chautauqua muskie (*Esox m. ohioensis*) is found from central New York State southward through the Ohio basin. The tiger muskie (*Esox m. immaculatus*) is found from Canada's Manitoba Province south through Minnesota, Wisconsin, and Michigan. The native range of all three subspecies is across the northern tier of the United States and through southern Canada, but muskies have been successfully introduced into lakes and rivers along the East Coast as far south as Alabama and as far west as Missouri. The fish have done so well that the states of Kentucky, Tennessee, North Carolina, West Virginia, and Pennsylvania now have muskie fishing that rivals that of Canada and the Great Lakes states.

Muskies are the largest and fastest growing of the pike family. Fish of twenty pounds are common throughout their range, and every year muskies in the fifty- to sixty-pound class are taken. Most fish taken are from five to eight years old. The oldest fish on record, which was also the largest, weighed almost seventy pounds, and an examination of its scales showed it to be in its thirtieth year.

When water temperatures rise to the mid-forties and the ice is out, female muskies move in feeder streams or shallow bays in preparation for spawning. Each female is followed by a group of smaller males, which will seek out and suspend themselves in quiet backwater eddies or shallow bays with a dark bottom. Spawning itself takes place at night when the water temperature reaches the mid-fifties, and will last for a week or more depending on the weather. A sudden drop in temperature will arrest the spawning and the fish will wait for the correct conditions before dropping their eggs. Most spawning takes place at night; during the day the fish return to the main body of the lake or to deep areas of the feeder stream.

Spawning is complete by the time the water temperature reaches 60°F, and the fish then leave the shallows and return to the deeper water, where they take up their residence.

In rivers the best muskie spots are usually in deep pools or holes at the point of entry of a feeder stream, or under the cover of brush piles, logjams, and undercut banks. The deep pools or eddies where a feeder stream enters a main river are potential hot-spots, especially if there is a large brush pile or logjam at the edge of the deep water.

A tip for finding muskies in rivers that has worked for me is to fish after a rain, when the feeder streams are muddy but the main river is slightly clearer. Under these conditions the fish will often congregate on the clear side of the mudline closest to deep water. It pays to fish these areas carefully.

In lakes, muskies can be difficult to find. Big ones are solitary and territorial fish, and stake out their turf with authority. They prefer water from about eight to twenty feet deep, and need more than five acres to meet their food needs. Once a big muskie is removed from its territory it doesn't take long for another to move in.

Among areas in which I have found muskies are the edges of weedbeds that parallel a steep dropoff. Areas around beaver lodges are also good because of all the brush the beavers bury in the mud and water as a winter food supply, and which also provide cover for forage fish. Beaver lodges located on rocky points are real potential hot-spots. I also fish narrow bays with rocky ledges that fall off into about twenty feet of water. Occasionally I have taken muskies over a hard bottom about ten feet deep if there are lots of reeds extending out from the shallows. A good sign that a reedy bar is the home of a muskie will be the absence of small fish in the area. But my favorite muskie haunts are rocky reefs about ten feet deep that are within a few hundred yards of a shallow bay on one side and have a deep-water dropoff on the other. When I'm muskie prospecting in new water, this is the first kind of terrain I look for.

It is difficult to be more specific about finding muskies. Some of my favorite muskie holes appear no different from many other spots with seemingly identical features. I have found my favorite spots by spending many days and weeks of fruitless casting before finally getting a follow or a strike. Many successful muskie fishermen claim that they have a kind of "sense" about their quarry and the places in which they're found, but muskies require time and patience to locate, and even after you have located a lair, catching the fish is another story.

TECHNIQUES FOR MUSKIES

My muskie outfit consists of a heavy five-and-a-half-foot rod and a good baitcasting reel with a smooth drag and a retrieve ratio of five to one. The high retrieve ratio helps in working certain kinds of lures, especially jerk plugs, and it is important that the drag on the reel work smoothly. The reel doesn't have to hold a lot of line, one hundred yards will be all you'll ever need, but all of your equipment must be in good working order because once hooked, a big muskie will strain it to its very limits.

I use twenty-pound-test monofilament line, but many muskie experts like Dacron line. Dacron doesn't stretch under pressure the way monofilament does, and many anglers claim they hook more fish when using Dacron.

In the spring my favorite muskie lure is a big bucktail spinner with blades that are large enough to create a lot of vibration. In the summer I switch to surface lures, and in the fall I go back to big spinners. Where it is legal, some anglers use live suckers up to twelve inches long for bait. I never use live bait because the muskie will inevitably swallow it, making it impossible to release the fish with any assurance that it will live.

When casting for muskies it is essential that you make many casts to any area you suspect holds a fish. For instance, if I'm working a rocky reef I'll drift over that reef and make at least twenty casts to the deep-water side. I then drift over the reef again and make the same number of casts to the shallow side. If I'm fairly sure that there is a muskie in the area because I've had a follow or have taken a fish on an earlier outing, I'll start the process all over again using a different lure. Ultimately, I may make as many as two hundred casts into the area with a single lure, and when I reach the point at which I'm sure I'm wasting my time, I'll change lures and start all over again. There have been more than a few times during muskie fishing when I have questioned my own sanity. After a few days my arm will be so sore from casting that I can barely pull the starter rope on my outboard motor and I have to keep reminding myself that if I don't have patience and perseverance I won't catch a fish. It's remarkable how quickly my fatigue vanishes when a five-foot-long torpedo appears under the lure and begins to follow it.

In some areas of the country trolling is a popular way of taking muskies. But while some anglers consider trolling relaxing, I would rather cast to the fish. If you prefer trolling, be sure to check the local fishing laws to determine that it is legal in the body of water you're planning to fish. Some states prohibit all trolling for muskies. If you're determined to troll, use two rods that are very well secured to rod holders. One lure should be trolled between forty and fifty feet behind the boat and the second should be dragged in the wake of the motor about fifteen feet back. Muskies are often attracted by the propeller vibrations, and fish are frequently hooked close to the boat.

Jerk plugs are my favorite muskie lures. One fishing companion of mine, strictly a bait fisherman, says that these lures are named after the anglers who use them. They are nothing more than oversized topwater lures that are jerked through the water with long sweeps of the rod. These big plugs weigh between three and four ounces, and a short, stiff rod is required to work them properly. Some anglers like short spinning rods and light saltwater spinning reels for working big jerk plugs, but I find it less tiring to use heavy baitcasting equipment. Regardless of your choice of tackle, you will know you have been working after a day of throwing and retrieving these big plugs.

Some jerk plugs have rounded noses and bodies and look like a piece of broom handle. Others have a flat body and a lip and are actually large floater-divers. Each lure has its own action and should be retrieved in a fashion that will bring out its maximum action. However, the most important thing is the length of the sweep of the rod; the lures are moved through the water with full sweeps of the rod, and it is impossible to work them too quickly. Depending upon the lure it may be jerked through the water for a distance of six feet on a single sweep.

When casting surface lures for muskies it is essential that you watch the lure and continually vary the retrieve. When I have been casting for hours without a strike I find it difficult to keep concentrating on the lure and to avoid falling into a consistent pattern or rhythm on my retrieve. Fast, erratic movements have always generated the most strikes for me, and it takes real stamina and concentration to work a jerk plug properly for the long periods of time required to arouse a big muskie.

Muskies will often follow a lure and even nudge it without striking. It can be maddening to have a big fish interested in your lure and not be able to entice it into striking. When you have a "follower" there is one technique that may produce a strike: When the lure is right at the boat, about eighteen inches from the rod tip, shove the rod into the water almost to the reel and move it in a rapid figure-eight motion. Sometimes an interested fish will make a pass at the lure as you're making the figure-eight and then turn away from the lure. Don't give up. Keep up the motion for at least two more minutes and the muskie may return and smash your lure.

The figure-eight motion should be done with all muskie lures. It is easiest to do with spinners and lures with built-in action. It is most difficult with a jerk plug. The only way to keep a "follower" interested in the latter is to keep jerking it while you make the figure-eight motion. This is not as easy as it sounds, and if you have not used jerk plugs with any regularity you should practice the jerky figure-eight motion with them. For some reason that I have never understood, the underwater movement of the rod close to the lure does not scare the muskies.

When you hook a big muskie at boatside, let the fish run from the boat before you start to apply pressure. A green fish close to the boat can easily wrap your line around the motor or even jump into the boat, and a big fish that is still full of fight can be very dangerous when thrashing around in a boat with a big lure full of treble hooks in his mouth. Once the fish has taken the lure, set the hook firmly two or three times and let the fish take line and fight him away from the boat. Don't try and stop the fish on the first few runs because you may break your line or your rod. Hold the rod high and try to maintain a steady pressure, especially when the muskie rushes toward the boat—one of their favorite tricks. Pick up line only when the fish will give it. A big muskie will eventually tire, and if you try to horse him in you'll bust up your tackle or your hooks will pull loose.

Muskie fishing is hard work but worth the effort. I try to take at least one muskie trip each fall; in 1981, in five days of casting, I had three follows and hooked only one fish, which I estimated to go about twenty pounds. I lost him on the first jump.

I have never killed a muskie. I have too much respect for them to kill one for the sake of having a mounted fish hanging on my wall. Catching a muskie is one of the fishing thrills of a lifetime, and I urge all anglers to release these fine fish unharmed to fight another day.

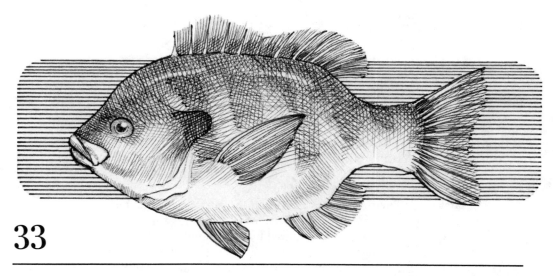

33

Bluegills

The sunfish family is composed of thirty species that are native to North America alone. They range in size from the tiny inch-long pygmy sunfish to the largemouth bass, but it is the bluegill (*Lepomis macrochirus*) that is the most popular of the family.

No freshwater fish is more readily accessible to the angler than the bluegill. It is abundant over all of North America, easy to catch, a scrappy fighter, and delicious in the skillet. In the North, bluegills are often considered kiddie fish and are not actively pursued by so-called serious fishermen. In the South, where they are called bream, many anglers specialize in catching (and eating) them to the exclusion of all other varieties of fish.

Bluegills thrive in quiet, weedy but not weed-choked waters. The young fish are found in cover near shores where there is an abundance of insect life, their primary food, and where they can find protection from larger fish. All warm-water game fish feed on bluegills; I have found many in the stomachs of largemouth bass.

Bluegills spawn in the late spring when the water temperature reaches 70°F. A shallow nest is dug in the sand near the shore, and into this the female deposits as many as forty thousand eggs. Under normal weather conditions the eggs hatch in two to six days. The male protects the fry for a few days and then leaves them to fend for themselves.

In colder northern waters bluegills grow slowly, about an inch each year, to a maximum of about ten inches. In the South they grow much faster, as many as four inches per year. The largest bluegill on record was taken in Alabama in 1950 and weighed four pounds twelve ounces.

Many lakes in both the North and South contain large populations of blue-gills big enough to be of interest to anglers. But unless you know where to find these larger fish you might believe that the biggest bluegills in the lake are six inches long. The biggest fish are found in water that is much deeper than many anglers suspect. In small, shallow lakes without large numbers of predator fish the bluegills tend to become stunted by overcrowding.

The biggest bluegills are males, and they school in deep water over a soft mud or clay bottom. You can tell if you have found a school of mature fish by their markings. When mature, bluegills lose their vertical stripes and become very dark, almost black in some lakes. If the fish you catch—no matter how large—have stripes, there are bigger bluegills to be found.

TECHNIQUES FOR BLUEGILLS

The biggest bluegill I ever caught weighed exactly two and a half pounds. I took it on a small yellow jig in almost thirty feet of water while looking for walleyes. I spent the balance of the afternoon fishing that same spot and landed over a dozen fine bluegills between one and a half and two and a half pounds. When I got back to the dock, that stringer of fish generated more excitement than if I had brought in a big bass or walleye. Many fishermen, even veterans of that lake, had never seen bluegills that large, and most of them didn't believe I had taken the fish in almost thirty feet of water.

Spots such as the one I found by accident can be discovered in most deep lakes, and are worth looking for. Once you have found the home of a school of mature bluegills, that spot will continue to produce big fish year after year unless the natural balance of the lake is altered.

The best way to prospect for big bluegills is to use ultra-light spinning equipment or any light outfit, and to fish at gradually increasing depths. My favorite baits are worms or crickets on a No. 10 hook, with just enough weight to be able to feel the bottom. Near shore there are always plenty of small fish. As you go deeper the fish will get bigger, after which you will stop catching anything. At that point you should move into slightly deeper water and keep parallel with the shore. I like to row or scull very slowly, probing the bottom as I go.

It is important to fish very slowly for big bluegills because these fish won't travel far to take a bait, and a large number will be schooled in a very small area. I concentrate on fishing deep weedbeds, sunken islands, and old creek channels, the same kind of water preferred by largemouth bass. In fact, should you ever catch a really big bluegill on a deep-running crankbait while looking for bass, mark that spot and try it with bait or tiny jigs and spoons. I have found some of my best bluegill holes while searching for bass.

Deep-water bluegills can be taken on a variety of baits and lures. Worms and crickets are among the most popular baits, but many anglers swear by catalpa worms, bits of shrimp, or mousie grubs. If you don't have a convenient supplier of live bait, a tiny one-inch triangle of pork rind, hooked lightly so it will flutter, is almost as good. Big bluegills will also take tiny spoons, spinners, and jigs.

Many expert bluegill fishermen favor a lightweight spinning outfit with a tiny jig tied directly to the end of the line and two or three droppers tied about a foot apart above the jig and fished with bait or small artificial flies. The rig should be dropped to the bottom and gently jigged up and down. When you find the fish, it is common to take two or three on each cast. Before you use this technique be sure to check local regulations to find out how many hooks can be legally used on one line.

In most lakes the big bluegills come to weedbeds near shore in the early morning and late afternoon. When the fish are in the shallows they can be taken on tiny fly-rod poppers or almost any wet fly or nymph, but my favorite for topwater fishing is a tiny sponge-rubber spider. Fly-fishing for big bluegills requires basic casting skill because they spook easily in shallow water. Your leaders should be long, at least 9½ feet, and your casts should be gentle.

In shallow southern lakes the best bluegill fishing is in the spring when the fish are bedding or spawning. Many anglers locate bream beds by their smell, a tactic I always thought was myth until I fished Lake Conway in central Arkansas with a veteran "brim" fisherman. He explained that the bedding fish disturb the lake bottom, releasing air bubbles that give off the musty-sweet smell of decaying vegetation. After a day of fishing I was able to find the bedding fish by smell, and using long cane poles and crickets dangled on a tiny hook about three feet under a small bobber, my companion and I caught all we could stand to fillet.

When the water temperatures drop in winter, bluegills stay in the deep areas of a lake. Even in shallow lakes they will go as deep as they can. Some of the best bluegill fishing I've ever had was on a very cold winter day in a large shallow southern lake. The bluegills were in twelve feet of water, just off the bottom in an old creek channel that was one of the deepest spots in the lake. I don't know how many big bluegills were concentrated in that channel, but in less than two hours I caught a freezer-chestful using bits of frozen shrimp for bait.

Ice fishing for bluegills is popular in some northern lakes. The fish continue limited feeding all winter, and never taste better than when taken from icy winter water. In the winter, bluegill anglers should fish the same deep spots they fished in summer for the biggest fish; the waters that were coolest in summer will be the warmest in winter. In the cold water the biggest fish tend to school even more tightly than in summer, and a bait that is ten feet from a school won't be touched. If you haven't marked summer spots, try your ice fishing over deep weedbeds or off the deep side of a weedy dropoff, and plan on cutting a lot of holes in the ice before you find the fish.

The most popular winter bluegill tackle is the ice-jigging rod, which can be purchased for a few dollars at any good sporting goods store. For deeper water, ultra-light spinning equipment is better because it is easier to use the reel to drop and retrieve the bait. Some anglers put a reel seat and handle on the tip of an old rod about eighteen inches long and use a spinning or even an old baitcasting reel.

Baitfishing is the most productive way to catch bluegills in winter, and my favorite bait is mousie grubs. I tie a weight at the end of the line and add three dropper hooks about a foot apart. It is interesting that at times I'll catch fish only on the top bait or middle one; in the cold water the fish won't move even a foot up or down to take a bait. Finding big bluegills in deep water at any time of the year is a matter of patience and persistence.

If you enjoy eating fish but have disdained fishing for bluegills, you're missing a real treat. I dip the fillets in batter and deep-fry them for just a few minutes until they are golden brown. The meat is flaky-white, firm and sweet. Just one meal will convince you that the bluegill is a fish well worth pursuing.

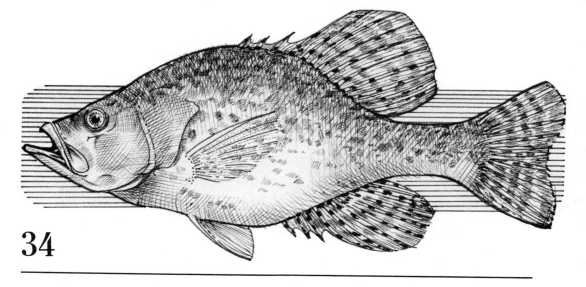

34

Crappies

Crappies are a popular panfish throughout most of North America. Their range is from southern Manitoba south to the Mexican border, and they have been introduced to the few areas where they are not naturally present. There are two varieties of crappie, the black crappie (*Pomoxis nigromaculatus*) and the white crappie (*Pomoxis annularis*), and the differences between the two fish are insignificant. Both fish grow to a weight of four or five pounds in suitable environments, but do best in new lakes and those of over five hundred acres in size. In smaller lakes crappies tend to become stunted by overcrowding.

Like most panfish, crappies go through cycles in their population. They may be caught in great numbers for a few years and then all but disappear for the same length of time. When spawning and food conditions are good, large broods are produced. If in following years the spawning is not successful, the mature fish eat most of their own young, resulting in a severe population decline. When the numbers of mature crappies become so small that they cannot eat most of their own young, the population increases dramatically and there will be a few years of excellent fishing.

Crappies spawn in the late spring or early summer, in shallow depressions scraped in the bottom near vegetation in water less than six feet deep. A mature female may deposit more than one-hundred-fifty thousand eggs, which ordinarily hatch within six days. The parent fish guard the nest during spawning but are the first to feed on the newly hatched fry. The fish grow from two to four inches in their first year and up to nine inches in their second year. Maturity is reached at two years, and crappies seldom live longer than six years.

I was introduced to crappie fishing by an elderly dentist who had lost his eyesight. As a kid I frequently went fishing with Doc and was instructed by my dad to help him in any way I could. Actually, Doc rarely needed any help, and usually ended up helping me. One of the lakes we fished was a public water supply that Doc was allowed to fish because of his disability. He was primarily a bass fisherman, but in the late spring we would concentrate on crappies, which we called calico bass. The lake had a tremendous population of bluegills, and after the young bluegills were off the nest in the late spring there were a few places in the lake where the water would be thick with their one-inch fry. Our favorite crappie spot was an underwater culvert that joined two sections of the lake separated by a road. Our fishing technique was simple: using an umbrella net I would make a single pass and collect a bucketful of tiny bluegills. Doc and I used fly rods, and would impale a tiny bluegill on a No. 4 hook and drop it over the edge of the culvert into the mass of swimming bluegill fry. As the bait drifted under the school of fry the tip of the rod would dip gently, and by setting the hook we would be fast to a big crappie— and they were big, a few running over three pounds. It wasn't until I was much older that I realized how phenomenal that spot had been for big crappie. In fact, I've never found better. One day while crappie fishing Doc hooked and landed a nine-and-a-half pound largemouth bass on his light bamboo fly rod. It was exactly one day before the opening of the bass season, and when Doc released the fish it was a bit too much for this seven-year-old. I cried all the way home.

Most states have no closed season and very liberal bag limits for crappie. Many biologists feel that there should be no bag limit, and that half of the crappies should be removed from any lake each year in order to keep the population from becoming overcrowded. Crappies are a fish that the angler doesn't have to worry about depleting, and once you find them the only problem you'll have is deciding when you have all that you feel like filleting.

TECHNIQUES FOR CRAPPIES

Most crappie fishermen concentrate on these fish in the spring, when they are easiest to find. Spawning begins when the water temperature reaches 65°F, at which time the fish mass in incredible numbers in the shallows. The techniques for taking spawning crapppies are routine wherever these fish are found. Like many anglers I like to use a fiberglass crappie pole, the kind with two telescoping sections and a permanent built-in bend in the tip. This bend may look strange to the uninitiated, but the poles are extremely sensitive and transmit the slightest nibble. No reel is used with the pole, most having a slotted bamboo handle around which the line is wrapped for storage.

When fishing for crappies in the spring I use minnows for bait. Early in the season I use small ones, about an inch long, because the crappies are foraging on newly hatched baitfish. As the season progresses I switch to larger minnows, and in the summer I use jigs almost exclusively. Finding the spawning fish is usually a matter of trial and error. I look for shallow brushpiles or beds of reeds in water from two to four feet deep. I tie a No. 4 gold-wire hook directly to my line, add a small splitshot just above the hook, and attach a tiny bobber at a point that will hold the minnow just off the bottom. I hook the minnow lightly under the back fin and move between brushpiles, dropping the minnow straight down into holes in the brush. Once I find the fish I can usually catch all I want.

Since in some lakes the crappies prefer to spawn in shallow, reedy areas and will not be found in the brush, it pays to try different kinds of shallow cover until you locate a school of fish. When the water is muddy I can occasionally find the fish by looking for them. Crappies are very active when spawning and I'll sometimes see swirls in the water that give the appearance of milk being poured into coffee. Under muddy conditions I have taken big crappies in water only one foot deep but always in brush or reeds.

In the spring not all areas of a lake warm at the same time to the preferred spawning temperature of crappies. Sometimes, because of sun exposure, the north shore of a lake will be five to seven degrees warmer than the south shore. It is best to look for spawning crappies on the north shore first, and as the weather warms to switch to the south shore. When the spawning is over on the south shore, look for shallow, reedy islands in the main body of the lake. It is possible to extend your peak spring crappie fishing by following the spawning progression around the lake. Each body of water will, of course, be different, and will warm at different times. You will have to explore and experiment on your own favorite crappie lakes to determine the different spawning grounds and the best times to fish these areas.

Crappies bite very gently, and can often suck a minnow off the hook without the angler knowing he has had a bite. When I see the slightest twitch of my bobber I lift the rod tip, and even when there is no movement of the bobber I occasionally lift the rig out of the water. Expert crappie fishermen fish with a continual gentle lifting and dropping of the line, and frequently hook fish that could not be felt biting.

As the water warms the crappies move deeper, but they are always found near brush or some other obstruction. Some anglers maintain that when the weather gets hot crappies stop feeding, but I believe that they feed continually and are just harder to find in the warm summer water.

The crappie migration to deeper water starts right after spawning. The fish spend a few days feeding on their own fry, which scatter and bury themselves in dense weeds or in water too shallow for the adult crappies to reach them. After the fry have scattered, the adult fish drift into water from about six to twelve feet deep, not far from their spawning grounds. Huge schools of fish may suspend themselves on the deep side of a dropoff just outside a shallow bay. At this time the fish may also congregate in the mouth of a narrow bay, especially if the shallow area is a big one where there is likely to be a current flowing from the bay into the main body of the lake. Crappies are hard to find at this time, but I have noticed that if there is a noticeable current flowing from the bay the schools of fish will tend to hold at distances of 50 to 100 yards out from the bay opening. If there is little current, I have often found them right in the bay opening or right over the dropoff that is present where the bay enters the lake. In the late spring the crappies will enter the shallows to feed at dawn and dusk. These forays into the shallows become briefer as the water warms, and eventually stop completely.

During the summer crappies are still found around obstructions, but sometimes a rockpile or bridge abutment in deep water will hold bigger fish than brush piles and weedbeds. I like to fish the deep edges of old creek channels that have stumps and stick-ups. Other spots where I have found the fish in summer are over rocky shelves between ten and fifteen feet deep that are surrounded by deeper water. The best shelves are those with a rockpile or submerged tree. A depthfinder and a good contour map of the lake you're fishing are helpful for finding the right combination of water depth and cover for summer crappies, and once the fish are located they can be caught.

A summer habit of crappies is to move around following schools of forage fish. If a spot that produced one day draws a blank on the next outing, try some of the other spots in the area that have always looked good but have not produced. Very slight changes in aquatic conditions prompt schools of small crappies to move, and when they do so the big crappies follow.

When fishing for crappies in the summer I use an ultra-light spinning outfit or a fly rod with a spinning reel, and I like to use jigs. The jigs must be small, and I prefer white or yellow ones weighing one thirty-second or even one sixty-fourth of an ounce with a gold-wire hook. Sometimes a yellow quarter-ounce spinnerbait will be excellent for the big "slab" crappies. It is essential that the jig or lure be worked slowly. I like to drift or quietly anchor over an obstruction in about ten feet of water and jig straight up and down, moving the lure very slowly and gently. Sometimes the fish will hang over the top of an obstruction, and when I take one I will add a bobber that helps me maintain the level at which they are concentrated. I reel in very slowly and twitch the rod tip to keep the jig barely moving, and answer any hesitation in the movement of the bobber, no matter how slight, by raising the rod tip.

When the water cools in the fall, the crappies migrate back into the bays that they occupy in the spring and once again cluster around brush and reeds. When the fish move back into the shallows I go back to my fiberglass crappie pole and minnows. In the fall I have also had good crappie fishing using my ultra-light spinning tackle, a plastic casting bubble, and No. 6 or No. 8 artificial nymphs, the same ones I use for trout. I fish these nymphs about three feet below the bubble and reel them in just fast enough to keep tension on the line.

In man-made lakes there will often be significant water fluctuations due to water draw-downs for power generation or irrigation. I find that crappies will often stop biting when the water begins to drop, while a rise in the water level will often turn them on. Sometimes, even in midsummer, a rise in the water level will send massive schools of crappies into shallow, brushy areas. These feeding sprees don't last long, but for an hour or so the fishing will be excellent and the crappies will hit almost any lure or bait that is passed near them.

Experienced crappie anglers chart their favorite lakes and eventually learn exactly where the fish will be found under different water temperatures and conditions. One friend of mine who is a crappie addict builds large brush piles on the ice in late winter. He weighs the piles down with stones and fishes them as soon as the ice goes out and they sink to the bottom. He maintains that crappies like new brush piles, and he points out that in summer every brush pile becomes the lair of a few big largemouth bass that enjoy eating crappies as much as he does.

I was shown a useful trick for catching crappies a few years ago when I was fishing in Missouri. A friend and I had taken a few big fish from a partially submerged brush pile, when they suddenly stopped biting. My friend took an oar from the bottom of the boat and started beating on the brush pile, and I mean he really beat on it. When we started fishing again we loaded up on crappies, most of which were bigger than the fish we had been catching before my friend beat on the brush. I've since tried this trick in many other lakes, both north and south, and more often than not it works.

In most lakes there are probably too many crappies. When you take your limit you are actually helping the population. Every spring I try to do my part to maintain the population balance in my favorite crappie lakes and, in the process, I stock my freezer with plenty of excellent crappie fillets.

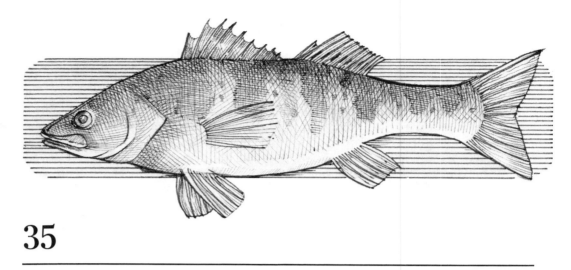

35

Yellow Perch

Yellow perch (*Perca flavescens*) are the most widely distributed members of the perch family; extensive stocking has extended the range of these fish to most of North America. Its natural range is from central and eastern Canada south to Missouri, and along the East Coast from Nova Scotia to South Carolina. While they are found in rivers, streams, lakes, and ponds, perch grow to their maximum size in large, cool lakes with a sand-and-rock bottom. The average yellow perch is about nine inches long and weighs about one-half pound, but some lakes produce fish averaging almost two pounds. The record yellow perch was taken in 1865 in New Jersey and weighed almost five pounds.

Perch are not nest fish, and when spawning the female spreads a gelatinous string of eggs up to six feet long over weeds or brush. A mature female produces over one hundred thousand eggs, and spawning occurs on early spring nights when the water temperature reaches 48° F. Under normal conditions about half of the eggs hatch within fourteen days.

Perch parents do not protect their young, and the schools of slow-swimming, newly hatched fry provide forage for predator fishes including walleyes, northern pike, pickerel, and bass. Young perch stay in shallow water near weeds, where they forage for insect larvae and zooplankton. They are slow-growing fish, averaging only two or three inches each year. The importance of the yellow perch as a forage fish is demonstrated by the fact that only ten of every fifty thousand of the newly hatched fry survive their first year of life.

As yellow perch mature, their food gradually changes from zooplankton to small fishes, including smaller perch. The fish stay in schools for their whole lives, and when they mature the school will inhabit deep water during the day while moving into the shallows to forage at dusk. A school of perch will always be composed of similar-sized fish, and some studies have found that males and females travel in separate schools for at least part of the year.

Perch often strike a small spoon or spinner so hard that the angler thinks he has a much larger fish, but after that first whack they give up quickly. What they lack in the water, however, they more than make up in the frying pan. Perch fillets dipped in batter and fried crispy brown are among the tastiest of all freshwater-fish dishes.

During their spawning run in the spring, perch are easy to find and catch. In some areas of the country, the rivers and streams that feed into Chesapeake Bay, for example, the late February spawning runs literally fill some of the smaller feeder waters. Anglers who are tired of watching television or staring at a round hole in the ice all winter line the stream banks and fill buckets and tubs with mature perch during these spawning runs. The taking of this many fish does not diminish the perch population. In fact, some biologists feel that without fishermen the perch in Chesapeake Bay would be much smaller as a result of stunting from overcrowding. Each stream has a peak run of from ten days to two weeks, and spring perch fishing is so popular that the Washington, D.C., newspapers run daily information on the creeks that are producing each day.

All lakes containing yellow perch will have a spawning run into their feeder streams, and many anglers are unaware that some of the best fishing of the early spring is right around the corner. If you're accustomed to thinking of perch as a fish taken only through the ice, you're missing the best perch fishing of the year.

TECHNIQUES FOR PERCH

I do most of my perch fishing with ultra-light spinning equipment and four-pound-test line. I tie a No. 6 hook directly to my line, pinch a splitshot, and add a bobber high enough to keep my bait about a foot off the bottom. I use live minnows or worms, but sometimes the bigger perch prefer artificials. I've stood in a spot catching half-pounders on every cast while the person fishing next to me catches one-pounders on a small spoon or spinning lure. But I like to watch a bobber, and I cast my worm or minnow into the brushy pools where the spawning perch congregate. If the perch are there the bobber rarely sits on the surface for more than a few seconds before it twitches and disappears.

Catching spawning perch is ridiculously easy. Almost any bait or lure will work, and I've taken perch on flies, spinners, spoons, and once—when I ran out of minnows—a plain gold hook. Spring perch fishing is a family affair, and is a fine time for introducing a youngster to the sport of fishing.

When the spawning is finished the schools of perch return to the lakes into which the spawning streams run, and are more difficult to find. The larger fish school in deep water, much deeper than many anglers would believe. I have taken most of my biggest summer perch over a sand or rock bottom in from twenty-five or forty-five feet of water. A good way to find a school of these fish is to jig or troll slowly using a small spoon or spinner, worms, or a small dead minnow. I look for rocky points and fish the deep water around a point. Other than at dusk, when they move into shallower water around weed-beds, I have never found schools of large perch in water less than twelve feet deep. But even at dusk I have rarely found the fish shallower than about ten feet.

Once you find a school of perch you will catch them easily, but the schools move constantly. If you find a school of big perch at, say, thirty feet deep off a rocky point, and the school moves, you should continue slow jigging or trolling at the thirty-foot depth around other rocky points. Eventually you will find another school of fish.

I have taken many yellow perch on flies. Once when I was fishing a large northern impoundment for rainbow trout, a large school of surface-feeding fish turned out to be big perch feeding on mayflies. Before the school moved on I caught a dozen nice perch of about two pounds each on a No. 6 brown nymph.

If it wasn't for the yellow perch, winter would become considerably longer for fishermen in the northern part of the country. While many species of fish can be taken through the ice, the perch is a winter staple. In winter these fish can be anywhere in a lake, and the challenge is to find the big ones. My method for finding big perch is to cut a series of holes in the ice starting about fifty feet from shore and moving right into shallow water. I check the depth with a sinker tied to a piece of line, and prefer water between fifteen and twenty feet deep. In winter I have never found perch at depths greater than about twenty-five feet, although when there is a lot of snow on the ice and little light is reaching the water I have found big perch in water as shallow as three feet.

Many winter anglers swear by three-inch minnows when fishing for large perch, but I find it easier and just as productive to use small jigs or spoons. I use a simple ice-jigging rod that can be bought for a few dollars in any well-stocked sporting-goods store, and my favorite lure is a tiny spoon called a Swedish Pimple. I jig this spoon about one foot off the bottom, and when I catch a perch I remove an eye from the fish and put it on the hook. When fishing for winter perch it is important to jig the bait or lure slowly and set the hook at any change of pressure on the line, because these fish take a bait or lure very gently.

When ice fishing for perch it is important not to spend a lot of time in a spot that isn't productive. If you haven't caught a fish in about fifteen minutes, try a new spot. If you are catching perch and the school moves on, try fishing at the same depth in a new spot.

One final perch tip for the summer angler. If you come across a school of small perch about three or four inches long, put on a red-and-yellow spoon or crankbait and work the edges of the school. Most freshwater game fish feed on perch, and I have taken some big walleyes, pike, and bass by following a school of small perch and tossing a lure that looks like a wounded member of the school.

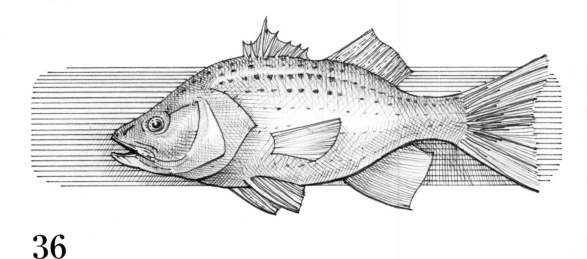

36

White Bass

The original range of the white bass (*Morone chrysops*) was from the Great Lakes to the Mississippi Valley, but their range has been extended to most of North America by continual stocking. White bass are found in large rivers in a few areas, but are primarily a lake fish, reaching their maximum size in lakes of over four hundred acres in size. The fish have taken particularly well in large, man-made impoundments with little turbidity, good water quality, and large populations of gizzard or threadfin shad.

White bass are a school fish and look very much like small striped bass, which belong to the same family. The usual size of the white is about one and a half pounds, although they may grow as large as six pounds. Any fish over three pounds is very respectable.

Whites spawn in May or June when the water temperature reaches 60°F. The female broadcasts up to 1 million eggs over a rocky bottom in from six to ten feet of water. The eggs hatch in a few days but are very fragile, and weather conditions must remain perfect during the incubation period for successful spawning. A change of just a few degrees in the water temperature is enough to keep the eggs from hatching, which is why populations of whites vary widely from year to year. After hatching the tiny fry immediately form into massive schools and become forage for every form of wildlife that feeds on small fishes. The fry feed on zooplankton until they become large enough to forage on small fishes and each other.

White bass grow quickly, as much as eight inches during their first summer, but their life span is only between two and four years. As they mature they feed in increasingly deep water during the day, but invade the shallows at sunset and throughout the night to forage on minnows. Occasionally they feed on the surface during the day, trapping schools of small shad against the top of the water; however, the schools of these feeding bass move so quickly that they are difficult to catch. This surface feeding action is identical to the surface feeding of striped bass, except, of course, that whites are much smaller fish and the lures used to take them are also smaller.

TECHNIQUES FOR WHITE BASS

My white bass rig is my ultra-light spinning equipment and four-pound-test line. Any silver spoon, spinner, or small plug will take the fish, but if I had to pick one lure for white bass it would be a quarter-ounce Little George, which is a small crankbait with a spinnerblade at its tail.

During the day throughout the year white bass hold in water from fifteen to forty feet deep, often along the edges of old creek channels. They can be difficult to find unless you know the lake well, and even on some of my favorite white bass lakes there are many days when I never find the fish. I always make a systematic search, casting into areas where I have taken fish before, and I cover a lot of water.

When going after white bass it is important to fish a lure or bait slowly near the bottom, with a stop-and-go retrieve that imitates a wounded baitfish. I sometimes add a streamer fly on a twelve-inch trailer line behind my spoon or lure to make a combination that can be very productive.

In winter one of the best fishing areas for white bass is below large dams on big rivers. Small minnows hooked through both lips are among the most popular baits, but sometimes jigs will work even better. I prefer a one-eighth-ounce white or yellow jig, and occasionally add a small minnow to the hook. Sometimes the whites will take a jig or bait that is cast into the current and drifted with no action at all, while at other times they prefer a fast, jerky retrieve. You will know when the whites are feeding below a dam by the large number of anglers casting for them. It's best to watch the other anglers and copy the lures and retrieves of those that are successful. A few white bass experts I know swear by small yellow plastic grubs and will use nothing else.

When fishing below dams I've had my best results when the water flow is moderate or low. I cast into eddies where an abutment or other obstruction creates a break in the current; whites usually like the faster-moving water. On occasion, however, I have taken big whites in a calm backwater below a dam when fishing a minnow under a bobber for crappie. Again, it pays to watch the fishermen who have stringers full of fish, and to copy their techniques.

When the river water is discolored, white bass find it easier to home in on the vibrations from a spinner. Any spinning lure can be productive, but I like a small Willow Leaf spinner tied about six inches above a live minnow. I cast the rig across the current and retrieve it just fast enough to keep the spinner turning.

The very best white bass fishing I've ever had was at night. I had taken a week off in January to fish some Texas lakes for largemouths, but winter seemed to follow me everywhere I went. I spent a fishless four days trying to keep warm as high winds buffeted my small van. On one very cold and windy day I pulled into a camping area on the shores of Lake Amistad on the Texas–Mexico border. I had decided to wait just one more day, and if it didn't warm up and calm down to head back to Little Rock. Having driven all night I slept most of the day, and when the winds died, after sunset, I took my light spinning rod and a plastic box full of lures and walked to the well-lit boat dock at the nearby marina. The temperature was very close to the freezing mark, but I had traveled a long way to fish and was determined to catch something . . . anything.

When I got to the dock I was surprised to find another fisherman, an elderly gentleman, casting from the stern of his large houseboat, which was tied to the dock under one of the lights that burned all night. I asked the fellow if he was having any luck and he told me that fishing was excellent. As we talked, a large school of white bass surged toward the dock and ripped into schools of minnows that had been attracted by the lights. They were big whites, averaging over two pounds apiece, and I caught a half-dozen on a Little George before the school retreated into the darkness. The old man told me that the fish would be back and invited me into the houseboat for a cup of coffee. As we drank coffee and warmed up we swapped fishing stories and ate a heaping platterful of excellent white bass fillets. We spent the whole night drinking coffee and eating fish, and occasionally moving out into the cold night to catch big white bass. We didn't have to watch for the fish because when they moved into the area we could hear their splashing as they chased minnows. When morning dawned the gentleman, with true Texas hospitality, invited me to share his luxurious (and warm) houseboat. For the next few days we spent the cold and windy days sleeping and playing cards, and at night, when the winds calmed, catching and eating big white bass. Texas hospitality and white bass turned what could have been a freeze-out into a memorable fishing trip.

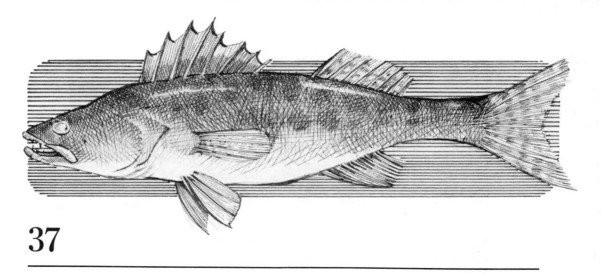

37

Walleyes

The walleye (*Stizostedion vitreum vitreum*) is called by many names including walleyed pike, doré, pike, jackfish, jack, and pickerel. But while the name walleyed pike is used in many areas, the fish is not a member of the pike family; it is the largest member of the perch family. The average size of the walleye is between one and three pounds, but in areas where they are abundant, walleyes over ten pounds are not uncommon. The largest walleye on record weighed about twenty-five pounds.

The walleye is not a great fighter, but any big fish on light tackle is a dogged adversary, and in the skillet this fish is a gourmet's delight. The savory flesh of the walleye is considered by most anglers to be the tastiest of all among North American freshwater fish.

The walleye was originally found only in the extreme northern United States and in Canada, but extensive stockings have extended its natural range to all but a few areas of the South and Southwest.

Walleyes are very prolific. The female produces up to twenty-five thousand eggs per pound of body weight. Spawning takes place in the spring when the water reaches 45° to 50°F. The preferred spawning areas in lakes are in water from two to six feet deep with a sand or gravel bottom. In rivers the fish spawn in shallow areas with a light but consistent current and a gravel bottom.

The fry of walleyes are not protected by the parent fish, and for the first few days of their life they drift with the current or wave action while absorbing their yolk sac and gaining strength. When the sac is completely absorbed they begin to feed on zooplankton. By the end of the first summer the young reach a length of about eight inches and feed primarily on small fishes.

In the second year, walleyes reach full maturity and a length of sixteen to eighteen inches. In the southern areas of their range, where the comparatively warm waters provide abundant forage, they grow quickly and live to an age of about ten years. In northern areas they grow slowly due to the shorter summer season. A count of the growth rings on the scales of one fish taken from Michigan's Lake Gogebic found it to be twenty-six years old. Thus, while walleyes may grow more slowly in northern areas, they live much longer there than in the South.

The walleye derives its name from its oversized eyes, which allow it to see best under low-light conditions and at night. The fish prefer comparatively clear water with good circulation; they are rarely found in dead-water areas such as sheltered coves and bays. They feed at water temperatures from just above freezing to almost 85°F, but their metabolism is most active at temperatures between 56° and 60°F. All these facts are important to the angler because the walleye is a relatively easy fish to catch when it can be found, although finding it can often seem impossible.

I have found it easier to find walleyes consistently in rivers than in lakes. When they make their spring spawning run into tributary rivers and streams they are so vulnerable that some states do not allow walleye fishing in April and May. Here again, as when setting out for any species of fish, you should always check local fishing laws.

Walleyes spawn at night over shallow gravel bars. During the day the fish congregate in deep holes directly up- or downstream from the spawning site. At this time they can be taken on a wide variety of baits and lures.

TECHNIQUES FOR WALLEYES

I use a light spinning outfit for almost all my walleye fishing. A long, light rod with a fast tip is best, and while fiberglass is good, graphite or boron is better. These space-age rods, discussed in Part One, have the exact sensitivity required for gentle-biting fish. I like an open-faced spinning reel with six-pound-test line that enables me to cast very light lures.

In the spring my preferred walleye bait is a live minnow about three inches long hooked through both lips on a No. 4 or No. 6 hook. I add enough splitshot to hold bottom, and cast the rig slightly above the hole nearest the suspected spawning site. When the minnow settles into the hole I retrieve it at a crawl over the bottom. It doesn't take long to catch walleyes if they're there, so if a spot doesn't produce within a half hour, try elsewhere.

As mentioned earlier, walleyes prefer clear water, and in the spring will often congregate in the clearest water in a river. During the spring freshet none of the water will be very clear, but some areas will have less silt than others. If you can find a hole near a gravel bar where a clear tributary stream enters the river, you may have found a spot that is full of walleyes.

If you aren't a bait fisherman you can fish the holes in a river with almost any slow-moving lure that hugs bottom. Small yellow plastic split-tail grubs will often produce as well as bait, although it's hard to beat a small jig carrying a live minnow hooked through both lips. A spinner attached about six inches above a nightcrawler or minnow can also be very effective, particularly in discolored water. Whichever bait or lure you use, I can't overemphasize the necessity of fishing slowly on or near the bottom. I've often had walleyes take a jig-and-minnow combination only when it was sitting motionless on the bottom. I am convinced that many anglers work their baits or lures so quickly that they literally take them away from the fish.

Walleyes take a bait or lure so gently that it can be hard to know when you're having a strike. A few years ago I was spring walleye fishing with a friend who had done a lot of bass fishing but had never tried for walleyes. We were anchored above a pool that had been a consistent producer every spring I had fished it, and which on that day was no exception. I took a three-pounder almost immediately and a four-pounder about fifteen minutes later. My fishing companion complained that he was having no strikes, but each time he would bring his minnow back to the boat it would be dead and look as if it had been scaled with a tiny knife. I watched him slowly retrieve his bait and could see strikes that he couldn't feel. His rod tip would dip very gently when a walleye took the minnow, and he would keep reeling in and pull the bait right out of the fish's mouth. When I pointed out the overlooked bit of tension on his line he started to connect and landed some fine fish.

When the spawning run is over, river walleyes enter a period of inactivity that lasts about two weeks, at which time they school and migrate to those areas where they will spend the balance of the year. A few specific areas in a river will almost always hold walleyes. One of the best summer and fall areas is where riprap, or a man-made rocky shoreline, has been constructed along the banks of the river to prevent erosion. The best riprap fishing is had where the rocks drop off into at least six feet of water and where there is a secondary break into deeper water with a consistent current. When the fish are active during the warm months, small crankbaits that run deep enough to occasionally bump bottom are excellent lures. I prefer to cast or troll them parallel to the bank, and to work them as slowly as possible. Strikes in warmer water tend to be pretty firm, and the fish will often hook themselves.

When the water begins to cool in the fall, riprap areas continue to provide excellent fishing, especially when adjacent to much deeper water. I prefer a jig-and-minnow combination because I can present it more slowly to the less aggressive cold-water walleyes. It isn't necessary to make long casts. Often I just make an underhand flip of about twenty feet and let the jig settle over the edge of the rocks. When it hits bottom I lift it a few inches and let it hang in the current. In cold water most walleye strikes are felt by the tip of the rod being drawn slowly and very gently downward.

Wing dams that extend into rivers to break the flow are other good walleye spots in the summer and fall. They should be fished in the same way as rip-rap. The best wing dams border the mouths of tributary streams, backwaters, or sloughs. If you know of a wing dam that borders a large tributary stream and breaks quickly and close to deep water, you have a spot that should contain some big walleyes. Try fishing these spots with minnows or a jig-and-minnow combination. For big walleyes a minnow six inches long is not too big. Work the minnow at a crawl along the bottom at the very end of the wing dam, and be prepared to hook some really big fish.

Dam abutments are also good locations for walleyes in the late summer and early fall. I like to cast my jig right against the abutment because the fish often lie with their sides right against the cement. A cast that lands even a few feet from the abutment will be ignored. Abutments near shore, especially those with a backwash current, have consistently produced for me.

Other spots on rivers that have been consistent walleye producers are locations directly above a dam where the water depth drops quickly from shore. Above almost every dam will be an area where small inlets are formed by water that is pushed back upstream by the force of the current striking the dam. The spot where the bottom of such an inlet drops off sharply into the main body of the river is a prime walleye location on any river, but it is often ignored by the many anglers who prefer the waters below the dam. Many rivers also have rip-rap along the shore immediately above a dam. These are potential hot-spots and should be fished in the same manner as rip-rapped areas below the dam.

Don't be intimidated by large rivers. Fishing carefully and slowly the areas I've described will produce walleyes big and small. Keep trying different spots until you find the fish. Once found, these spots should continue to produce year after year.

Walleyes can be difficult to find in lakes since they are migratory fish that move in and out of feeding areas: into shallower areas at dusk and at night and back into deeper water during the day. They are rarely found far from small forage fish, and in many lakes, small yellow perch make up the bulk of their diet. In some lakes they also feed extensively on sucker fry, leeches, bloodworms, and large hatches of insect larvae.

In the early spring, lake walleyes can be found in water from three to six feet deep. After spawning on shallow gravel bars the fish recuperate for a few weeks. The males tend to hang around the spawning area while the females usually go immediately to deeper water. Fishing is difficult right after spawning because the walleyes are not very active.

After a week or two of resting after they spawn, the fish move back into shallow water near some kind of cover that offers shade and protection. But while the fish seek shade in the springtime, they will not be in water too deep or cold to hold forage fish. Emerging weedbeds, logs, and boulders that adjoin the spawning area are good places to fish. Live minnows or the traditional jig-and-minnow combination fished slowly around shallow, thick cover can be very productive, particularly at dawn and dusk.

One time during the summer when walleyes can often be found in shallow water is between eight P.M. and midnight. I've found the best night fishing to be along a shoreline where the deep water is close to shore, and over shallow bars that are adjacent to deep water. Slow trolling or casting a floater-diver such as a Rebel or Bang-O-Lure along the shore is a good night-fishing tactic. When night fishing it is important to troll with a long line and to make a quiet approach to the areas you'll be casting over. Walleyes are very wary: any disturbance or light shining on the water will immediately spook them.

Large lakes contain two distinct populations of walleyes: those that are weed-oriented and those that prefer deep water. The deep-water fish are rarely found at depths greater than twenty feet except in winter, when they may be at forty feet or deeper. These fish migrate between distinctive kinds of structures such as reefs, rock shelves, and dropoffs in ten to twenty feet of water. They travel erratically and may cover only a few hundred yards in a single day. The one consistency in their movement is their attraction by weak lake currents that lure schools of forage fish. Therefore, because it is the wind that creates the currents in a lake, knowledgeable walleye anglers fish windy areas.

Many fishermen believe that walleyes taken from weeds have migrated there from deeper water. It is difficult to convince these deep-structure anglers that a large walleye population spends the entire summer and early fall in the weeds. Extensive research has established the existence of these weed-oriented walleyes, and some fisheries biologists suggest that they may be a subspecies.

I like to fish for deep-water walleyes by back-trolling; this differs from traditional trolling in which a lure is dragged behind a moving boat. When back-trolling I use my electric trolling motor and move the boat backward very slowly. Jigs are easy to fish when back-trolling, and I use a jig-and-minnow combination heavy enough to hold bottom at the ten- to twenty-foot depths at which I fish. I let the jig sink to the bottom directly behind the boat. When it hits bottom I take in line until the rod tip is about a foot from the surface of the water. I then lift the jig a few inches off the bottom and slowly move the boat backward about three feet, causing the jig to swing under the boat like a pendulum. When the jig is once again directly under the rod tip I let it hang motionless for a few seconds before dropping it to the bottom to be sure the depth is correct. I then lift the jig once again and move the boat another three feet and repeat the process. Back-trolling is the best way to cover an area slowly and thoroughly, and I have taken more walleyes with this method than with any other.

Walleyes have an excellent sense of smell, and often a nightcrawler or leech hooked on the jig will produce more fish than a jig-and-minnow or jig alone, especially when the waters warm and a greater variety of food becomes available. However, I have taken many big walleyes on empty jigs and plastic grubs. Good baits to use by themselves are minnows, nightcrawlers, crawfish tails, leeches, and a V-shaped piece of yellow perch belly where this is legal. These baits can be back-trolled by adding enough weight to bounce bottom about twelve inches above the hook.

Most large lakes stratify into three distinct layers during the summer. The top layer is called the epilimnion; its sun-warmed waters contain limited oxygen. The cold bottom layer, the hypolimnion, also contains little oxygen. But the middle area, the thermocline, is composed of cool, oxygen-rich water, and it is this area that attracts and holds most species of game fish and the forage upon which they feed.

When seeking summer walleyes, you must concentrate your efforts on the thermocline layer. I fish locations where the thermocline and bottom structure come together in about twenty feet of water. A live minnow is an excellent way to determine if you are actually fishing the thermocline. If the minnow comes to the surface dead, with its gills flared, you are fishing either too shallow or too deep. When you find a spot where the minnow stays lively when fished on the bottom, and where there are rock shelves and dropoffs at about twenty feet, you're in the thermocline and prime walleye territory. These areas should be fished slowly and methodically.

One time when walleyes may be found near shore is during periods of strong winds. Under windy conditions I like to wade the shoreline casting a jig-and-minnow. I fish the areas most disturbed by the action of the waves, working the rig parallel to shore in about three or four feet of water. It is important, as always with walleyes, to work the jig very slowly and to let the waves impart most of the action. Although wading the shallows is usually best on a cloudy day, I have also taken fish in less than three feet of water on bright windy days.

When the fish are in the shallows, day or night, they can be taken on small crankbaits as well as a jig-and-minnow. I prefer long thin crankbaits that have their maximum action when worked at a crawl. Lures such as the Flatfish and Rapalas, which have a wide, lazy wobble when barely moved, are the best.

In the fall and winter, walleyes will be found in deeper water than at any other time of the year. I begin a day of winter fishing by trying off deep points or over sunken islands with a rock or sand bottom in at least twenty-five feet of water. If these areas don't produce I move to steep dropoffs adjacent to very deep water, especially those with shallow flats nearby. I use a six-inch minnow hooked lightly through both lips and dropped slowly to the bottom so as to let it become accustomed to the pressure. The change in pressure will kill a minnow that is dropped too quickly into deep water.

An angler fishing deep water for walleyes may have difficulty detecting strikes. When I'm fishing a large minnow and feel additional pressure on the line I back my boat directly over the fish and gently take up slack line. I then slowly lift the rod tip until I can feel the fish, set the hook firmly, and move the fish up quickly to keep from disturbing the rest of the school. If you catch a walleye at thirty feet, for example, and the fish then stop biting, don't immediately move to a new area. The school may have dropped to forty feet or may have moved up to a shelf at twenty feet. It pays to work different depths in any area where you have taken fish before giving up and moving on.

In shallow lakes where walleyes are stocked each year and there is little natural reproduction, and in deeper, more traditional walleye waters where fishing pressure over deep structures is extreme, the best fishing is in the weeds. Deep-water anglers wrongly argue that shallow aquatic growth is not the natural habitat of walleyes. Weeds provide forage, cover from the sun, and oxygen. Many lakes contain huge populations of weed-oriented walleyes that bass fishermen take by accident.

Walleyes living in the weeds display a wide range of behavior. At times they will be inactive, lying deep under the vegetation, while at other times they will travel between weedbeds for many days and cover many miles. Tags placed on weed-oriented walleyes have shown that no matter how far the fish travel they eventually return to a single specific weedbed.

Summer is the best time to fish for weed walleyes, which stay in the vegetation until the fall turnover when the weeds die off. At that time the fish move to deeper water and more traditional walleye structures. Dawn, dusk, and night are the best times to take the weed-oriented fish because they cruise the surface over the submerged weedbeds or move to the shallow side of the vegetation seeking forage fish. During these periods of dim light, shallow-running crankbaits cast over the weeds or trolled along the edges will often be hit very hard.

I have taken some of my biggest weed walleyes in water from six to twelve feet deep where coontail and cabbage weed create an underwater forest. The best of the weedbeds grow over a sandy bottom that gradually tapers to deeper waters and where these weeds contain no brown, slimy algae. The absence of brown slime is due to continuous underwater currents with enough movement to discourage the growth of algae. These currents also attract forage fish for the walleyes.

Other areas to try when fishing weeds are sharp turns along the outer edge of a weedbed, which indicate a dropoff; areas where slow-tapering weedbeds break up into clumps of vegetation; and depressions in the middle of weed-beds. These depressions are difficult to find; a key to their presence may be hardly more than a spot in the middle of the bed that contains less growth. Because they are often the best walleye locations in a lake, these dips and depressions in the weeds are well worth looking for.

It is, of course, much easier to fish areas where the weeds are thin or clumpy rather than areas in the middle of the thickest weed growth in a lake. But the biggest fish are invariably right in the middle of the salad, lying on the bottom. It is almost impossible to use live bait in this heavy cover; minnows get torn right off the hook. I prefer to use a one-eighth- or one-quarter-ounce jig with some yellow plastic for garnish. Small plastic worms or split-tail grubs are excellent for this kind of fishing. I use medium-weight spinning tackle with ten-pound-test line. Ordinarily, equipment this heavy isn't necessary for walleyes, but a large fish hooked in dense weeds will be impossible to land on lighter tackle.

I cast the jig right into the heaviest cover and let it sink to the bottom. Sometimes I have to jiggle the rod tip to allow the jig to work its way to the bottom. Once the jig hits bottom I let it lie there motionless for a few seconds. Occasionally a fish will have taken the jig while it was falling, or will suck it off the bottom while it is lying motionless. If I feel any pulsation I immediately set the hook. Strikes in the weeds are often difficult to detect, usually being just a slight nudge or twitch of the line. It is important to set the hook any time you think you have a strike, and when a fish is hooked it should be moved quickly out of the weeds with authority.

If the jig has been sitting on the bottom for a few seconds with no strike, move it gently through the weeds. When it gets hung up, a snap of the wrist will generally tear it through the growth. Let it settle to the bottom once again. With patience and practice it is possible, if not easy, to fish weeds that are considered unfishable by many anglers.

If you're a walleye angler who hasn't been doing very well fishing traditional deep structures, I urge you to try the weedbeds. Weed fishing can be frustrating to someone accustomed to fishing deep water with few obstructions, but once you start bringing home large stringers of big fish, you'll be convinced that it's worth the effort.

When it comes to walleyes, I believe the most important thing is to know the waters you're fishing. It is better to invest your time on one lake that you know contains a good walleye population than to run all over the countryside looking for a better body of water. Learn the locations of shoals, reefs, dropoffs, and gradually sloping weedbeds. Find the depressions in the weeds. Keep a notebook of where and when you took your fish and the conditions under which you took it, including such factors as wind direction, wave action, and water clarity. Before long you'll know your lake and the habits of its walleye population, and you will then know where to find the fish under a wide variety of conditions.

Once you find them, there are no easier fish to catch than walleyes, and no matter how they are prepared, they make a delicious dish.

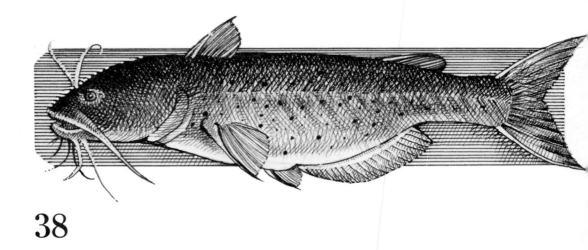

38

Catfish

When I lived in Arkansas I had a favorite barbecue restaurant not far from one of the locks and dams that dot the Arkansas River. Many of the men who worked for the River Authority frequented the restaurant and I could usually find a group eager to swap fishing tales. Two of the men were divers whose job it was to clear debris from the intake pipes above each of the dams. Every time the talk would turn to catfish, these fellows would tell the story of the diver who quit his job one day when the river was clear enough for him to get a good look at the catfish clustered around the intake pipes looking for food. The divers maintained, and never backed down on their story, that many of these cats were longer than a man, and that the fellow who quit did so because he was afraid of being attacked and drowned by one of the monstrous fish. I suspect it was just another big catfish story, but I'm not all that positive. Every year there are stories from southern catfish anglers about fish over seven feet long that they hooked and lost, and there is a report in Captain William Heckman's book, *Steamboating Sixty-five Years on Missouri's Rivers*, of a three-hundred-fifteen-pound blue catfish that was taken from the Missouri River just after the Civil War.

The catfish family is a large one, ranging from the tiny madtoms that average less than four inches long, through the bullheads, and to the catfish themselves, some of which grow to weights exceeding one hundred pounds. Bullheads can be distinguished from the other catfish by the shape of their tail, which is rounded, while the tails of other catfishes are forked. The only other exception to this is the flathead catfish, which has a rounded tail but also has a distinctly flattened head and a longer, more slender body than a bullhead.

All catfish have tiny eyes and depend on their sense of smell to find their food. The fish have over one hundred thousand food sensors located all over their bodies, most of which are in their chin barbels, or whiskers. As they swim they gently fan the bottom with the barbels and home in on vibrations and food scents.

Few bodies of water in North America get too warm for catfish. Enzyme action in the stomachs of these fish doubles with each eight-degree increase in temperature, and the hotter it gets the more they feed. Water temperatures must approach 100°F before their feeding begins to slack off. Catfish also prefer a dark habitat, and during hot, sunny weather do most of their feeding at night. I've consistently had my best fishing for all species of catfish between sunset and midnight.

BULLHEADS

The black bullhead (*Ictalurus melas*) is found over most of North America. It is a smaller member of the catfish family and rarely weighs more than about three pounds, although the largest recorded bullhead weighed over eight pounds.

Bullheads deposit their eggs in the spring into shallow nests or depressions, or sometimes on plants or underwater debris. All members of the catfish family guard their young until the latter grow to about an inch long. Bullhead parents have been observed to chase their roaming youngsters, take them into their mouth, and gently deposit them back in the nest.

Of all the members of the catfish family, bullheads are the most tolerant of water pollution, turbidity, and lack of oxygen. In ponds all but devoid of oxygen I have seen them cruising the surface, taking their oxygen directly from the air, and as a kid I dug bullheads from dry pond bottoms that looked like a huge puzzle of cracked earth. Under those conditions the fish were in the center of large lumps of dried mud. When the lump was opened it was similar to breaking an egg; each bullhead had constructed a small cell slightly larger than its body and lined with a mucuslike substance from the skin of the fish. This substance apparently allowed air into the lump but did not allow the interior moisture to evaporate. When dropped into water, these bullheads immediately swam away, apparently unharmed by many weeks without water.

Bullheads are bottom feeders, scavenging whatever they can from the mud. During the day they school in deeper water, in holes and channels, and while they feed all the time, they don't travel in search of food during the day the way they do at night. At night the fish roam and can often be found very close to shore, especially if wave action has muddied the water along the shore.

Bullheads have the reputation of being garbage eaters, and the traditional baits used to catch them are supposed to smell so bad that only a bullhead or bullhead fisherman could love them. The fact is that the fish are extremely diversified foragers, feeding on plants and crustaceans, crawfish, minnows, and small aquatic insects. Occasionally, bullheads are taken at night by bass fishermen using surface lures.

BULLHEAD TECHNIQUES

While I have used awful-smelling baits to catch bullheads, I have done as well with nightcrawlers as with anything else. I like to use live nightcrawlers on a No. 4 hook tied directly to my line, and to add just enough splitshot about sixteen inches above the bait for easy casting. I use spinning tackle because I find it easiest to use at night, but any kind of equipment will suffice, and probably as many bullheads are taken on hand lines as in any other way. I cast into the area I have chosen to fish, prop my rod in a forked stick, and watch the rod tip. When I see any movement at all I gently pick up the rod, being careful to keep the tip pointed toward the fish so that it won't feel any additional resistance. When I feel a solid tug I set the hook and immediately bring the fish in. Bullheads are not hard fighters, but if given the opportunity will roll around on the line, creating an awful tangle.

Usually that's all there is to bullhead fishing, but even these omnivores get choosy at times. On some nights the fish will pick up the bait only once, drop it, and move on. When they are dropping the bait I try reeling in slowly, in which case the bullhead will sometimes strike the moving bait and immediately swallow it. On other nights the fish will run with the bait and drop it without getting hooked, which is usually a sign that I'm using too much weight and the fish can feel the resistance. A smaller sinker or a light slip sinker will usually correct this situation. When the fish are feeding close to shore I don't use any weight at all; the nightcrawler alone provides enough weight for short casts.

The flesh of bullheads is dark red before cooking and has a consistency that reminds me of swordfish. Early in the season bullheads are tender and sweet tasting, but as the summer progresses their flesh may soften in the warm water and develops a "muddy" taste. For this reason I do most of my bullheading in the late spring. The fish can be prepared in almost any fashion, but I prefer them as fillets dipped in egg, rolled in cornmeal, and fried hot and fast. Another way to serve bullhead is to cut it into one-inch cubes, parboil it for about five minutes, and then use the cubes in any recipe calling for lobster or crabmeat. I consider bullhead newburg as tasty as lobster newburg.

Cleaning bullheads can be troublesome and painful if you get stuck by any of the sharp spines on their fins. I clean them by driving a large nail through a flat board, turn the board over, and impale the head of the fish on the nail. I slit the skin all the way around the base of the head, take a flap of skin near the cut with a pair of pliers, and pull off the entire skin, all the way to the tail, in one continuous movement. After this bullheads can be filleted like other fish.

FLATHEAD CATFISH

Flathead catfish (*Pylodictis olivaris*) range from the Mississippi Valley south into Mexico. They are called yellow cats and shovelheads throughout much of their range, and grow to be among the largest members of the catfish family. In some rivers the flatheads average over twenty pounds, and many fish approaching one hundred pounds have been landed. The flathead is easily distinguished from the other catfish by its rounded tail, long slim body, and unusually flat, wide head.

Flatheads are found in deep, slow pools in large rivers, where they spend the daylight hours near or under some obstruction on the bottom. These big fish like to lie against a big boulder, under a submerged log, or in a cave or hollow beneath an undercut bank or ledge. During the day the fish lie quietly, waiting for small fish to come near. Large flatheads are almost exclusively fish eaters, but smaller ones feed on crawfish, and grasshoppers seem to be a favorite flathead food in some rivers. The fish have been observed lying on the bottom with their huge mouths open, and small fish taking refuge in this "cave" are quickly eaten.

TECHNIQUES FOR FLATHEADS

Many big catfish are taken on trot lines and by jug fishermen, but some anglers specialize in wrestling these big fish on a rod and reel. For the really big cats saltwater equipment is required. Most anglers use heavy, two-handed surf rods about nine feet long, 1/0 or 2/0 reels, and line testing at least forty pounds. The hooks used must be heavy and strong, and I find that No. 4/0 or 5/0 hooks hold best. The rig is a simple but substantial one. The large hook is tied to a heavy leader about two feet long. A four- to six-ounce slip sinker is threaded on the line and a heavy brass swivel is tied to the end of the line. The swivel serves to hold the sinker above the hook and to attach the leader. I prefer flat or pyramid-shaped sinkers that will not roll along the bottom in the current.

Among the baits used for flatheads are cut shad, crawfish, grasshoppers, or shrimp for the smaller fish, but the biggest fish are taken on live bait. I prefer a live eight-inch sucker for really big flatheads, but many catfish experts swear by a live one-pound carp. When I'm fishing in water with a current I hook the bait through both lips, and when fishing in deep quiet pools I hook it under the back fin.

The best flathead fishing is at night, when the fish roam and feed all over the river, but if you know a deep hole or rockpile off the current, they can be taken during the day. Big flatheads return to their lair in the morning and spend the day lying on the bottom. They do feed during the day but they won't move very far, so the daylight flathead angler must be fairly certain he is fishing a hole containing the fish, and he must be patient.

A big flathead takes a bait slowly and deliberately, mauling and crushing it before swallowing it. Considering the size of these fish their strike is very gentle, often being seen as little more than a slight bobbing of the rod tip. All of this changes when you set the hook. Flatheads fight deep, making long, powerful circles. Sometimes a big fish can be coaxed from the bottom quite easily, but when it decides to go home it does so with authority, and nothing can stop it. In one of my favorite flathead holes I have hooked a fish that I believe would go well over fifty pounds at least once each summer for the past three years. The last time I hooked the fish I was using forty-pound-test line. I raised him off the bottom, turned him in my direction, and took in about ten feet of line before he decided that he'd had enough. When he headed for the bottom I couldn't stop him, and the line broke on what I believe is a sharp piece of ledge. I don't own any tackle heavy enough to land that fish.

These big catfish are dangerous. The pectoral spines on a big shovelhead can be over six inches long and are covered with mucus. On the few times I've scratched myself on one I've always developed a nasty infection, and there are stories of anglers being seriously injured by big catfish thrashing around in the bottoms of boats. Most of the catfish anglers I know won't let their young kids fish alone for the really big cats, and I think they are wise. A youngster alone in a boat or on a river bank could easily get tangled in his own line and be dragged into the river and drowned by a big catfish.

BLUE CATFISH

Blue catfish (*Ictalurus furcatus*) have a wider natural range than flatheads, being found from southern Canada to Mexico. These fish also prefer faster water than flatheads, and do most of their feeding in rapids and swift-flowing chutes. The tackle and baits for blues are about the same as those used for big flatheads, except that blues grow larger than the rest of the family and many anglers use line testing sixty or seventy pounds.

TECHNIQUES FOR BLUES

I've caught my share of blue catfish—fish running up to about fifteen pounds —but only once have I ever had a real monster on my line. A friend of my dad's had invited me to try for a really big blue cat at a spot he knew in the Missouri River in South Dakota, below Gavins Point Dam. We were both using stout seven-and-a-half-foot boat rods fitted with 1/0 reels and sixty-pound-test line. Our baits were live eight-inch white suckers, fished on the bottom at an entrance to a fast-moving chute near a massive logjam. My instructor had taken a fish over thirty pounds the first day we fished, and I took one about half that size in the afternoon, but it was just after I finished my peanut butter and jelly sandwich at about five thirty P.M. that the fish started chewing on my bait. I fought that cat for about ten minutes before it finally wound me around something and broke off, and I was almost glad it had gotten away. My arms were shaking so much from the strain of the fight that a half hour later I could barely hold a cup of coffee without spilling it. I never saw that fish, but my fishing instructor said that it would have been in the ninety- or one-hundred-pound class. I would at least have liked to have gotten a look at it.

Some blue cat anglers I've met while fishing Kentucky Dam on the Tennessee River use 120-pound-test line and still have fish break off. But these days anglers complain that the monster blues are gone. The big rivers have been dammed and channelized, and blue cats like swift chutes and big-river water fluctuations. Commercial fishermen say that the numbers of small blues remain excellent, but that catches of really big fish are probably a thing of the past.

CHANNEL CATS

The channel catfish (*Ictalurus punctatus*) ranges from mid-Canada to Mexico, and has been stocked throughout all of North America with varying success. It is among the most popular of the catfish, and tolerates the greatest variety of water conditions. Channel cats do best in lakes, streams, and rivers that have large areas of sand-and-rock bottom. They are infrequently found in great numbers over mud bottoms or in dense vegetation. In rivers and streams the fish are often found in areas with a rocky bottom and a swift current.

Channel cats in big rivers lose the scattered black dots on their sides and begin to look like blue catfish, but are much smaller. A channel cat over five pounds is a good one, and the all-tackle record is about fifty-eight pounds. The channel cats in streams run smaller than those in rivers, averaging between two and three pounds and being called "fiddlers." Many anglers consider fiddlers to be the very tastiest of all catfish.

Channel cats are not primarily bottom feeders. In most bodies of water live baitfish are their preferred food, but they also feed on a wide range of organic materials. On one fall day I watched a school of small channel cats feeding on the surface on wild grapes that had been blown into the river by gusty winds. My fishing companion said he was going to tie up a bunch of flies he would call "grape floaters" and be the first to take a channel cat on a dry fly. I don't know if anyone has taken a channel cat on a dry fly, but I have taken them on spinning lures and bucktails when casting for trout.

Good catches can be made from spring through fall, but channel cats are warm-water feeders and the hot months provide the best fishing for them.

CHANNEL CAT TECHNIQUES

Like other catfish, channel cats stay in deep holes during the day. For this reason they are easier to take during the day in small streams, where they can be caught by drifting a nightcrawler or a minnow below riffles. In the summer grasshoppers make excellent channel cat bait in smaller streams.

When fishing for channel cats I prefer lightweight spinning tackle, a No. 4 hook, and enough splitshot to feel the bottom. I cast across a riffle and let the bait drift naturally downstream. I don't close the bail on my spinning reel, holding the line on the reel by draping it across my finger. This permits me to release line to keep the bait deep in the drift. Most strikes come as the bait leaves the riffle and drops into the pool. Channel cats, like trout, stack up in feeding lanes where the current delivers a continually changing food supply, and they sample a wide variety of drifting items. Worms, cheese, grubs, and even marshmallows will also take these fish.

The best channel cat fishing in big rivers is between sunset and midnight, and at night the angler has the advantage of being able to pick almost any spot with a current and know that sooner or later the fish will come to him. Channel cats roam and cover a lot of water during the night. They usually follow the currents, and when the water level in the river has held constant they tend to follow similar feeding migrations each evening. For this reason your favorite channel catfish spot may not produce at different water levels, and under high- or low-water conditions you may have to find yourself a new location.

On big northern rivers cut bait such as shad or chub produces well. These baits are fished in the current and allowed to bounce along the bottom and settle downstream. I set my rod in a forked stick and I don't wander far. When a channel cat picks up the bait he usually moves off with it in his mouth and there is no need to wait before setting the hook. Frozen shrimp that have been allowed to ripen in the sun are another popular channel cat bait on some big rivers.

Unlike many species of fish, catfish are not spooked by lights, which is fortunate because a lantern is essential for rigging, baiting, and unhooking fish. A lantern gives another advantage by casting enough light to allow you to use a live minnow hung under a white-topped bobber that is clearly visible in the lantern light. I have taken some of my best channel cats fishing a live four-inch minnow on a No. 2 hook about four feet below a bobber. I cast the rig upstream and let it drift downstream within the circle of lantern light until it is out of sight; I then carefully retrieve it and follow the same drift. I don't catch as many channel cats drifting a live minnow as I do bottom fishing, but those taken by drifting are ordinarily larger. Channel cats take a live minnow hard and fast, and I set the hook as soon as the bobber goes under.

In large, shallow lakes it can actually be easier to find channel cats during the day than at night. At night the fish spread out to roam the shallows, while during the day they cluster in the deepest water they can find. In a few large southern lakes I have found that deep summer locations that yield big bream will often also yield channel cats. On hot summer days when I can't seem to find a bass I have taken dozens of two- to four-pound cats by dropping live minnows into the deepest holes I can find. There aren't many bass waters that can provide such action in the middle of a hot summer day.

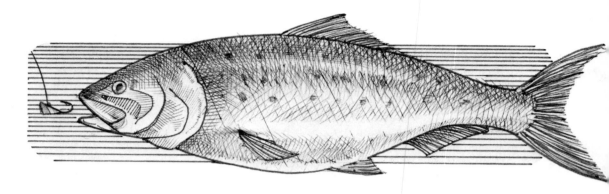

39

Shad

During the winter of 1776, General George Washington's troops were near starvation. Food was scarce and the Continental Congress hesitated to appropriate funds for what looked like a lost cause. But spring brought the annual shad run up the Schuylkill River, which flowed near the encampment at Valley Forge, and armed with pitchforks the soldiers set upon the fish. Some historians believe that supply of fresh fish helped win the war, but that may be a revolutionary fish story.

Shad played another role in our history. In the 1870s the United States Fish Commission wrestled with the problem of how to move fish from one part of the country to another. Special railroad cars were designed to carry fish eggs and fry. One of the earliest successful shipments on a "fish car" consisted of sixty thousand shad eggs from Maryland's Susquehanna River that were carried to Portland, Oregon. The eggs hatched in transit and were thriving fry by the time they reached their destination for stocking in the Columbia and Willamette rivers. That single stocking became the basis for a thriving West Coast shad fishery that now extends from Kodiak Island in Alaska to the Mexican border.

Shad belong to the herring family, which includes the small threadfin and gizzard shads that are popular bait and forage fish in the South and Southwest. It also includes the alewife, a common forage fish in the Great Lakes, and the skipjack and blueback herrings, which are not considered valuable because of their small size and extremely bony flesh.

The American or white shad (*Alosa sapidissima*) and the hickory shad (*Alosa mediocris*) are the basis of the East and West Coast sport and commercial fisheries. Both of these fish have similar life cycles.

Like the salmon, white and hickory shad are anadromous, spending their lives in the ocean and ascending coastal rivers only to spawn. These fish are approximately five years old when they make their first spawning run, and about 35 percent return to the sea and become repeat spawners. White shad live up to ten years and reach weights of up to seven or eight pounds. The largest white shad on record was netted at the mouth of the Connecticut River and weighed thirteen pounds. Hickory shad are smaller, weighing up to about five pounds, and prefer small tributary streams for spawning. White shad spawn in main rivers and rarely enter tributaries.

It is difficult to distinguish between the two fish without examining their jaw structure. The hickory has a long lower jaw that extends beyond a shallow-notched upper jaw. The lower jaw of the white shad is entirely enclosed within the upper jaw when the two are pressed together. Most fishermen make little distinction between the fish, although it is generally acknowledged that the white shad is better eating.

Much of the life of shad while they are at sea is unknown. It is believed that they feed exclusively on krill (tiny shrimp) and plankton, and follow deep, cold ocean currents north in the spring and south in the fall. They have been taken by commercial trawlers over two hundred miles from shore and at depths of over four hundred feet.

Biologists speculate that shad do feed in fresh water, but only on microscopic plankton that is too small to detect in their stomachs. Fishermen have long speculated on why the fish strike darts, spinners, streamer flies, and brightly colored beads while making their spawning run. No one knows the answer, but they do strike small shiny objects, at times with savage vehemence.

Shad spawn when the water temperatures in costal rivers reach about 55°F. The fish return to their natal waters guided by changes in the light intensity of the sun and their ability to smell or taste the familiar chemical make-up of individual rivers. Because of water pollution and the construction of dams that block the spawning run, shad migration has been a problem in some areas, but improving water quality and the construction of fish ladders have greatly improved the outlook for these fish, especially in the Northeast.

TECHNIQUES FOR SHAD

There are probably as many individual shad fishing styles as there are shad fishermen, but the basic techniques are identical on both the East and West coasts. For shore fishing most anglers use medium-weight spinning tackle and six- or eight-pound-test line. It is essential that the drag on the spinning reel be working smoothly and that it be set a bit on the light side. Shad have wide bodies, and when they turn their sides to the current they can pick up great speed. If the drag is not working smoothly or is set too tight, the lure will inevitably pull out of the fish's soft mouth.

When fishing from shore you should cast slightly upstream and allow the current to carry your lure just off the bottom. When the line pauses during the drift, the rod tip should be gently lifted to free the lure from the bottom. It is best to start with short casts and gradually lengthen them. Once you hook a fish, the exact drift used on that cast should be fished over and over again. Since shad are school fish you will frequently get a strike on every cast once you have located them.

While shad will take a fly or lure with a solid yank on the line, they will sometimes be remarkably gentle in their strike. I have stood on a high bank watching other fishermen and have seen a shad take a lure from behind, drift with it in its mouth for a few seconds, and then drop it. The angler never knew he had a strike. Any faint tap on the line should be answered by raising the rod tip, and you will often find yourself fast to a shad that seems determined to make it back to the ocean.

Shad will take a variety of lures; shad darts are the universal favorite. These are tapered jigs that weigh from one-eighth to one-quarter of an ounce. Many are adorned with a white or yellow tail, usually bucktail, but jigs without tails produce just as well. Red and white and red and yellow are the most popular colors, but I believe that color is not as important as finding the fish. Once you locate a school of shad they will usually hit any small shiny object that drifts by them. I buy blank jigs and enjoy painting them with lustrous, quick-drying nail polish. Sometimes when designing darts I get carried away and come up with bizarre colors and designs, all of which catch fish. A color rule for successful shad fishing may be that brighter colors produce best on dark days and duller colors on bright days, but no matter which colors you choose you should have a good supply of darts. Casting from shore will result in frequent hang-ups, and it's common to lose a dozen or more darts in an afternoon.

Many anglers claim that shad strike better in the early morning or late afternoon than at other times of the day. The fish may be more active in the morning and evening, but I've taken as many at midday as at any other time. I believe the answer is in finding the fish. There have been days when my

favorite spots haven't produced a single strike while anglers up and down the river will have quit because their arms tired from fighting fish. If one spot doesn't produce, try another, but don't give up. Sometimes a school of fish will appear seemingly out of nowhere, and a placid shore scene can turn into confusion as dozens of anglers find themselves attached to hard-fighting, leaping shad.

Fly rods and ultra-light spinning tackle are used by many shad fishermen. Shad flies can be as traditional or as bizarre looking as darts. Every spring I tie a handful of weighted red or yellow bucktails with a silver body on a No. 4 gold hook, and these colors have been consistent producers.

Fly- and ultra-light fishing is easiest from a boat where there is plenty of room to play the fish. Casting with very light tackle from shore will result in tangled lines and frayed tempers. I like to anchor my boat above a channel or the rim of a deep pool, or at any spot where the currents change abruptly. It is a simple matter to cast the fly or dart across the current and let it drift downstream below the boat. Ordinarily the current will work the fly or lure for you, but sometimes the fish respond better if a slight jigging action is added during the drift.

The fly-fishing equipment for shad need not be fancy. Any fly rod fitted with a reel that will hold the line and at least fifty yards of monofilament backing will do. I use a level, six-pound-test leader about five feet long, and rather than casting, I lower my fly over the side and let the current take it downstream behind the boat. I allow the fly to hang in the current and I twitch it back and forth. When a shad hits the fly you must resist the urge to set the hook, because that will ordinarily tear the fly from the fish's mouth. Most of the time shad will hook themselves, and all you will have to do is keep the rod tip high and hang on.

Shad make long runs and spectacular jumps, and their fighting ability has won them the nickname "poor man's salmon." I find it interesting that when taken on a fly rod these fish will often come to net faster and easier than with spinning equipment. The long, limber fly rod apparently tires them more rapidly than a shorter rod with more backbone.

When fishing from shore you may carefully drag your shad onto the bank. In a boat, a net is a necessity for landing these fish. If you are fishing from a boat with a companion, have him slip the net quietly into the water downstream from the fish. The shad should then be brought just over the net and the tension on the line released. Most of the time the fish will dive directly into the net.

I release all the male shad I catch and keep the females for their delicious eggs and for baking. You can tell a roe (female) from a buck (male) by gently running your hand down the fish's stomach. If it is a buck, white milt will flow from the anal opening. In the early stages of the spawning run the eggs and milt may not have developed or matured, and you may have to judge the sex of the fish by its conformation. Bucks are usually smaller and much thinner than roes.

One tip for shad fishing: I have found that if I scrape a few scales from the fish I have on my stringer and let them flutter downstream into the area I'm fishing, they will often arouse the shad. So if you have a few shad on your stringer and the fish suddenly stop biting, try scaling a fish. Sometimes this will immediately start the shad hitting at anything that floats by.

Shad are quite bony fish and few people seem able to fillet them. I've tried but haven't found a method for removing the rows of tiny Y-shaped bones that fill the fish. However, I have found a way around the bone problem. I put a few cut onions and carrots into the body cavity of a cleaned fish, wrap it tightly in foil, and bake it at 250°F for about six hours. The slow cooking dissolves the tiny bones, leaving lots of fine tasting fish. One good-sized shad will easily feed four people.

Shad roe (eggs) is one of my favorite meals. I take one roe sack (there are two in each female fish) for each person and carefully split it down the middle. I dust it with breadcrumbs and fry it in butter at a heat just low enough to keep the eggs from "popping." If the roe is cooked at high heat the tiny eggs react like popcorn and fly all over your kitchen.

If you live on either coast of the United States, you aren't far from good shad fishing. Almost all coastal rivers have a shad run, and the best fishing is usually before the waters warm enough for other freshwater gamefish. Shad fishing is an excellent way to open the fishing season.

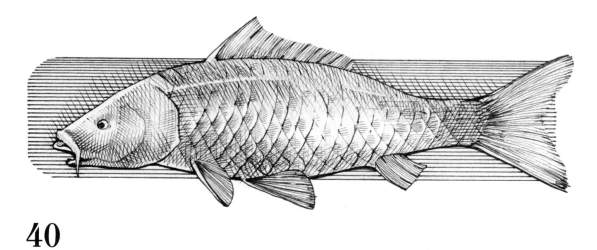

40

Carp

The carp (*Cyprinus carpio*) was introduced into North American waters from Germany by the U.S. Fish Commission in 1876. Carp have long been a favored food throughout Asia and Europe, and few French farms are without a carefully tended carp pond. In Greece, carp roe, called *taramosalata*, is considered a delicacy. Jewish cooks use carp as the basic ingredient in the delicious gefilte fish. Izaak Walton called the fish the "queen of waters" in his *The Compleat Angler*, and Aristotle made early reference to the carp as a food fish in 350 B.C.

At first carp were greeted with enthusiasm in this country and stocking the fish was an official policy of the U.S. Government. As a result, in a very few years carp were found in almost every body of water in North America. It wasn't until the fish were firmly established, however, that it was discovered that they had negative impact on many native species of fish. The carp is an omnivore and will eat almost anything. In the process of feeding they root in the mud and disrupt water conditions by spreading silt throughout the lake. In many bodies of water carp have eliminated native fish by eating their eggs and destroying their spawning sites. The carp is one exotic import that we have been forced to learn to live with.

Carp survive under a wide range of conditions, but prefer warm rivers and lakes with shallow, muddy bottoms that contain abundant organic material. They can tolerate extremes in water temperature, from the freezing point to almost 100°F. In the heat of summer they can utilize atmospheric oxygen in waters that will support little other fish life. In winter they bury themselves in the mud and enter a condition of semihibernation.

Carp spawn in the shallows in April or May, when the water temperature reaches 65°F. The spawning activity is marked by violent rolling and splashing as the female broadcasts her eggs. The eggs sink to the bottom or adhere to plants and hatch in four or five days. A thirty-pound female carp produces over 3 million fertile eggs.

The abundance and size of carp have made them a popular quarry in many areas of the country, and while many anglers consider them "trash fish" a big carp's size and strength make for a battle on any fishing equipment. Carp weighing over twenty pounds are common throughout their range. The rod-and-reel record is over fifty-five pounds, and fish of almost one hundred pounds have been taken commercially.

The best carp waters are warm and contain a lot of aquatic vegetation. Good catches can be made any time from spring to fall, but the best fishing is usually right after spawning when the fish eat the equivalent of 20 percent of their body weight in food each day. The major portion of their diet consists of mollusks, crustaceans, green algae, and other plants, but they will eat almost any organic material.

TECHNIQUES FOR CARP

Carp are occasionally taken on lures and artificial flies, but most are taken on bait. Canned kernel corn, worms, and doughballs are the most popular baits. In some waters big carp feed on crawfish, and the largest I've ever seen, which weighed over forty-four pounds, was taken by a bass fisherman using a large crawfish for bait.

The fish can be taken on any kind of equipment. I have landed a few on a fly rod and a few more on ultra-light spinning tackle, but these light outfits are good only where the water is free of brush and other obstructions. For most of my carp fishing I use medium-weight spinning tackle with eight-pound-test line, and I still lose many fish to snags.

Carp can be as wary as trout, and while they are often seen in shallow water I find it easier to catch them in water from six to twelve feet deep. The deeper water holds bigger fish, and in the deep water the carp are not spooked by movements on shore or even the thrashing of a hooked fish.

Finding carp is usually more difficult than catching them. Every lake or stream that contains these fish will have some big ones, and I fish the quiet deep backwaters in rivers and shallow dropoffs near the shore in lakes. When trying new waters for carp your best bet is to ask other anglers where they have seen or caught big ones.

My carp fishing rig is a simple one. I tie a No. 8 hook directly to my line. I pinch on a light splitshot to provide casting weight, and put two kernels of corn on the hook. I cast into an area that I have "seeded" by tossing out a handful of corn and then prop my rod in a forked stick and wait. I don't move far from my rod, and if I'm going to take a walk for any purpose I always open the bail on my spinning reel and put a small stone on the line. There have been a few times when I have forgotten to open the bail and only a diving catch has saved my spinning rod from being pulled into the water by a big carp. It shouldn't take long for the carp to find the corn you've thrown out, and if you don't get a fish in an hour, try a new spot.

Don't expect hard strikes from even the biggest carp. Sometimes the line will barely twitch and the bait will be gone. Usually the line will just start to go out, and when you lift the tip of the rod to set the hook it will continue to go out—only much faster. Once hooked, a carp will inevitably head for deep or fast water or the nearest brushpile, and you will have a good fight on your hands. Carp fishing is an excellent way of learning to play a big fish on light tackle.

When fishing for carp it is important to use the lightest sinker that will give you casting weight. These fish have sensitive mouths and will quickly drop any bait that offers resistance. Where long casts are necessary, or where weight is needed to keep my bait in a current, I use the lightest sliding sinker that will hold bottom. The slip sinker can be kept from sliding to the hook by adding a tiny splitshot to the line about eighteen inches above the hook.

Once you have landed a fish, be sure to seed your fishing area with another handful of corn and cast back into the same spot. While carp are not school fish they do seem to swim in "pods," and I have rarely taken a solitary fish.

Carp from unpolluted water are excellent eating. The fish can be baked, pressure-cooked, fried, or made into a chowder. Without a doubt the most exotic of all carp recipes comes from Izaak Walton's *The Compleat Angler*. It is a classic that deserves repeating.

Take a carp, scour him and rub him clean with water and salt, but scale him not; then open him and put him with his blood and liver, into a small pot; then take sweet marjoram, thyme and parsley, of each half-a-hand-ful, a sprig of rosemary, and another of savory, bind them into two or three small bundles and put them to your carp, with four or five whole onions, twenty pickled oysters and three anchovies. Then pour upon your carp as much claret wine as will only cover him and season your claret well with salt, cloves, mace and the rinds of oranges and lemons; that done cover your pot and set it on a quick fire till it be sufficiently boiled; then take out the carp and lay it with the broth in a dish, and put upon it a quarter pound of the best fresh butter, melted and beaten with half-a-dozen spoonfulls of the broth, the yolks of two eggs, and some of the herbs shred; garnish your dish with lemons and so serve it up. And much good may it do you.

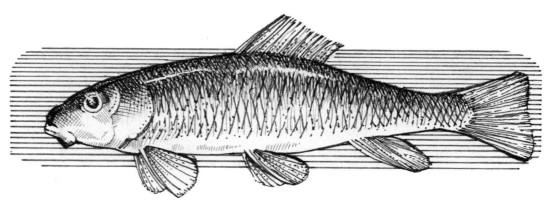

41

Suckers

Most anglers don't fish for suckers. The reasons I have included them in this book are that they are common throughout all of North America and they are excellent eating during the spring spawning run, when their flesh is firm and palatable. Each year a group of my fishing friends and I take an early spring day and hold our Annual Sucker Fest. We always catch a freezer-chestful of the fish, which we fillet, dip in egg, roll in cornmeal, and deep-fry. There are never any leftovers.

The white sucker (*Catostomus commersoni*) is the most common of all of these fish. It is found from northern Canada to Mexico and west to the Rocky Mountains. It is tolerant of extremes in water conditions and can live in water low in oxygen.

White suckers are bottom feeders and prefer aquatic insects, larvae, crustaceans, and various forms of algae. Unfortunately, many anglers consider them trash fish, and even though they run up to six pounds and fight very well on light tackle, some anglers throw them on to the stream bank rather than returning them to the water. It would be hard to convince these anglers that they are throwing away some fine eating.

In early spring white suckers move into feeder streams of all sizes, where they spawn at night. The fish deposit their eggs over shallow gravel bars and cover them lightly with a vigorous fanning of their tail. During the spawning the male sucker changes color, becoming olive-colored on the back and developing a lateral band of red along the side. The eggs hatch in a week and the young suckers gradually work their way back to the lake from which their parents came. Young suckers are a favorite food of both northern pike and lake trout.

No fancy equipment is needed to catch suckers, and they are easy to find. In the spring, from March through May, the first few hundred yards of any feeder stream entering a lake containing suckers will be paved with the fish.

I use a light spinning outfit, a No. 8 hook tied directly to my line, and enough weight for easy casting. The fish will take corn, doughballs, worms, or bits of shrimp, but a piece of nightcrawler is my preferred bait. I cast into the holes near the shallow spawning areas, set my rod in a forked stick, and watch for the gentle dipping of the rod tip that signals a strike. I let the fish mouth the bait until he swims away with it and then set the hook. Suckers fight very well on light tackle, and there have been many times when I have been trout fishing in the spring that a "big rainbow" taking line from my spinning reel has turned out to be a big sucker.

Sucker roe is also excellent eating, at least as tasty as shad roe. The roe should be sautéed in butter over heat just low enough to keep the eggs from popping. The roe can also be parboiled for a few minutes and scrambled into eggs with some diced onions.

I fish for suckers only in the early spring. Later in the season their flesh tends to become soft and isn't as tasty.

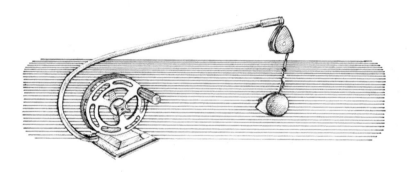

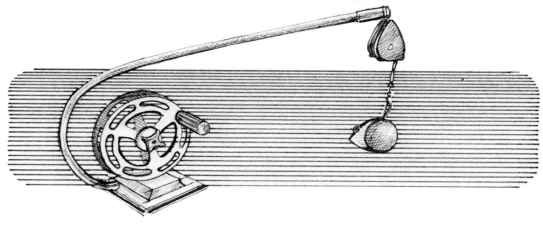

PART THREE

42

Trolling

Trolling is more than dragging a bait, lure, or fly behind a moving boat. Many anglers refuse to troll because they consider it a fishing technique requiring no skill, but that isn't so, and I learned the necessity of trying different trolling techniques many years ago when I was fishing a large northeastern impoundment. The huge lake contained many fine rainbow trout, but the only time I was able to catch them was right after the ice went out in the early spring. My technique was to troll a large Grey Ghost streamer about fifty feet behind the boat over shallow bars or at the mouths of feeder streams. It was always slow fishing, but if I had the patience to stick with it, I would usually take at least one good rainbow.

That particular day I trolled for over four hours without a strike. Then I tried casting spinning lures and even bottom-fished nightcrawlers, all to no avail. Back at the dock all I heard were complaints. None of the other anglers had been able to find the fish. I winched my boat onto the trailer and was waiting for the water to drain from the tail lights before I plugged the wiring into the truck when an elderly man pulled his boat onto the beach. I asked if he had had any luck, expecting the same answer I'd heard many times over. He smiled and held up a stringer with three fine rainbows between twenty and twenty-four inches long. He told me he took the fish trolling a Grey Ghost streamer. I expressed my disbelief and explained that I had dragged a Grey Ghost behind me for over four hours without a strike. The old man asked how far back I had trolled my fly, and I told him about fifty feet. He told me that he had been trolling his fly about fifteen feet behind the boat in the wash of the propeller. The next day I was on the lake bright and early, and while I took only two trout, the largest weighed almost five pounds. Both fish struck the fly right behind the boat in the wash of the motor.

SURFACE TROLLING

Surface trolling is most effective in the spring and fall, when water temperatures are substantially the same throughout a lake. Trout and salmon feed near the surface under these cold-water conditions, but pike, muskies, walleyes, and bass can also be taken. In the cold water the fish can be anywhere in the lake, and trolling gives the advantage of allowing you to cover a wide variety of waters. Most surface trolling is done off the mouths of feeder streams, over shallow bars and ledges, and around rocky points. Once the fish are located, you can cast to them or continue trolling the area.

For trout and salmon I prefer to troll a Grey or Green Ghost streamer. I use a sinking fly line, a level, eight-pound-test leader the same length as the rod, and an old, soft, fiberglass fly rod. When trolling flies the fish usually hook themselves, and I find that the softer fiberglass rod hooks many more fish than the stiffer graphite or boron rods.

When trolling streamers it's a good idea to experiment with different line lengths. I usually troll about fifty feet back, but as I mentioned earlier, the fish occasionally prefer a fly trolled on a short line in the wash of the motor. I've also found that it is best not to set the rod in a holder when trolling streamers. Trout and salmon like a fly with a darting action, and I have many more strikes if I work the fly with long sweeps of the rod. The fish invariably strike just after the forward sweep of the rod, when the fly hesitates in the water for a second.

Although at times trout and salmon will prefer a fly that is trolled right on the surface of the water, they most often prefer a fly that is traveling a bit deeper. The difference between working a fly on the surface and working two feet deep can be significant. To troll deeper, I slow the speed of the boat and add a few splitshot to my leader. I find that if I use a piece of sandpaper to remove the oxidized lead from the splitshot, and put the shot about eighteen inches in front of the fly, I get many more strikes.

Small minnowlike plugs, wobbling spoons, and rigged minnows can be trolled for trout and salmon. I use a light spinning rod to fish these baits and work the rod with long sweeps exactly as when I troll a streamer. A good ball-bearing snap swivel should be used to eliminate line twists, and the drag on the spinning reel should be set on the light side to keep the hooks from pulling out when a fish strikes.

Except for trout and salmon, the only other surface trolling I do is for muskies and largemouth bass. Almost any large topwater can be trolled for muskies, and I have taken most of my fish by dragging the lure at least sixty or seventy feet behind the boat. There are many theories about why a muskie will hit a trolled lure and not one that is cast, but muskies like to follow a lure before striking. When you cast they will frequently follow it to the boat and then turn away. Trolling gives the fish all the time it needs to study the lure and decide that it is edible. If you aren't having strikes when casting for muskies, or you have a persistent follower that continually turns away at boatside, try trolling the same area. However, be sure to check local fish and game laws before you start trolling; trolling for muskies is illegal in some places.

The idea of trolling a surface lure for largemouth bass is repugnant to many die-hard bass-casters. But I have found that trolling a topwater will some-times succeed when everything else fails. In the late spring, just after the post-spawning recuperation period, bass often suspend themselves in deep water. When they first start to feed, they don't travel far, and trolling at topwater can be the most effective way to find and catch these suspended fish. I have found surface trolling for largemouths to be most effective on cloudy, windy days.

In the summer, there are days when at dawn and dusk I can see bass chasing minnows but on which even a well-placed cast will not produce a strike. I believe the reason for this is that the bass are very skittish in the warm water, and the mere presence of the boat or the sound of a lure hitting the water is enough to send them scurrying for cover. For some unknown reason, the consistent sound of an outboard motor doesn't disturb them, and I've taken some big fish by slow trolling a jitterbug on a long line, at least fifty feet, along the outside edges of weedbeds.

MID-DEPTH TROLLING

Mid-depth trolling can be used for every species of freshwater game fish. It is also effective at every season of the year if the lure is run at the depth pre-ferred by the species of fish you are pursuing. Mid-depth trolling requires a basic knowledge of the habits of the fish, and for this information anglers are referred to the chapters of this book dealing with the different species of freshwater game fish and their habits and locations at the different seasons of the year.

I like to troll at mid-depths with a spinning lure or small spoon to find schools of yellow perch or white bass. I have also found mid-depth trolling effective for locating concentrations of crappie, especially in the summer when they tend to suspend over structures in comparatively deep water. Once I locate a school of fish, I stop trolling and cast, using the techniques discussed in the chapters on the different species of fish.

Mid-depth trolling is also an excellent way to find walleyes, largemouth and smallmouth bass, and pike and pickerel. It would be impossible to discuss the different lures and baits used for trolling—every troller has his favorites—but small or medium-sized crankbaits are my first choice. The size of the bill or lip will determine how deep the lure will run, as will the length of line and the speed of the boat. I usually start with a shallow-running crankbait, especially on cloudy or windy days, and gradually work deeper until I find the fish. Most of the time I stop trolling and cast when I find fish, but there are days when the fish, regardless of species, are widely scattered. Under these conditions I keep trolling.

There are three aspects of mid-depth trolling of which you must remain aware: the speed of the boat, the course of the boat, and the length of the line. Most trolling is done at a speed of between one and two knots, about the same as that of a brisk walk. Many times the fish will show no interest in a lure that travels in a uniform path, even if that path is at the level at which the fish are located. Often a lure that rises from below to the level that contains the fish or drops to that level from above will generate more strikes. One easy way to accomplish this is to rev up your motor for about ten seconds before dropping back to your normal trolling speed. Increasing the speed of the boat causes the lure to run higher in the water, and when the boat is slowed the lure will drop to a deeper level. If you're trolling and having no success, don't maintain a constant speed; mix it up.

Another way to vary the depth at which your lure is running, and to add some erratic action, is to avoid running the boat in a straight line. This can be difficult or impossible if you are trolling a comparatively straight line along the outside edge of a shallow weedbed, but when trolling over submerged islands or humps try running your boat in a lazy-S pattern. The lazy-S is simply a wandering course from port to starboard in gentle curves. This causes the trolled lure to move at different speeds and depths even though you maintain a constant speed. On each turn of the boat, sinking lures will drop and floating lures will rise. There have been many days of trolling on which the only strikes I got were on turns of the boat.

As mentioned earlier, the length of your line can make all the difference in catching fish when trolling. A longer line ordinarily carries the lure deeper than a short one. On bright days I start by trolling a fairly long line; on gray days I begin with a shorter line. But like all general rules, there are exceptions to this. Sometimes on a bright day the fish will strike only when the lure is trolled on a short line, and there have been overcast days when I have had to bump bottom to find the fish.

DEEP TROLLING

Not many years ago, deep trolling was done using heavy weights or lead-core line on heavy rods and reels. This technique took plenty of fish, but the equipment was so heavy that the sporting aspects of the catch were lost. Many times the angler didn't know if he had a fish or some debris until it was brought to the surface. The downrigger has changed all of that.

Downrigger fishing was developed by West Coast salmon fishermen about thirty years ago and it is only in the past few years that the technique has become popular in freshwater. A downrigger is a metal weight of about two to ten pounds that is lowered or raised on a light metal cable with the help of a small winch. Attached to the weight is a quick-release pin. The angler clips his line to the pin and lowers the weight and his bait or lure to the desired depth. When a fish takes the lure, the pin releases the line and the angler is free to fight the fish. The advantage of using a downrigger is that lures and baits can be trolled deep without heavy weights, lead-core lines, and stiff trolling rods. With a downrigger, spinning tackle, a baitcasting outfit, or even a fly rod can be used to troll deep.

Downriggers are particularly effective for species of fish that stratify at specific depths determined by water temperature and the availability of forage. Trout and salmon in large lakes are a natural for this technique, and the freshwater use of downriggers originated with Great Lakes anglers seeking these fish. A depthfinder is required for downrigger fishing in deep water. The depthfinder locates schools of fish or their forage, and the downrigger is set to run at that depth.

Downriggers are now being used all over North America and do not require very deep water to be effective. The downrigger will hold a lure or bait as precisely at fifteen feet as it will at sixty feet, and I know many anglers who use them to catch suspended largemouths. The rig can also be used with great success for walleyes and muskies, and the downrigger in combination with a depthfinder has made the taking of striped bass from large impoundments a year-round affair. By allowing access to deep water that was beyond the reach of the light-tackle angler, the downrigger has added hours to the midsummer fishing day. No longer do you have to wait for dawn and dusk, when the water is cooler and the fish feed near the surface. With a downrigger you can probe the depths during the middle of a hot summer afternoon and add many potentially productive hours to your fishing.

If you're considering the purchase of a downrigger, there are many from which to choose. There are a few efficient, inexpensive, hand-crank models that are best suited for fishing down to about thirty feet. There are also expensive electric pushbutton rigs that are popular for depths up to one hundred feet or more. If you're going to be trolling deep impoundments, you should consider the purchase of a depthfinder to help locate the fish you're after or the schools of forage fish on which they feed. How much you decide to spend on these rigs depends on your involvement in the pursuit of fish, but once you become familiar with your rig and the body of water you're fishing, your downrigger and depthfinder will become two of your most valuable fishing aids.

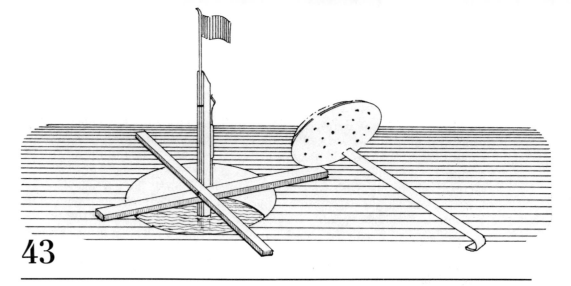

43

Ice Fishing

I'm not a rabid ice fisherman; I don't go out when the temperature is below zero or on very windy days. But on a calm sunny day there are few more pleasant ways to spend a winter afternoon. Many warm-weather anglers living in the north spend the winter waiting for the ice to melt. They're missing some fine fishing. Species such as trout, pike, pickerel, walleyes, and panfish can be caught all winter long, and they never taste better than when taken from icy winter water.

Ice fishing depends entirely on finding the fish, and while the techniques vary for different species, the same basic equipment is used everywhere. For cutting a hole in the ice I prefer an old-fashioned ice spud. This is a large chisel that will easily cut through more than a foot of ice. During a very cold winter when the ice gets quite thick, I switch to a manual ice auger. Both ice spuds and small augers are inexpensive and will last indefinitely if treated properly. In areas where the ice gets very thick, many anglers use a gasoline powered auger. These units are heavy and expensive, but when there is three feet or more of ice on the lake, drilling holes by hand becomes a real chore. Forget about using an axe to make a hole in the ice. It won't work and in the process you will get soaked with cold water.

For sweet-tasting panfish like perch, bluegills, and crappie you need very little equipment. I use a short one-piece ice-jigging rod with four-pound-test monofilament line. These rods can be purchased at most sporting-goods stores for a few dollars and are excellent for jigging tiny spoons and fishing bait in comparatively shallow water. If I'm going to be fishing in water deeper than about twenty feet, I use a home-made rig that consists of the tip of an old spinning rod fitted into the handle of an old baitcasting rod and an old bait-casting reel spooled with four- or six-pound-test line. This rig allows easy fishing at almost any depth but has the drawback of the line's freezing on the spool of the reel if the weather is very cold.

For bluegills I like to use mousie grubs, which are the larvae of the syrphus fly, a type of fruit fly. When I can't get mousie grubs I do as well using bits of shrimp, goldenrod grubs, maggots, waxworms, and mayfly nymphs, which are called wigglers.

In winter I look for bluegills in the same spots in which I have found big ones in the summer: over vegetation or debris in water about fifteen feet deep or deeper. In winter the bluegills school even tighter than in summer and won't move far to feed. If you don't catch any in about fifteen minutes, try a new spot. The fish often suspend at different depths in the cold water, making it even more difficult to find them. I use a No. 10 hook and a single mousie grub, add a splitshot, and lower the bait to the bottom. I add a light quill bobber so the bait will hang a few inches from the bottom, and jig it very gently and not very far. A bite is usually a gentle increase in pressure on the line or a few taps. If I don't take a fish within five minutes I raise the depth at which the bait is hanging to about eighteen inches off the bottom. Often a change of depth of a foot or less will make all the difference.

For crappie I use the same equipment as for bluegills, except that I use a No. 4 hook and a live minnow for bait. I place a splitshot about twelve inches above the hook and put on a two-inch minnow hooked lightly under the back fin. With this setup I've taken crappie two feet under the ice and a few minutes later right on the bottom in over fifteen feet of water. It pays to try many different depths before giving up and moving to a new spot. Crappie are always gentle biters and in winter they are gentler still. With a bite, a light quill bobber will often drift very slowly across the hole in the ice as if it were being pushed by the wind. Winter crappie fishing requires real concentration.

Once you find a hot crappie or bluegill spot, it pays to mark it exactly with a piece of brush so that you can find it when snow covers the ice. Sometimes one hole will produce big fish all winter long while holes cut just a few feet away produce nothing.

Yellow perch are taken easily in winter because they remain active in the cold water; however, as with the other panfish, finding them can be difficult. I've caught them right on the bottom in thirty feet of water and the next day only six feet below the same hole in the ice. They usually feed within two feet of the bottom, but in the cold winter water you can never tell exactly where they will be. When you find the fish you will catch all you want, but it is a feast-or-famine game.

Many anglers use small minnows as bait for perch, but I think that small teardrop jigs or a Swedish Pimple are just as good and much easier to use. The Swedish Pimple is a silver spoon about an inch long fitted with a small treble hook and a tiny silver tail that vibrates when the lure is lifted and lowered. I jig with a Swedish Pimple until I catch a perch, and then I put a perch eye on one of the hooks. I find this combination impossible to beat for winter perch. The jig should be lowered slowly and given a flip now and then as it is sinking. Perch will often hit a lure as it is sinking, and when I flip the rod up I often find myself fast to a perch I hadn't felt bite.

In winter, schools of panfish tend to consist of fish of a similar size. If I find a school of small perch or crappie I move until I find larger fish. When looking for winter panfish you have to be willing to do some prospecting.

Walleyes are also easy to catch through the ice if you can find them. They roam in cold water, and I often have the feeling, especially when I'm tired from cutting holes in the ice, that I have spent the day cutting holes just behind a school of big walleyes. On many days all I get is a badly needed winter workout. When ice fishing for walleyes, the same deep structures and weedbeds that were productive in summer are your best bets. If I'm not familiar with the lake I move around a lot and pray. I use only live minnows for winter walleyes, and prefer them about three inches long. I hook them lightly under the back fin on a No. 4 hook and add enough splitshot to keep the minnow within about three feet of the bottom.

Because walleyes do so much roaming in the winter, my walleye rig is a simple one, and I set out as many as the law allows. I cut a willow limb about seven feet long and shaped like a heavy fly rod. I tie eight-pound-test monofilament to the base of the limb, leave about ten feet of slack, and thread a loop of line over the tip of the limb. I set the limb in the ice at about a forty-five-degree angle so that its tip hangs directly over the hole and the line drops straight down. I then thread half a playing card on the line. The card flutters in the wind and keeps the bait moving, an essential for attracting winter walleyes. A strike is nothing more than a gentle sinking of the tip of the limb. In winter walleyes tend to stay in one spot while they swallow a bait, then sit still or swim slowly in a circle. I have never had a walleye of any size break a limb, and most of the time they don't even pull the loop of line off the tip of the limb. The gentle pressure of the willow limb seems to be enough to hold them in one spot, and they just wait to be pulled in.

When ice fishing for pickerel and pike, most anglers use tip-ups that have a built-in indicator that shows when a fish has taken the bait. The most popular tip-ups are X-shaped wooden crosses that span the hole in the ice. Attached to the X is a spool of line that hangs beneath the water. Attached to the spool is a trigger mechanism that releases a flag when a fish turns the spool of line. Good tip-ups cost about five dollars each; local fishing laws determine how many each angler is allowed to use.

I prefer fifty-pound-test squidding line on my tip-ups. Line this strong isn't necessary, but what is necessary is line that is thick enough to be easily handled with cold, numb fingers. I use about three feet of ten-pound-test monofilament for a leader, although I may use up to thirty-pound test when I'm seeking big pike.

Minnows are my preferred pike bait. I hook them under the back fin and drop them to within about two feet of the bottom. An eight-inch minnow is not too large for big pike. Smaller minnows usually attract smaller fish, and many will swallow a small bait, making their survival questionable after they are released.

In most lakes pike and pickerel spend the winter in shallow water. I look for pickerel along the edges of weedbeds. Pike seem to prefer the shallow side of a dropoff on either side of a river channel or areas where springs and streams enter a lake. These same areas may contain patches of weak black ice and the angler must be cautious not to fall through.

When using large minnows for big pike, I find that the fish will run some distance before stopping and turning the minnow in its mouth. When a flag goes up, I go to the hole and look down at the spool of line before I touch anything. If the spool is turning I wait until it stops before I pick up the tip-up and set the hook.

The only additional equipment you will need for ice fishing is an ice strainer to skim ice from the holes as it forms, a small tropical fish net to use for getting minnows from the bucket without having to plunge your hand into the icy water, and a Styrofoam minnow bucket. I don't use a metal minnow bucket, because they tend to freeze over quickly on a cold day.

Since the gear for ice fishing tends to be bulky, I have fitted the top of an old sled with a large, covered wooden box. The box holds my tip-ups, jigging rods, bait bucket, ice spud, and anything else I'll want, such as my lunch and a jug of hot coffee. It is easy to pull the sled from hole to hole when rebaiting, and the box gives me a convenient place to sit when I get tired of standing.

It isn't a good idea to just toss your fish on the ice. They will quickly freeze, meaning that you'll have to wait for them to thaw before they can be cleaned, and refreezing thawed fish is unsafe because of bacterial contamination. Some anglers wrap their fish in newspaper and bury them in a snowbank, which will keep them cold but unfrozen. To keep my fish I prefer to use my ice spud and make a basin in the ice about eight inches deep and three feet square. I then cut a hole in the ice about a foot away from the basin and make a small channel from the hole to the basin. The basin will fill with water, making it an excellent place to keep fish alive until it is time to head home.

If you have done some ice fishing and haven't had much success, try being more mobile and fishing many different spots. In winter, finding the fish is the hard part, but you have the advantage of being able to walk all over the lake. If you haven't tried ice fishing, and you spend the winter months complaining and waiting for ice-out, you're missing some fine winter sport and a sure cure for cabin fever.

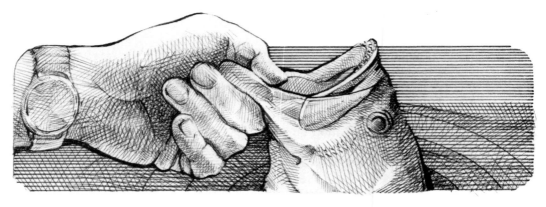

44

Catch-and-Release Fishing

For many years I believed the oft-heard statement that anglers using traditional fishing techniques could not deplete the natural fish supply of a body of water. Unfortunately this is not so, and sadly it has taken extremes of water pollution to help prove the point.

There are many examples of fish depletion by sportfishing from all over North America. In 1975, for example, the state of Virginia banned the taking of fish for human consumption on the lower stretches of the James and Chickahominy rivers and their tributaries. The reason was high levels of Kepone, a toxic pesticide known to be damaging to human beings. The fish in these rivers were found to contain very high levels of this substance and were becoming more toxic each year. Fortunately, the source of the pollution was discovered and corrected, but Virginia's Kepone Task Force estimates that the rivers may be expected to remain contaminated for up to two hundred years.

Sportfishing was not banned in the rivers, and some anglers felt that without harvesting the rivers would soon become overcrowded and stunted fish would result. Nevertheless, since 1975 most fish taken by anglers have been returned to the rivers, and rather than overcrowding and stunting resulting from this, fishing has become nothing short of phenomenal. Before the catch-and-release policy, a good fishing day would see six or seven bass in the boat. The fish averaged about two pounds. Now, catches of fifty bass per day are common and the fish average over four pounds each. On the James the fish are running even larger, and largemouths between five and ten pounds are taken with regularity.

While the contamination of these two rivers was a tragedy, the fishing in them has now become sensational. There is no longer any doubt that the reason is the no-kill policy.

The implications of the Virginia experience have been carefully studied, and many states, even those without obvious chemical contamination problems, have imposed regulations to limit fish harvesting for the purpose of improving fish populations and the quality of sportfishing. But in the last analysis, the quality of our sport depends upon the individual angler's releasing, unharmed, the majority of the fish he catches. The benefits of catch-and-release fishing are obvious. What isn't as obvious is the fact that there are some definite guidelines to follow in the playing, handling, and releasing of a fish if that fish is going to survive.

The act of fighting a fish creates a tremendous strain in its body. During the fight, the fish uses oxygen at an abnormal rate and, if the fight is prolonged, excess lactic acid builds up in its muscles. Once the fish has been landed, the location in which it has been hooked, how it is handled, and how quickly it is returned to the water will all determine its chances for survival.

Oxygen is one important aspect of catch-and-release fishing, particularly in summer when waters are warm and contain their lowest oxygen levels of the year. When brought to shore or boatside, a fish caught in the summer is in a condition similar to that of a sprinter who has just finished a race. Its need for oxygen is extreme, yet at this critical time the angler takes the fish from the water, completely eliminating its ability to satisfy that essential need. For this reason it is important to keep a fish in the water while removing the hook. If the hook can't be removed immediately, the fish's gills must remain covered with water during the unhooking process. The difference between holding a fish out of water for fifteen seconds or for two minutes can determine if it survives or dies. The fish held out of water for two minutes may quickly swim away, but if it has gone for too long without oxygen it will die in a few hours.

Lactic acid builds up in the muscles and blood of all living creatures during muscular activity. A good example of the effects of too much lactic acid in a human being is the sore muscles that follow extreme physical exertion. The soreness is caused by an excessive build-up of the acid. If a human being is in good physical condition, and the muscles used in a specific activity are strong, the lactic acid is quickly absorbed by the body and the muscular soreness does not last long.

There is no way a fish can condition its muscles for the process of being caught. For the fish this is a life-and-death struggle, and its exertion is maximum. If the fight goes on for a long time, lactic acid will build up to such an extent that the central nervous system of the fish becomes depressed, the acidity of its blood increases, and the fish dies of shock. Again, the fact that the fish may swim quickly away after a prolonged fight is no guarantee that it will survive.

The problem for the angler is that he cannot know how long a fish can be fought before the onset of lactic acidosis. The thing to remember is not to overplay a fish you plan to release. This means that light and ultra-light equipment should not be used on large fish that are to be released. One objective of catch-and-release fishing must be to bring the fish in quickly so that it can be released quickly, with a minimum of exertion and damage. Thus, you should use your heavier equipment for catch-and-release fishing. If a fish is brought to the shore or boatside after a long battle and is so exhausted that it is literally belly up, it should be kept for the frying pan because its chances for survival are minimal at best.

Where a fish is hooked and how much damage has been done by the hooks are other determinants of its survival when it is released. In all living creatures, excessive bleeding lowers the blood pressure. If too much blood is lost, the creature goes into shock and can die.

Fish hooked in the lips or near the front of the mouth will probably live when released. Those hooked in the gills, esophagus, and back of the tongue, where there is ordinarily excessive bleeding, will probably not survive.

There is a common belief that if the angler cuts the line and leaves the hook in a fish, the fish's digestive juices will eventually dissolve the hook. Unfortunately, there is no way of knowing if this theory is correct. However, since I have taken many fish with other people's hooks still in their mouths or stomachs, some fish carrying hooks do survive. My rule of thumb is that if there is little or no bleeding from a deeply hooked fish, I cut the line and leave the hook in the fish. Again, if there is extensive bleeding, I keep the fish.

I am a believer in barbless hooks, not because they do less damage than hooks with barbs but because they are much easier to quickly remove from a fish. For instance, when catch-and-release fishing for northern pike I use spoons from which I have removed the treble hook and replaced it with a single, large barbless hook. This hook can often be easily removed from a pike with long-nosed pliers without even taking the fish from the water. I land almost as many pike on these single hooks as I do on treble hooks.

There will be many fish that because of the hook location, type of lure, and hooks on the lure will have to be taken from the water prior to release. How these fish are handled during the unhooking process is essential to their survival.

The eyes of a fish are among its most sensitive organs. Fish have no eyelids, and regulate the amount of light entering their eyes by finding places in the water where the light is comfortable for their needs. The retina of the eye also requires an extremely high level of oxygen. Removing a fish from the water and holding it in direct, bright sunlight at a time when its oxygen demands are greatest can cause permanent damage to the eyes and blindness. If a fish must be removed from the water, it should be held in the shade during the unhooking process. Never pick up a fish that is to be released by putting your fingers in its eye sockets.

The gills of a fish are also extremely fragile. If there is bleeding from the gills, even if it is minimal, the fish has little chance of surviving. One popular landing technique that should be eliminated is inserting the fingers under the gill covers to get a firm grip on a fish. Simply touching the gills can damage them or cause fungus infections on the sensitive gill tissues, which will eventually kill the fish. A better way to get a good grip is to use the entire hand to grasp the fish just behind (not under) the gill covers. A couple of fingers might overlap the gill covers, but the pressure needed to lift the fish should be applied by the fingers behind the gill covers and not on the covers themselves.

Using a net to land a fish eliminates many of these problems, especially when the fish is large or of the toothy variety such as a pike or muskellunge. I like to net a fish and not lift the net from the water. This lets me work on removing the hooks without having to exert extreme pressure on the fish, so that it won't flap around on me. Having a companion hold the net or letting the mesh of the net hang over the gunwale of the boat immobilizes the fish in the water. Rubber-mesh landing nets are best because they are softer than rope nets and won't scrape off the fish's protective body slime. If the protective slime is removed, the fish is subject to fungus infection, especially in places where scales have been removed or where the fish has suffered cuts.

If a fish is allowed to flop around on shore or on the deck of a boat it is likely to suffer any of the following conditions: scratches on the eyes from sand and grit, the loss of protective body slime and scales, injury to internal organs, suffocation, and lactic acidosis.

A pair of long-nosed pliers can make the unhooking job a lot faster and easier, resulting in a shorter period before a fish is returned to the water. Once the fish is returned it should be held gently in the water to give it time to regain some of its strength. It should not be moved back and forth to pump water through its gills. Moving a fish backward forces water into the gills from the rear, and the gills do not function in this fashion. A fish moved backward through the water will quickly suffocate.

The survival rate for a fish that has been on a stringer is impossible to determine. It may swim quickly away only to die days later. No matter how a stringer is used it will do more damage than will releasing a fish, and dragging a fish around a lake on the stringer is always fatal. You must make an immediate decision after you land your fish whether you are going to keep or release it.

Tired fish can sometimes be reconditioned in a boat live-well, but only if it circulates new water and is well oxygenated, cool, and dark. If the live-well does not circulate new water, even if it has an aerator, the temperature of the water will get too warm, wastes will build up, and the danger of suffocation and fungus infections will increase.

All of this careful handling and the many potentially fatal stresses that accompany the landing process make it appear that fish are much more fragile than they are. They are amazingly resilient creatures, and if brought quickly to the boat or bankside and the hooks quickly and gently removed, most of them will survive the experience. But there is no way of telling which fish survive, and I've often wondered how many tournament fish survive after going through the catching process, extended confinement in a live-well, the weigh-in, and eventual release in an unfamiliar, overcrowded area of the lake.

Some fish are going to die no matter how carefully they are handled; it is inevitable. But most of us like to bring home some fish for the frying pan. These days I find that most of the fish I bring home are those that have been injured during the catching process and are unlikely to live if released. A problem results when the injured fish is a bit too small to meet legal requirements. Unfortunately, these fish must be returned to the water even though their death is inevitable.

In these days of increasing fishing pressure and the development of sophisticated equipment and techniques, the quality of our sport will suffer if more fish are not released. That is simply a fact. I believe that catch-and-release fishing symbolizes the best qualities of the modern angler. It illustrates that the fisherman has an understanding of, and respect for, the fragility of the natural system that surrounds us, and that he has an understanding of his role in that system.

Index